The Association of MBAs
Guide to Business Schools

D1823917

The Association of MBAs
Guide to Business Schools

Tenth revised edition

Editorial commentary by Godfrey Golzen

Reference matter collated and revised
by the Association of MBAs
with the assistance of Laura McGeary

Published with the Association of MBAs

Pitman Publishing
128 Long Acre, London WC2E 9AN

A Division of Longman Group UK Limited

First published by Macdonald & Evans Ltd 1970
Second edition 1973
Third edition 1976
Fourth edition 1979
Fifth edition 1981
Sixth edition 1985
Seventh edition 1988
Eighth edition 1990
Ninth edition 1992
Tenth edition 1993

© Macdonald & Evans Ltd 1970, 1973, 1976, 1981, 1985
© Longman Group UK Ltd 1988, 1990, 1992, 1993

British Library Cataloguing in Publication Data
A CIP catalogue record for this book can be obtained from the
British Library

ISBN 0 273 60340 X

Typeset by Land & Unwin (Data Sciences) Limited
Printed in England by Clays Ltd, St Ives plc

Contents

Foreword by the Secretary of State

As the next century approaches, Britain faces new challenges to organisational, national and international competitiveness in a rapidly changing world economy. Increasingly, enhanced performance depends on improved management of economic, physical and – most of all – human resources. Effective management is vital, not only in industry and business but also in the public and voluntary sectors.

This Government is committed to lifetime learning targets to raise national levels of participation, achievement and skills. Management education at all levels has a vital role to play in individual and organisational motivation and success. Britain's business schools have responded to the demand for high quality management education by developing innovative, flexible learning programmes, informed by closer business links, to meet a wide range of needs.

Prospective students, faced with choosing from the wealth of courses available, will find this 10th edition of AMBA's Guide to Business Schools a most useful tool. Now well-established, the Guide is testimony to AMBA's continuing mission to raise standards and awareness of management education. I commend it to you.

The Rt. Hon. John Patten MP
Secretary of State for Education and Science

Preface: MBAs and their Association

The degree, Master of Business Administration (MBA), is by far the fastest growing postgraduate qualification in the UK. A recent report in the *Wall Street Journal* states that Britain's current output of nearly 6000 MBA graduates a year is more than the rest of Europe put together. Though still a long way behind the USA's 77,000 a year, that is nevertheless a huge jump from the total of 2000 in 1985/6. According to Roger McCormick, Director-General of the Association of MBAs, the UK output of MBAs has increased by a compound 18% a year since 1990.

Variation in the quality of the places that offer MBAs is an almost inevitable side-effect of growth of that order. It has to be said that money and 'me-tooism' have played a part in the establishment of some of the MBA courses now on offer in 92 schools in the UK. The MBA programme, which runs for either one or two years (overwhelmingly the former) for full-time students and for a minimum of about two years for part-time and distance learners, is a useful revenue generator for financially hard-pressed tertiary institutions. Apart from that, the high visibility of the MBA concept increasingly makes them feel that they have to be able to offer an MBA to be taken seriously in the community and even in the academic world. The result is that while, until quite recently, just being able to put the letters MBA after your name was sufficient to give you a competitive advantage in the career stakes, commentators now increasingly report that employers look at where the degree was earned. A survey conducted among Warwick Business School MBAs makes the following typical comment: 'Because of the recent proliferation in new courses, employers were starting to differentiate between different MBAs: "an MBA – from where" was the key question.'[1] Some MBAs,

it is becoming clear, are more equal than others. Consequently monitoring standards has become one of the key roles of the Association of MBAs (AMBA).

The Association of MBAs and quality control

The Association of MBAs (AMBA) was founded in 1967 as what was then the Business Graduates Association by a group of British graduates who had returned from studying at some of the leading US business schools. Their initiative had two main objectives. One was a belief in the need for some kind of pressure group to promote the idea of management education itself, at a time when it scarcely existed in the UK in a formal sense. There were, for instance, no management schools awarding the MBA in the UK before 1965 and the influence of AMBA members in important positions has played no small part in the expansion of business education in the UK since then.

Their other motive was more social. Experience of the Alumni associations of the American schools had shown that they had much to offer their members. The founders of AMBA wanted to extend the concept of continuing social contact, informal networking, and exchanges of information through periodic workshops and members' meetings, strong among business school graduates in the USA, to the UK.

Both these themes continue to underpin what AMBA does, but they have been joined by a third one that has become equally important: that of quality control of MBA-awarding bodies through a system of accreditation. Currently 28 out of the 92 institutions conferring the MBA in the UK are accredited by AMBA. The value attached by schools to AMBA accreditation is confirmed by the fact that business schools on the European Continent are now also beginning to seek it.

The criteria are rigorous and themselves offer a kind of consumer protection for intending students. Here are some of their principal features:

- the school should have its own discrete identity and physical facilities within the institution of which it is a part
- it should have graduated at least two 'cohorts' (graduating classes)
- the faculty should be big enough to ensure strength in depth – AMBA believes that around 40 staff is the minimum needed to provide adequate contact with students during the course
- the staff should be credible in terms of their academic qualifications, their ability to teach business at postgraduate level, the quality of their research and the extent of their business contacts and consultancy activities
- admission standards for students must be high and based on work experience as well as academic criteria
- the student body must be large and varied enough to form an intellectually critical mass
- the curriculum must cover core business skills: marketing, the economic and legal environment of a business, accounting and quantitative methods, organisational theory and interpersonal skills, the processes and practice of management
- examination results must be the principal though not the sole measure of attainment.

In addition, accreditation is based on such factors as the availability of language teaching, library and computer facilities, international contacts, and the content and quality of assessment of the project/thesis/dissertation which, towards the end of the course, integrates what has been learned and relates it to a real situation. Also considered is the extent to which student reactions are taken into account in the continuing process of course design and improvement.

AMBA membership services

One of AMBA's major roles is to act as a clearing house for enquiries from intending MBAs or from those who are thinking of doing an MBA. In fact its staff deal with some 1500 letters and telephone calls a month. However, one area where it is hesitant to give advice is on matters of opinion. It is, in particular, difficult to judge whether one school is 'better' than another, or to provide rankings of schools.

AMBA takes the view that the accreditation process in itself provides a broad measure of quality assurance. After that it is up to the individual – or the company thinking of sponsoring an employee to take an MBA – to pursue their own investigations by making personal visits or talking to other sponsors or to graduates of the institutions in which they are interested.

However, it does provide very significant services on concrete issues. It runs regional and national events for AMBA members, such as evening and lunchtime meetings with nationally prominent speakers which also give members the opportunity for informal networking, it advises on a range of career matters and it has negotiated special terms for members with a number of business and social bodies. Another valuable contribution is in the field of publications. Apart from two Reports produced in the last year, to which we will refer in more detail later in the text, it publishes a regular Newsletter and an annual Handbook containing names and addresses of AMBA members.

From the point of view of prospective MBAs its most valuable service is probably the operation, in conjunction with Barclays and the National Westminster Bank, of the Association's Business School Loan Scheme. We will give more exact details of this later in the text, but the importance of the Scheme can be judged from the fact that in the year ending June 1992, 1398 applications were processed, totalling £18.5 million.

This is a decrease from the previous year, both in numbers and in the total sums being lent, which is partly a product of the recession and partly reflects greater prudence by applicants in the extent to which they commit themselves to borrowings. But the fact that, in the current economic climate, so many people are prepared to do so on what is still an impressive scale is an indication of the ever-growing demand for the MBA qualification.

It also shows that most of those seeking it are funding at least part of their course themselves and are prepared to invest time and money on their own development. This is a lesson that is not lost on prospective employers.

The revenues generated by the Loan Scheme also benefit the Association's members in other ways. Notably, it enables it to offer all these wide-ranging services without charging a joining fee, though there is thereafter a flat rate, tax-deductible annual subscription of only £35 per annum. AMBA currently has around 7500 members. Membership is growing at around 15% a year and is well on target for the Association's next goal of 10,000 members.

Business Schools and the recession

The 10% drop in applications to UK business schools which has been noticed this year is undoubtedly a reflection of the recession – delayed because of the time lag between making the decision to take the course and actually joining a programme. It is therefore possible that a drop in numbers will continue to feed through the system for two or three years to come. However AMBA Director-General Roger McCormick pointed out in a recent article in Banking World that demand for places is nevertheless running at 90% of last year's level, indicating 'a pause rather than a reversal of quite exceptional figures of historic growth'. Wisely, schools accredited by AMBA have not lowered their admission criteria, although certainly competition to attract students has become sharper. Many commentators have also noticed a growth in part-time courses, as people become unwilling to take the risk of leaving the job market.

The question has been asked whether some of the drop in applications should be attributed to the backlash against MBAs that has been commented on in the press. To judge from the increasing number of recruitment advertisements that express a preference for MBA graduates, it would seem that this had very little impact. It is significant that, according to a recent report in *The Independent* [2] 'This year record numbers are using redundancy as an opportunity to enrol at a business school and enhance their job prospects by doing an MBA.'

However this does call for a cautionary note. As the *Wall Street Journal Europe* has pointed out, Britain has a potential over-supply of business schools. Many cities have two or more and London has over ten. The *Financial Times* thinks that 'smaller, less-known providers may have to withdraw from the MBA market.' [3] Alternatively the weaker ones, while managing to keep going, may find that they do not have the resources to fulfil enough of the criteria set out in Chapter 3 (Choosing A School). Which is why careful perusal of the Guide is advisable for those considering doing the MBA.

The scope of the Guide

'The decision to take an MBA is overwhelmingly an individual one,' reported the former Council For National Academic Awards. [4] For that reason it is also, as stated earlier, predominantly individually funded, either in whole or in part.

'At a good school,' warns *The European Education Yearbook*, 'the MBA does not come cheap.' [5] Basic fees hover around the £5000–£6000 range, to which have to be added living costs in the case of a full-time course, plus the cost of earnings foregone. It is estimated that the total outlay on a one-year, full-time course is not likely to be much less than £18,000–£20,000, and can be as much as £25,000 at a leading school abroad. One is talking, therefore, of a very considerable sacrifice in terms of money, time and, possibly short-term career opportunities. Even those taking a part-time or distance learning MBA will have to take their eye off the promotional ball if they are to get through what is universally seen as one of the most demanding of all academic courses. The question is then: is it really worth it?

It is a difficult one to answer for the same reason as AMBA finds it difficult to answer qualitative questions – so much depends on the individual, on individual circumstances and business environments. But one of the chief objectives of the Guide, which having been largely re-written for the 9th Edition, has now been revised and updated, is to provide readers with enough information about key aspects of the MBA to enable them to draw their own conclusions about whether or not taking the MBA is the right decision for them.

Thus it begins by examining some of the expectations that might lie behind a decision to take the course and whether these are likely to be met by so doing. Is it, for instance, likely to enhance your career prospects or should you see it more as a question of personal development?

In either case, what does it actually involve? That may depend on the mode of study. The choices lie between full-time, part-time, and distance or open learning options. The first is a short and extremely intensive course of study in a primarily academic setting. The others are longer courses, covering the same ground but spun out over at least two years, that will enable you to carry on working – and apply on the job what you are learning – but will place perhaps even greater strains on your time-management skills and possibly on your private life. We will discuss the pros and cons of each method.

But apart from the question of whether it is worth it in career terms, what are the risks of doing the course in the first place? What are the chances of failure? How difficult is it all? We hope you will get some idea of this by reading about what is actually involved, but there is one overriding and consoling feature which we would like to point out right away: the hardest part may be getting admitted in the first place. The

consensus of opinion is that if you can get past the admission procedures, notably the dreaded Graduate Management Admission Test (GMAT), the chances of anyone with reasonable determination finishing up with an MBA are very good indeed. Because of the importance of GMAT we will devote a special section to that.

The other question that is often asked is whether it is all worth it from a career point of view. Certainly the last year or so has seen a backlash from employers, voiced in such publications as *The MBA Question: Perception and Reality in the UK*.[6] It is the belief of AMBA that criticism of MBAs is very largely unjustified and that in so far as the anti-MBA brigade among employers have a case, the business schools have already taken steps to counter their objections ('too academic, not relevant to business needs, too compartmentalised in the way subjects are taught' etc.) in the design of their courses.

The telling fact is that rising young managers – most MBA students are in the age range 27–35 – are voting for the MBA with their feet. They are right to do so because if the future of businesses is as learning and knowledge organisations – and it is impossible to envisage any other future – then the MBA qualification must be the keystone of that kind of structure.

Notes

1. MBAs Still Undervalued, *THES*, 20.12.91
2. Masters of Destiny, 12.11.92
3. Successful To A Degree, 30.12.92
4. Review of the Master of Business Administration, CNAA, 1991
5. Published annually by The Whitehall Press, London
6. *The MBA Question: Perceptions and Reality in the UK*, Saxton Bampfylde International plc, 1990

PART ONE

1 Thinking it over

In the case of most postgraduate qualifications you can move straight on from a first degree to a postgraduate course. While it is not absolutely impossible to take an MBA in this way – some non-UK schools do not list work experiences among their admission requirements – it is generally regarded as inadvisable. In the words of Roger McCormick, writing in the *European Education Yearbook*:[1] 'The MBA is not only a postgraduate degree; it is also strongly post-experience and the length and quality of a student's working background are of high relevance in securing admission to a good school.' Thus few, if any, MBA students in the UK are doing the course without a practical grounding of some kind, though it need not necessarily have been in a business role. Profiles of recent and current cohorts of students at a typical leading school show, apart from line management in a wide variety of sectors, backgrounds that range over law, engineering, the armed forces, journalism, financial services, teaching, consultancy, helicopter flying and television production.

One reason why work experience is important is, as Sheila Cameron writes in the *MBA Handbook*[2] because 'students who have worked as managers tend to be far more excited by their studies than those who have not.' This seems to be particularly true of those who take the course part-time or by distance learning – we will deal more fully with the various options and what they involve in the next chapter. 'Part-time and distance learning courses,' she goes on to say, 'offer splendid opportunities for practice for those already in managerial jobs.'

That conclusion is borne out in conversations with MBA students. For instance, Carl Conn, taking a part-time MBA at Warwick Business School to widen his selling skills into those of consultancy and general management, is typical in talking of his excitement at finding what he is learning on his course to be instantly applicable to what he is doing in his job as Business Development Manager at IBM's Midlands Marketing Centre. Indeed Sheila Cameron believes that part-time and distance learning courses are 'most effective if you can practise the skills in parallel with the course.' By contrast, full-time MBA programmes tend to have a more theoretical orientation. They may therefore be more suitable for those who want to upgrade work experience, say in a specialist or functional capacity, into a future role in general management.

MBA students: characteristics and profiles

To mark its 25th anniversary, the Association of MBAs carried out a wide-ranging survey of the characteristics, expectations, motivation and careers of some 2000 members who had taken full and part time MBAs.[3] The findings may point readers in the direction of options appropriate to their own situation. There were, for instance, significant differences in the ages, marital status and work experience of full and part-timers.

On the question of funding, no details are available on employer funding of full-time students, but it is likely to be low since AMBA's research shows that 75% of those entering a full-time course had resigned their jobs to do so. By contrast, 50% of part-timers who were employed during their studies had all their fees paid by their employer. Others were supported by employers in a variety of ways, ranging from some financial assistance to time off work.

	Full-timers	Part-timers
Age	25–29	35–39 (almost 28% were over 40)
Percentage of Women	23%	18%
Marital Status	44% Married	75% Married
Ten or more years work experience	27%	47%

However, in other ways, the differences between full and part-time students were only minor. In both cases, around 80% had a first degree and around 50% had achieved a first or upper second. A significant statistic here was the preponderance of those with some kind of science/maths/engineering/accounting background. This underlines the point, made by several course directors, that for all the shift towards 'soft' management subjects in the MBA (e.g., interpersonal skills such as communication, negotiation, teamwork etc) students with poor levels of numeracy would be likely to find the course very difficult.

There were were no marked differences in the employment background of the two groups, except that more full-timers than part-timers came from consultancy, whereas the reverse was true of those who came from the public sector. Other interesting features were the wide spread of job disciplines in students' background, and their relatively high previous levels of responsibility – 35% had been handling budgets of more than £100,000 (indeed 18% had been in the £1 million plus budget range) a statistic which ties in with the findings about work experience. 65% of the MBAs in the survey had worked for six or more years when they started the course. This is encouraging because such a large part of the learning process comes from mixing and exchanging views with fellow students from different backgrounds but with comparable levels of responsibility and experience.

Some further points about students' background emerge from the CNAA (Council for National Academic Awards) Review of the MBA. This shows that full-timers are most likely to be self-funded and of UK origin, though the latter characteristic seems to be changing. Some schools contain a very sizeable overseas contingent. That may be a laudable move towards internationalisation, but it may also reflect a policy of active recruitment in countries where UK fees seem less daunting and where the status of a UK MBA has an added cachet. In one school, overseas participants make up 90% of the MBA cohort. AMBA regards this as disproportionately high. Sitting in on classes with a large contingent of non-native English speakers, language difficulties became immediately obvious to the writer.

Student expectations and motivation

Opponents of the MBA often cite the salary demands made by MBA graduates as a reason for their suspicion of the qualification. While it is true that MBAs often expect to, and do, increase their earnings after they graduate (see Chapter 7 for further information on this) – they are after all adding value to their business skills and have made considerable personal and often financial sacrifices to do so – the evidence is that money is not a prime motivation for those taking the MBA. Research undertaken by the former CNAA, as well as evidence gathered by the Association of MBAs for the 25th anniversary survey previously referred to, show that improvement in overall job prospects is the main motive.

There seems to be little difference here between the expectations of full- and part-time students. However it appears that sponsored students are more interested in improving their skills as managers within their current organisation, whereas self-funded students are thinking in terms of career or job change. But only a minority of all students give 'making more money' as a reason for doing the course, though this may be a case of the motive that dare not speak its name.

So the evidence is that career strategy is the centrepiece in the mix of reasons why people do an MBA. In their controversial report, *The MBA Question*,[4] the headhunters Saxton Bampfylde established some broad characteristics of what lies behind these strategies. They may give prospective MBAs some explanation of their own, sometimes unarticulated motives and the chance to examine whether doing an MBA is the right career move for them in the light of that:

- **The Big Game Planner** is described as 'often a very driven individual' who may be planning to use the MBA to assemble a set of skills and a network of contacts for some future entrepreneurial activity. Big game planners should be aware, however, that while the MBA does contain a great deal of practical content, it is not a vocational course on running a business.
- **The Natural Next Stepper** often comes from a business like banking or consultancy where possession of an MBA is the norm for their peer group. But in a setting where most people have an MBA, where it was obtained is likely to be very significant. Saxton Bampfylde warn, however, that the content of some MBA courses is more readily transferable to another business sector than others. This is particularly true of moves from financial services to manufacturing line management.
- **The Disillusioned Functionalist** is generally a person trying to move out of a specialism with limited access to general management. Engineers and those seeking a change of career direction fall into this category. Engineering, say Saxton Bampfylde, is the 'single most important professional provenance for MBAs', though accountancy must run it close. While people with a numerate background, it is generally agreed, do enjoy a considerable advantage on parts of the course, they should be aware that literacy is equally important. So are interpersonal skills, the development of which is becoming an increasingly important feature of MBA courses.

- **The Searcher** is someone with high, but perhaps unarticulated, career expectations who sees the MBA as a way of exploring directions their career might take. Such people are often looking to the MBA to provide a route to a new career direction, though some have reported this to be more difficult than they had imagined. For instance, a graduate who had won a scholarship to INSEAD acknowledged to be one of Europe's top schools, reported that she was finding it extremely difficult to move from the financial services sector to line management in industry. Relevant experience, it seems, still counts – even for those who can point to an MBA in their CV.
- **Moving Up At 35**. The mid-30s are widely seen as a crucial career stage. If you are going to get anywhere in senior management, that is when it has to start. At this point an MBA – generally taken part-time or by distance learning – can provide an invaluable reinforcement to experience and an enhancement of existing skills. The problem is that doing an MBA while holding down managerial responsibilities obviously imposes additional strains both in work and in study. Those who have followed this course all stress that it requires a good deal of understanding on the part of one's family and employers in order to keep up with the workload.
- **The Cop-out** falls into the category of the perpetual student. Bright enough, he or she is not likely to experience too much difficulty with the intellectual challenge of the course, but is lacking direction and more concerned with study as a way of postponing a career decision. Such people are likely to benefit least from an MBA. While it is not a vocational course, it is not meant to be a set of abstract intellectual exercises either.

Employer expectations – and fears

Since most people take the course in order to advance their careers, either within their own organisation or by changing jobs, the perception of employers of the value of an MBA is crucial. Except in sectors like consultancy and financial services, which have always been appreciative recruiters of MBAs, it is somewhat mixed. But attitudes are changing as a younger generation of managers comes to the top and as the value of a global perspective in business issues – now a regular feature of the MBA programme – becomes more evident. The CNAA Report cites a marked shift towards more positive feelings about business schools on the part of executives 'who have actually experienced the support and teaching of academics.'[5]

The fears and prejudices of the rest have been fairly well publicised. There have been ill-informed criticisms of MBAs as aggressive, egotistical, job-hopping, know-it-alls with unrealistic expectations of their immediate prospects. Hostility along these lines is reported be most marked among the more traditional and less progressive kinds of UK manufacturing firms. Saxton Bampfylde sums up their attitude as regarding MBA courses like a 'finishing school for management consultants.'

To some extent this can be put down to the anti-intellectualism in some quarters of British business. The generation gap and fears about job security from older, less well-trained people also play a part. The MBA is the business equivalent of a Commando course and there is a temptation, natural among people who have gone through an experience of this kind, to be 'cocky' towards those who have not had it.

The business schools are aware of this problem, which is why interpersonal skills now form an important part of the course. But what is it that the more forward-looking employers expect to gain from hiring MBAs? And, by the same token, what qualities should an MBA expect to come away with, having taken the course? The Saxton Bampfylde survey, conducted among major employers of MBAs, comes up with an interesting picture:

- a breadth of business understanding of management principles across the key concerns of organisations
- specific tools for analysing strategic issues and options
- the ability to identify priorities in courses of action
- presentation and communication skills.

It will be noted from this that implementation and line management ability do not figure here. Indeed firms are quoted as saying that MBAs are not automatically 'great line managers'. Many of them feel that the real worth of an MBA course is to add value to in-company training. However, the

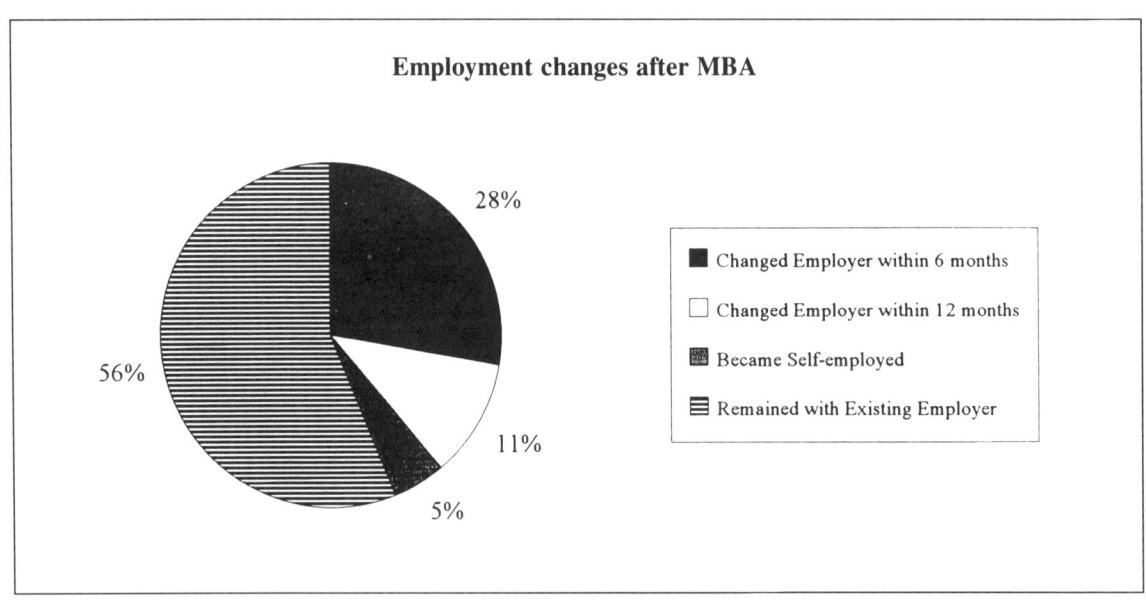

Employment changes after MBA

28%

56%

11%

5%

- Changed Employer within 6 months
- Changed Employer within 12 months
- Became Self-employed
- Remained with Existing Employer

fact that an increasing number are incorporating the MBA in their internal schemes – a matter which we shall discuss at greater length in the next chapter – indicates that there can be a congruence between the MBA qualification and employer expectations.

What about the charge of job-hopping, though? The notion that at any level, training is something provided for the benefit of the next employer, is often the underlying, if unstated, reason for not supplying it or regarding it as something employees must provide in their own time and at their own cost.

The AMBA Survey might be regarded by some as slightly ambiguous on this point. It did, however, emerge that 72% of those who had all their fees paid by their employer remained with them for at least a year.

Employers must also recognise that to some extent whether, and for how long MBAs stay with them, depends on them providing settings and opportunities that will encourage longer-term commitment. Often that is not the case. The Report on *The MBA Experience*[6] warns that: 'MBAs recruited in some companies are under pressure to perform and produce results fast.' Trial by ordeal is also a way of losing them fast.

It can also be argued that investment in training is simply a matter of public interest, which falls into the sphere of the growing emphasis on the importance of corporate ethics.

Getting it together

In the absence of direct company involvement in course design, the aims of prospective MBAs and organisations are most likely to meet if both have a clear understanding of each others' views and motives. That means that MBAs must be realistic about the ways in which they can add value to an employer as well as to their personal career aims.

From the employer's point of view, it is important to buy into the notion of lifelong learning and to see its benefits from a corporate point of view. Central to that is using the qualities that MBA graduates can bring to bear. The Economist Intelligence Unit's survey, *Which MBA?*[7] says that many companies have found that using new MBA graduates initially as internal consultants is the best way of tapping into what they have learned. But it adds that 'trying to show traditionally reluctant companies to use MBA graduates effectively' is a key task. The implication is that whether it is worthwhile taking an MBA as an individual – or sponsoring it as a company – depends on the organisation as much as the individual.

Notes

1. op. cit.
2. *The MBA Handbook*, Sheila Cameron, Pitman Publishing 1991
3. Beard, P., *The MBA Experience*, AMBA 1992
4. op. cit.
5. op. cit.
6. op. cit.
7. *Which MBA? A Critical Guide to the World's Best Programmes*, EIU 1992.

2 Choosing the options

Deciding to take an MBA is, as we have seen, primarily a career-building decision. Few people embark on it to pursue knowledge for its own sake; according to Professor David Weir, as with any career decision, it must start with a consideration of one's personal circumstances, lifestyle and values, as well as one's objectives. For instance, the choice between taking a full-time course and a part-time or distance learning option, may depend on whether you can afford to take a year off work. Within these two latter modes, whether you can operate on the basis of distance learning or whether you need the stimulation of fellow students and regular face to face contact with tutors, will depend on the workstyle which best suits you.

However, schools increasingly recognise that students' circumstances may alter during their period of study. There are a number of reasons why this may happen and one change that has occurred since the 9th Edition is that there is now more flexibility about changing, say, from a part-time to a distance learning mode. We will deal with this in more detail later in the chapter.

When it comes to objectives, whether you feel that you would like to continue your career with your present company or intend to look further afield after completing your course may determine your choice between doing an employer-sponsored MBA and doing it on your own. That boils down to a question of weighing up the financial advantages of the former against what would be at least moral strings attached to staying with the organisation that funded your studies. Let us now look at the various modes in more detail and see what they entail.

The Full-time MBA

Originally, most full-time courses were two-year programmes, based on the example of the MBA in the United States. The London Business School, Manchester and a couple of Continental European schools still offer the two-year version or a period of study very close to two years, but 12 months has become the norm in Europe. In fact the INSEAD MBA runs over only 10 months.

The one-year model is based on the length of time it normally takes to do a master's degree in other academic disciplines, but beware of assuming too much from the parallel. Whereas other master's courses will build to a large extent on your first degree, the MBA will involve a lot of skills that are entirely new to you. This is true even in the case of those who start with an advantage because of the nature of their previous qualification and/or experience. An accountant, for instance, will not previously have had much exposure to marketing, management strategy, organisational behaviour, or human resource management, all of which are part of the core programme all students have to go through. Conversely, a young general manager may not previously have had to get to grips with finance or quantitative methods at the level required by the course.

The common pattern of study events for a generalist MBA – irrespective of the mode by which it is taken – is that the first part of the course will consist of a crash programme covering all the basic business skills. This is followed, or in some cases accompanied by, electives which allow students to focus on subjects that particularly interest them – they may, for instance, have some bearing on their future career direction – or where they can bring their expertise best to bear. The final part of the programme is usually a project, carried out within a company – possibly their own employer in the case of a sponsored student. That is, or should be, more than a token gesture towards practicality. Students are given access to people and data. They are then expected to undertake a thorough analysis of the problem and to produce an action plan support by quantified research.

But when all this has to be crammed into a year, it follows that study is very intensive. There is little time to stand back and relate it to your previous experience or to see where it applies to everyday management, and this may have some bearing on the criticisms about the MBA being 'too theoretical'. The schools are well aware of this and combat it in a number of ways. One is to use case studies, simulations and role play in their teaching. Another is to ensure that the various subjects are taught in an integrated way, showing how each topic relates to other disciplines, for instance that a marketing decision will also have financial management implications. Some schools take this as far as teaching through themes – say the management of change – rather than by discipline.

A third way of keeping in touch with the 'real' world is through the project which comes in the final part of the course. In some cases this may involve seconding students to an employer, helping him (we will generally use this personal pronoun in a unisex sense in the Guide, though the proportion of women on MBA courses averages around 18%–20%) to solve a problem or manage a project in a quasi-consultancy role and writing a dissertation based on that experience.

One rapidly growing trend is the development of opportunities to take one or more electives abroad or to undertake projects with a company outside the UK – or, in the case of foreign students, to come to Britain for that purpose. A number of schools offer a direct link with sister bodies on the European continent which are facilitating what is likely to be a growing trend to extend internationalisation of the MBA from the classroom into the delivery of the practical work, thus reflecting the globalisation of business itself.

Because it involves a career break, the full-time MBA is less attractive to managers who are already well-embarked on their careers. That is indicated by the younger average age of full-time MBA: around 25–28. It is also considered by some commentators to be more suitable for those who want to switch career direction and to equip themselves with the conceptual management tools they need to do this; for instance to switch from a functional specialism like engineering to general management or to move from the armed forces into a civilian career.

The disadvantage of such intensive exposure to theory in an academic environment has been well voiced by Sheila Cameron in *The MBA Handbook*.[1] It may be, she writes, 'that if the more difficult techniques are not practised while 'fresh', there will be insufficient impetus ever to make the effort of applying them. By the end of a year's full-time study a students's head may feel completely stuffed with all that has been covered.'

There is, however, one big plus point that is widely reported by students as emerging from the pressure-cooker atmosphere of the full-time MBA. It produces a very good campus atmosphere, based on a spirit of practical teamwork – exactly the direction management is now heading in practice. Students are supportive of each other. 'The group saw to it that nobody fails,' some recent alumni commented at a meeting with the writer. 'For instance, if there is someone in the group who is particularly strong on information technology, he or she takes over the leadership of any project associated with it and brings the group through.'

Though such networking patterns are easier to develop in the full-time mode, they are not unique to it. For instance, even in distance learning, some schools encourage the formation of study groups of students who are geographically close to each other. The view is that networking is not only valuable to organisations as a method in itself, but that it can also lay the foundation of future working relationships along the career track. It is also, of course, one of the fundamental concepts behind the Association of MBAs.

Part-time courses

UK business schools which offer full-time MBAs also run part-time MBA courses. In talking about part-time programmes, one has to distinguish among a number of species and two particular varieties:

- The Executive MBA is essentially a part-time course which might be taught evenings, weekends or via day release attendance at a business school. The term, Executive MBA, is used by some schools merely to denote their part-time course, the implication being that 'executive' is the level of competence required or achieved. Other schools, for instance Bradford, employ the term to denote a company-sponsored MBA programme which is delivered on a part-time basis.
- The Modular MBA could be described as the management equivalent of a block release course. It involves full-time attendance, over extended periods and on numerous occasions, at a business school chosen by the employer. The Modular MBA is therefore usually, though not exclusively, a sponsored form of study.

Modular, in this context is, or should be, written with a capital M to distinguish it from another sense in which the term is used: that of teaching material packaged in such a way that it can be digested in conveniently sized chunks, or modules.

Both these modes of delivering the MBA are structurally similar to the full-time course and identical in the content of the core material. The main differences are firstly that they take longer and secondly that they may offer a smaller range of electives. The usual length is 18 months to two years for a Modular MBA and two to three years for the Executive MBA. Of the two modes, the Executive MBA is by far the most popular.

- Distance or Open Learning. Its most familiar form to the public at large is that of Open University courses and this school's MBA is now the largest of its kind in the UK, though the Henley distance learning MBA is the longest established and has the bigger worldwide enrolment. Distance learning courses can be undertaken by students at their own initiative, but they require enormous application as well as support from employers, at least in terms of keeping the normal workloads of one's everyday job down to manageable proportions. Nonetheless they are proving extremely popular. For instance, according to *The Independent On Sunday*, the distance learning course at Heriot Watt University Business School, started only two years ago, already has 4000 students in 40 countries.

The difference between open and distance learning is somewhat blurred. Some schools say there is none and indeed both Henley and the OU have been known to refer to their distance learning course as 'open learning'. AMBA distinguishes between the two types in saying that open learning courses include at least some elements which call for mandatory attendance by students in person. According to AMBA, distance learning courses do not impose an obligation on students to attend the residential elements, whereas such an obligation does exist in open learning. Peter Calladine of AMBA says that 'open learning' in its full sense could be described as a distance learning/part-time hybrid. However, it is fair to say that in the case of distance learning programmes such as that offered by Henley, there is at least very strong pressure to attend residential courses and face to face meetings with other students and staff where this is at all feasible.

AMBA does not at present accredit distance learning courses, but a change in this policy is under active consideration in the light of the fact that distance learning courses are growing rapidly in popularity, at any rate with overseas students. UK numbers were actually down last year, but a number of schools are successfully marketing their courses in British Commonwealth countries.

Overall, part-time courses are attracting students at a faster rate than the full-time MBA. The part-time MBA falls into a number of sub-categories, each of which have pros and cons from the point of view of career objectives. They tend to be more favoured by employers which may indicate that some of their modes offer greater advantages to the organisation than to the individual. For instance, company-based MBAs, though designed to be extremely relevant to the needs of the sponsor company, have been accused of having limited transferability if you want to switch employers. But let us look at the various categories in more detail.

The Executive MBA

Professor Leo Murray, Director of the Cranfield School of Management, has described this as 'a triangular relationship between the school, the individual and the sponsoring company'. The course responds to the development needs of the individual, but it does so in the light of the skills and competencies required by his or her sponsor. Thus the latter has a good deal of input into the Executive MBA to ensure that corporate needs are taken into account and that the course content reflects what is happening in the 'real' world of business. Generally company representatives are encouraged to visit the school on a regular basis.

One advantage of that triangular relationship is that traffic runs both ways. The process of consulting with the school helps the sponsor to define strategic aims, while keeping the school in constant touch with corporate needs 'outside'. The student is the beneficiary of both aspects.

However, anyone who takes an executive MBA will need to be certain of company support at every level – not just the financial one and not just at the top. Your immediate boss will need to be understanding about your need to take time off for study and will, on occasion, have to distribute your workload to allow for your commitment to the course. Some superiors, particularly those who are sceptical about the value of the MBA or who fear for their own career prospects when you have got your qualification, may be hard to convince.

There may also be practical difficulties about doing a part-time Executive MBA in individual cases. It would not, for instance, be a suitable mode of study for someone whose job involves a lot of travel.

But given that commitment to the concept of the part-time MBA on the part of the organisation exists, the schools are nervous about the possibility that he who pays the piper may wish to call the tune; in other words that academic integrity may be impaired. The fear is that schools which come to be too heavily dependent on direct or indirect sponsorship may be pressed by sponsors either to lower their admission standards, or to make the degree easier to get, or to make the MBA a glorified form of vocational training rather than an intellectually rigorous business qualification. Here again the accreditation criteria set out by AMBA will help in keeping the triangular relationship an isosceles one.

The Consortium MBA

One of the main criticisms of the MBA by employers has been that it is too general and not relevant to their needs and that therefore they are not willing to fund it, directly or indirectly. In the words of a study by the training consultancy Harbridge House,[2] 'Much of what is taught is simply not seen as relevant and companies are reluctant to pay for a manager to take a degree in these circumstances, especially when or she often demands a considerable salary increase on their return.'

Some organisations have tried to set up single in-company MBA programmes instead – we will come to them in a moment – but among the objections to these have been that students do not get the intellectual stimulus from them that comes from mixing with people in other organisations. A compromise solution is therefore offered by many business schools: the so-called Consortium MBA, where a number of organisations club together to fund an MBA that is structured around their needs, though the business school which awards the degree maintains a grip on the academic content.

The organisation is able to assess more directly and immediately the effect of the course content on individual performance, while the interaction between students from a number of different companies does maintain the mix of backgrounds that is regarded as adding value to the academic content of an MBA. Examples of Consortium MBAs are those conducted by Warwick Business School (which calls this programme The

Integrated MBA) involving among others BP, The North-West Thames Water Authority, National Westminster Bank, and British Telecom; and the City University Business School one founded by American Express, The International Stock Exchange, Sainsbury PLC, Lloyds, Tektronics and the City and Hackney Health Authority.

In-company MBAs

The Harbridge Report states that 'the company-specific nature of a programme helps to build interest in the company, as what is learned is applied in the company.' That is even more true of single company, or tailored MBAs. Like the consortium variety, these are run by a business school in conjunction with a sponsor, but they have had a mixed reception. 'Tailored May Not Be Best', was the headline given to a *Times* article on the subject by Marion Devine,[3] which went on to point out some of the drawbacks of the in-company mode. The principal ones are that students do not get much of a view of what happens outside their company and they do not meet colleagues from other companies. That makes the in-company MBA simply harder to transfer to another organisation: good for the sponsors, much less so as an individual career strategy. An in-company MBA from a very large and well-diversified organisation, both internationally and in the range of its activities, would certainly have some value but most of the larger UK business schools have steered away from this mode.

Distance and Open Learning

The Open Business School (the business end of the Open University) and Henley have over 12,000 distance learning MBA students between them. They represent both ends of the spectrum in terms of the length of time for which they have been established: the former is a fairly recent arrival on the scene, while Henley has been the pioneer of running MBA courses by distance learning. Other schools who are recognised as major players in the sphere of the distance learning MBA are Warwick,

Durham, Strathclyde, Aston and Herriot-Watt. A growing number of other business schools are also now offering such MBA courses. According to a recent article in *The Guardian* [4] those graduating via this mode of study will soon account for more than a third of the total UK output of MBAs in the UK.

Gaining an MBA by distance learning normally takes at least three years. The students doing it are often self-funded – though reportedly a high proportion of them are funded wholly or partly by their employers – and they include a considerable number of expatriates. In fact distance learning is particularly suitable for those whose jobs are mobile or who cannot make a commitment to specific periods of study, as in the case of the part-time MBA, or who simply live too far from the nearest business school in the UK. However, some distance learning MBAs assume that you can apply and relate what you are learning within an organisation. That can be a problem for those who do not have a context within which to do this.

The content and, broadly speaking, the structure, of the distance learning MBA is exactly the same as for other modes but the method of delivery is obviously very different. The course will provide you with all the materials you need and a lot of it will have been specially written for the course. The words of Sheila Cameron's MBA Handbook cannot be bettered as a succinct explanation:[5]

Good distance teaching materials look very different from textbooks . . . teaching objectives are made very clear so that the student knows what should be achieved by the end of the part of the course being worked on, material is broken up into 'chunks' which can normally be studied at a single sitting, a study calendar is provided so that the student knows what should be achieved by each point of the course and the material should be as interactive as possible, asking the student at regular intervals to think about what has been read, and apply it to his or her own job context. There should also be regular exercises and self-test questions, with answers provided, so that the student can check understanding of one part of the material before progressing to the next.

This last point goes some way to answering a question which the writer overheard at one of the distance learning exhibits at an MBA Fair. The questioner was very typical of someone interested in this MBA mode: an export manager who spent a good deal of his time abroad. He wanted to find out how, working on his own, he would know that he was really grasping what he had read. The answer is that each student has a personal tutor who can be contacted when required, either about the subject matter itself or about problems such as difficulties in keeping a deadline. That may itself be a problem, however, for students in locations abroad with poor communications.

They may also have a problem with the residential element in the so-called open MBA version, where occasional weekends at which students get together are mandatory. In that case employer sponsorship may be necessary. For instance, the Standard Chartered Bank, which runs a company-based distance learning MBA with Henley, pays for flights from as far away as Australia.

Advances in information technology may well overcome some of the practical difficulties of distance learning. Material, including videos can be transmitted electronically, though costs are very high at present. Developments like video conferencing could cut down on some of the needs for face-to-face interaction.

Whatever the course technology takes, though, it will not overcome the psychological difficulties of distance learning. Though there are conflicting reports of drop-out rates on such courses, there is no doubt that distance learning requires larger doses of self-discipline than courses which call for regular attendances at set times.

It is noticeable that a number of UK schools are actively marketing distance learning in newly industrialised and third world countries, where the prestige of a European or American MBA is likely to be much higher than that of the local product. Bearing in mind the management population of, say, south-east Asia and the appetite for education evident in the bookshops there, this could be a huge growth area.

Transferability

Questions are often asked about the transferability of modes of study, say from part-time to distance learning, or between one management school and another – sometimes in different countries.

In general, there are no problems if you want to transfer between modes in the same school. It is not uncommon, for instance, for someone on a part-time programme to be relocated by their employer to a place from which attendance at once a week evening classes becomes impractical. Distance learning then becomes the only option. Another situation which schools are now encountering is when a student on a part-time or distance learning programme loses their job during the course of it. They may then seek to speed the completion of their degree – and possibly enhance their value in the job market – by switching to the full-time mode, sometimes with financial help from their employer as part of their severance package.

Schools are now very flexible about this, and as we indicated earlier, some foresee that MBA courses might in general adopt different modes of delivery for different parts of the programme and to meet individual circumstances. Bradford, for instance, already has a 'full-time' programme which can be taken at the rate of one term a year over three years.

The difficulty arises when students want to transfer from one school to another – for instance from a part-time MBA at one school to another one that offers a distance learning programme; not all do. In theory the Credit Accumulation Transfer Scheme (CATS) allocates transferable credits for each part of the MBA course and there is indeed a European Credit Transfer Scheme operated by the Erasmus Bureau in Brussels. In practice, the schools do not accept them as admission criteria on their own. They take the view that there are differences, ranging from the subtle to the substantial, in the content and quality of the course material at each school. It is this which decides whether or not a student wishing to transfer between schools will be accepted, though the quality of the work he or she has already done would be taken into account. Therefore, a move between schools requires advance planning and it would be advisable, even at the application stage, to consider the possibility that your circumstances might change over the three years of a part-time course. You cannot assume that because you have completed two terms at School A, School B will accept you for the final part.

This is also true of the transferability of CATS credits gained for other business courses, such as the Diploma in Management Studies, to MBA programmes. In theory, the 70 credits obtained for a DMS could be applied to the 120 which are required for an MBA, but in practice these are widely seen as two quite different fields of study. However, at least one business school, Durham, offers the possibility of a transfer from the first year of its Diploma in Business Administration to its MBA course. This is because the first year DBA programme is identical to Stage 1 of the Durham MBA. Henley takes a similar view of the DMS; in some circumstances it is prepared to count it as equivalent to the first stage of its distance learning MBA.

Notes

1. op. cit
2. *The Company-Based MBA, A study of In-Company and Consortium-Based MBA Programmes in Great Britain*, R W Baston, Harbridge Consulting Group Ltd. 1989
3. The Times, 5.92
4. 'Companies warm to distance learning graduates', 15.2.93
5. op. cit

3 Choosing a school

One of the questions the Association of MBAs is most frequently asked is: which are the best schools? There are also variants of this: 'I have been offered a place at X, Y and Z, which is the one you would recommend?' Or: 'I am thinking of applying to B – is it any good?' Such questions reflect the growing importance of the provenance of one's MBA, but there are good reasons why it is difficult to give a meaningful answer to them.

The situation is more straightforward in the USA where ranking lists of the top 10 or top 20 business schools are published from time to time in magazines like *Business Week* or *Fortune*. The most recent *Business Week* survey – it comes out every two years – was produced in October 1992:

Why is there no similar ranking for Europe, or at any rate none that has achieved any degree of acceptance? One reason is that the US experience

TOP UNITED STATES SCHOOLS

Business Week produces a ranking of US Business Schools every two years. The ranking below was published on 26 October 1992.

Rank	University	Name of School	Location
1	Northwestern	(Kellogg)	Evanston, Illinois
2	Chicago		Chicago
3	Harvard		Boston
4	Pennsylvania	(Wharton)	Philadelphia
5	Michigan		Ann Arbour
6	Dartmouth	(Amos Tuck)	Hanover, N.H.
7	Stanford		Stanford, California
8	Indiana		Bloomington
9	Columbia		New York
10	North Carolina		Chapel Hill
11	Virginia	(Darden)	Charlotesville
12	Duke	(Fuqua)	Durham, N.C.
13	MIT	(Sloan)	Cambridge, Mass
14	Cornell	(Johnson)	Ithaca, N.Y.
15	NYU	(Stern)	New York
16	UCLA	(Anderson)	Los Angeles
17	Carnegie Mellon		Pittsburgh
18	California	(Haas)	Berkeley
19	Vanderbilt	(Owen)	Nashville
20	Washington	(Olin)	St Louis

has been that since there is a commercial value in being a ranked school – they get both more applications from students and more consultancy assignments for the faculty – vigorous lobbying by PR firms can have an undue influence. The other is that, as with restaurants, the quality of whose cooking depends on who is in the kitchen, the quality of a business school is related heavily to who is on the staff. The loss – or gain – of one or two key professors can change the standing of a whole institution. It can certainly have a considerable impact on your choice if they are working in the fields in which you are most interested.

The other factor is that judgements about business schools are not only subjective from the point of view of the person making the report, but also from that of the prospective student. The question is not: how good is the school. It is: how good is it in the light of your career development needs, work situation, personal circumstances and preferred learning styles.

Looking at choice from that point of view there may, for some people, even be a case for considering a non-AMBA accredited school, provided that they meet some of the broad criteria set out in this section. A self-funded person who wanted to enhance their general management skills – perhaps in order to run their own small business more effectively – who had rejected the distance learning mode and who did not live near an accredited school, might well consider a local, unaccredited one. It might not carry much weight in the job market, but if that was not your object, it would undoubtedly help you to be a more effective manager. In such cases, incidentally, it would be important to look at the electives as well as the core programme. Do they correspond to your needs and are they offered by faculty members with a credible track record in that field?

The question of what you, personally, hope to get out of it also casts some light on another aspect of choice about which AMBA is often asked. What are the relative merits of going to a business school in the USA or in Continental Europe, as compared to the UK? There is no absolute answer to such questions, except to say that going to a US school would have an obvious value if you were planning to work in the USA or with an American company.

However, an increasing number of commentators are asking for how much longer, in a world of global trading and IT-based techniques and corporate strategies, we can really think about business education in national terms. On both sides of the Channel, and to some extent the Atlantic as well, an increasing number of schools are establishing a variety of links with their counterparts in other countries. Manchester Business School, whose MBA is one of the longest established in the UK, also claims to have the most extensive network of contacts abroad.

Such relationships are becoming increasingly formalised. The European Network Of Business Schools, set up in October 1991, between Strathclyde, The University of Bayreuth, Groupe ESC Atlantique and the Universidad Commercial de Deusto in Bilbao is an example which may herald the shape of things to come. Participants do one term each in Spain, France and the UK, taking courses in the language of the country and doing projects with local firms. Just how international this can get is illustrated by the example of a Norwegian-born graduate of the European Network. During his term at Strathclyde, he undertook a project relating to activities in Scotland for the Brussels office of Hertz, the American car rental firm!

Other schools are going down the collaborative road with varying degrees of directness. One major problem is the difference between the structure of education in different countries, so that, for instance, it takes very much longer to gain a first degree in Germany than it does in Britain.

However some very close relationships with European partners are already in existence, which in the case of Bradford goes as far as offering a Bradford MBA through a Dutch partner, the Netherlands Institute for MBA Studies. Another variant is the double French and British MBA offered by Cranfield and Groupe ESC Lyon. A more common route, however, is that of completing the core programme at home, after which participants can spend one or even two terms of their course as exchange students in another country, mostly within the EC, though.

London Business School's exchange network, to take another instance, covers the USA, Latin America, the Far East, and Australasia, as well as a number of countries on the European Continent.

It is very likely that various forms of the 'multi-centre MBA' will expand among all European business schools. Part of that process can take the form of a company attachment or work on a project with a local company. One of its main attractions from a career point of view is that it gives students access to the job market in more than one country. There can, however, be other good reasons for doing an MBA abroad. Asked why she took her MBA in France, one recent graduate said she thought it would be more fun and also a good way of improving her French.

Some objective criteria

Nevertheless, having taken subjective factors into account, there are some objective criteria which can also be applied. Some are those used by AMBA in its accreditation policy, which we have mentioned in the preface. These criteria are roughly similar to those laid down in the USA by the American Assembly of Collegiate Schools of Business (AACSB) which puts forward standards for the academic qualifications of the faculty and the range and quality of the programmes. In the end though, it is a question of applying one's own set of comparisons. The Economist Intelligence Unit Report, *Which MBA?*,[1] suggests that one should look at the following factors:

Size and culture
Programme content
Quality both of faculty and the student body
Facilities
Location
Internationalism
Published surveys and rankings

One should add to that list:

Administrative efficiency (particularly in the case of distance learning courses)
Success/failure rates

Career placement record
The alumni network
Fees
The selectiveness of its entrance requirements
Nature and quality of the school's research activities
Reputation – the status of a particular school's MBA among employers and recruitment intermediaries

Let us now focus on some of these factors in more detail.

Campus size and culture

The importance of the 'fit' between your own values and the culture of the organisation has received growing attention in career literature. It is equally crucial in the case of choosing where to study for your MBA – particularly in the case of the full-time and part-time modes.

In the first place it is essential to visit the place and talk to students and the faculty. Do you actually like the people there? Are you in tune with the way they talk, dress and behave? What can they tell you about the teaching style? Some places are competitive and confrontational, others have more of a collegiate culture. A good question to ask any students with whom you feel a rapport is whether, given the chance, they would choose that particular school again, knowing what they now know about it. Many would say that an informal visit is advisable even where a school also holds formal off-site receptions, as many do.

From the point of view of personality and temperament, it would be a great mistake to think that a business school is just a place where you learn a set of functional skills and mind your own business the rest of the time. Group and project work is a key part of the course, so interpersonal relationships are important. Admittedly you cannot forecast the configuration of your cohort of students from the current one, but the percentage mix of ages, genders, nationalities, business experience and educational qualifications in the current cohort will give you a fair idea of the nature of the student population and the school's admission policy. This can be compared with research produced by AMBA on the 'Areas of Major Qualification Before Business School':[2]

The size of the cohort is also important. The CNAA does not think that it is possible to run a proper course with less than 30 students, but how big is the maximum? Most full-time and part-time MBAs seem to have about 100–150 students in each year, though some of the big US schools have cohorts running into several hundreds. The key question though, irrespective of whether courses are part-time or full-time – or even in relation to the residential element in distance learning courses – is how big the working groups are in seminars and study groups. Numbers running into double figures become increasingly hard to manage effectively and may suggest an inadequate staff:student ratio.

So do over-large classes. The general opinion is that they should be no bigger than 30–50. Schools with larger cohorts than this solve the problem by breaking them up into streams, so these have nothing to do with ability, as in the school system.

Programme content

Though they may attach different terms to the concepts involved, MBA programmes consist of a core programme of basic business skills, which take up on average one-third of the course. They are followed by electives from which you can make your own choice, though in some schools certain mandatory subjects run on into the elective phase. In the final part there is a project on which you will be asked to prepare a report. Together they form the 'credits' which are the building blocks of the course. The CNAA report[3] examined 74 programmes and found the great majority contained the following compulsory core courses:

Accounting and finance
Quantitative analysis
Information systems
Business policy
Marketing
Operations
Human resource management
Organisational behaviour
Economics

Though what is taught may be coloured by the tendency of a school to build up a reputation in a particular functional discipline or in relation to a particular sector of business activity these topics are not, or at any rate should not be, taught as separate subjects. Business schools have been accused by their critics of breaking up management topics as if they were distinct academic disciplines. Many professors will admit privately that this may have been the tendency at

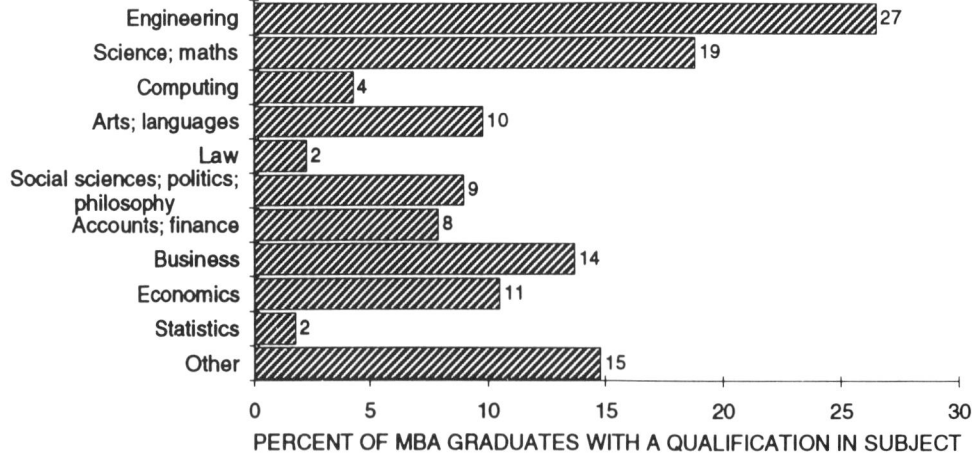

AREAS OF MAJOR QUALIFICATION BEFORE BUSINESS SCHOOL

PERCENT OF MBA GRADUATES WITH A QUALIFICATION IN SUBJECT

Some respondents had major qualifications in more than one subject (Numerate readers might otherwise be puzzled by the fact that the percentage addes up to 121%!)

one time, but the emphasis nowadays is very much on integration; looking at the implications of decisions in one sphere of the business for its other components. As we stated earlier, some schools are considering the idea of teaching core themes (e.g., the management of change), rather than individual disciplines.

The electives can cover an enormous range of subjects, though students should check that these relate to those they are interested in. Some schools have been accused of offering electives that reflect the research interests of their faculty, rather than what students want.

Given the number of schools and the variety of methods of delivery of the MBA, it is of course impossible to lay down any platonically ideal structure for the course. In particular, there are differences in the way the one- and two-year MBA is structured. There are also differences in the way part-time courses are delivered. Some schools have a dedicated part-time path. In others, part-timers simply attend the full-time programme, but over a longer period.

Distance learning MBAs have a similar structure, but here it is important to look at the way the content is delivered. How much of the course material is specially written? How often is it revised and is feedback from the students taken into account when this happens? How good is it? And where non-dedicated texts are used, how much guidance do you get in the way of study notes? How frequent are the residential courses? How many students are assigned to each tutor? What is the turnaround time when you send in completed assignments to tutors? How much critical guidance do you get from them and how good is it? These are basic questions the answer to which may depend, above all, on how much experience the school has had in the field of distance learning.

The faculty

A criticism that is sometimes made of some of the top US schools is that the star teachers and/or management gurus who are billed as one of the attractions of the place may seldom be seen by students; or when they are, it is as small figures on the podium of a large lecture theatre which also contains numbers of students from other faculties who want to hear what the guru has to say.

This is less true of the UK. What you see is what you get, and though you will find that most of the faculty have consultancy or research assignments, they generally do their fair share of classroom teaching and project work. In fact the usefulness and relevance of teaching is generally considered to be in close correlation to the amount of consultancy undertaken by the teacher. Not only is it a sign that he or she is taken seriously by the business community, it is also ensures that they keep in touch with the real world. Another advantage is that when part of their consultancy is in the field of management development and training, their material is likely to be both high quality and up to date. Business school students benefit from the real life feedback of private courses and consultancy; increasingly, too, from the depth of faculty members' international experience.

However, if you have gone to a school with the express purpose of sitting at the feet of a particular guru, it is as well to check that he or she is more than a name on the faculty list. Again, current students will be a valuable source of information on this, as well as on whether the guru in question is as good as you hope they will be. Notoriously some great thinkers are very poor communicators.

It is also important to check that the teaching staff are 'dedicated' to the business school; not in any psychological sense, but in that of being attached to the school itself, not to another faculty. This is a particular drawback of small, newly established business schools. They are apt to draw part or at least some of their teachers from other faculties within the institution of which they are a part. Some MBA students in this situation would say there is nothing less useful to a manager than being taught economics by someone from the economics faculty, rather than the business school!

The student body

The average age of students is reported by business schools to be between 28–35 and to be lower in full-time courses than in part-time and distance learning modes.[4] Generally students will have had at least three years of work experience. Indeed some schools specify this as an admission criterion, though others will accept a professional qualification and a few take people straight from a first degree. However, Professor Carnall, writing in his book *MBA Futures*,[5] expresses a widely held view in saying that 'real work and managerial experience are a vital 'resource' the member brings to the course'. Without them he lacks credibility with other members and he may not be able to derive full benefit from the interchange of ideas with other participants which is said to be almost as important a part of doing an MBA as its formal elements. Other criteria to apply to the student body are their career histories, their functional disciplines, their industry sectors and their nationality. Many schools publish an annual book of profiles of their students which contains such information. Though mainly intended as a marketing tool to send out to recruiters and potential employers, it would also give someone considering an application to a particular school a good idea of the kind of students it attracts.

Facilities and location

Location is said to be one of the key elements in the success of an enterprise. Big city business schools like London, Manchester or Strathclyde do benefit from being in a metropolitan area, but this has more to do with their physical proximity to contacts in business and industry than to the bright lights.

The fact is that the intensity of the MBA course means that students have very little opportunity to sample these. Indeed some would say that schools that are not particularly conveniently situated, like INSEAD or Cranfield, are good places to focus on one's studies; real-life examples of Michael Porter's theory of competitive advantage arising out of what can appear to be unfavourable environments. But for full-time residential students what is then important is that suitable accommodation is available at a reasonable cost, reasonably close to the campus; and that the school can facilitate finding this. For part-time students, though, convenience and proximity to

their workplace is important.

As far as facilities are concerned, you should look at the range of literature in the library and whether it can access the databases you are most likely to be interested in. The size and condition of lecture theatres and seminar rooms, the convenience and general state of care and maintenance of public areas – what might loosely be described as the general look of the place – are all signs of the morale and well-being of the school.

Internationalisation

Internationalisation is one of the buzz words of management education in the nineties and rightly so. But what does it mean in practice? Some schools take it to mean having an international student body and a faculty drawn from the nationals of many countries. The prime example of this view is INSEAD, where study groups are intentionally made up of students from many different countries. Critics say that overcoming the language and cultural barriers inherent in this approach slows down the process of learning the core skills it is meant to impart.

Most UK and continental schools now do include foreign students, but the general view is that internationalism is best transmitted through exchanges with schools in other countries and the multi-centred MBA referred to previously. The other valuable clue to how seriously a school takes internationalism is in its approach to foreign languages. Some places offer an MBA closely tied to a foreign language, such as Manchester's MBA with a diploma in Japanese or Bradford's mandatory foreign language in the core programme. In general, one has to echo the words of the CNAA Report: 'Learning a new (or half-forgotten) language as an adult is difficult, but any school serious about becoming more international should at least make the opportunity available to staff and students.'

Published surveys and rankings

Rankings and surveys are less prevalent in Europe than in the USA and have generally been attended by fierce controversy when they have appeared. What, to take just one difficulty, is being measured: teaching or research?

Since career development emerges as the main reason for taking an MBA, the most useful rankings may be unofficial: how the school is perceived by employers and headhunters in the sector which is most relevant to you. Barry Tuckwood, a Strathclyde MBA, suggests that a good test of a school is whether blue chip or significant public sector organisations encourage staff to take a course there. Another measure of quality is the criteria for admission. The best known schools also require the highest GMAT scores.

Administrative efficiency

Administrative efficiency matters most in distance learning. How quickly material is sent to you, relative to the schedules that have been laid down is important, as is the turn-round speed by tutors of the work you send in and whether residential courses are properly structured and organised.

In full-time and part-time courses, efficient scheduling of classes is important – and by no means easy when you may have several streams going through the same year. Students at one school said that the staff at times rationalised what looked to them like inept scheduling by saying it was part of the pressure MBAs had to learn to take!

Another important test of efficiency arises in project work. It is not always easy to get businesses to take on an MBA student for this purpose. Efficiently run schools have proper procedures for doing this. For others it is more of a scramble. The usefulness of the exercise will be very limited if the employer concerned is reluctant or unsuitable.

But how do you know whether a school is efficiently run or not? As we said earlier, the look of the place is often significant. Professor Carnell of Henley Management College suggests another measure: how promptly the school replies to your initial enquiry.

Success/failure rate

Business schools all say that their failure rate is very low. That is because the pre-selection process seems to be highly effective. Though the Graduate Management Admission Test (GMAT) or its equivalents are not the only criteria used for admission, if you achieve the score demanded by the school of your choice, it means that in theory you can cope with its MBA course. We will deal in more detail with GMAT in the next chapter.

Business school faculty maintain that the very small percentage of students that fail do so because they have, for one reason or another, lost the motivation to put in the work the course requires. When this happens, it is often the policy of the school to persuade the student to discontinue the course: that way no stigma attaches when they apply for jobs, since a decision to break off one's studies can be ascribed to any number of reasons. However, procedures on this point are worth checking on, if you feel you might be a marginal case. So are the criteria of what constitutes failure. Some schools will award the degree on overall performance, even though you have not passed in every subject. In other cases there may be a consolation prize; at least one school offers a Diploma in Business Studies to those who have successfully completed significant parts of its MBA programme.

First degree graduates should note that success is measured differently from first degree processes: there are no firsts, seconds or thirds, though some schools end up with much the same effect by placing MBAs in 'quartiles' on completion of the course. There may also be special recognition for outstanding performance, such as the London Business School's award of distinctions to the best students. In some other schools outside sponsors award prizes, usually for the best performance in some subject in which the sponsor has a particular interest.

Job placement record

Sponsored students generally go back to their organisation – at least for a while, but schools are becoming conscious of the importance of helping those who have financed their own studies to get back into employment. Some form of career management service should be in place, not only advising students on career opportunities, but also proactively marketing its graduates to business and industry. That has become increasingly important as the demand for MBAs from such previously reliable sectors as management consultancy and financial services has come under pressure with the recession.

You should know whether the career management service, or placement service as it may also be called, provides individual counselling on career possibilities, and on job search mechanics such as CV preparation and interview techniques. It should also have active and systematic contacts with recruiters, headhunters and influential alumni. But the old boy network, powerful though it can be, is not really enough these days. It has to be backed up by a database through which prospective employers can search for MBAs with specific skills. In many cases this is provided as hard copy in the form of a book of profiles of the current cohort (worth looking at, incidentally, by prospective students, because it gives a very good overall picture of the sort of people they are likely to be meeting). There also has to be a proper programme for presentations by key companies and appropriate interview facilities.

In the end, though, the proof of the pudding is how a school is viewed by potential employers. As we have stated earlier, there are no established rankings of UK business schools, though as Professor Carnall writes in *MBA Futures*,[6] 'people in the know perceive certain institutions as being of high status.' That status is the informal product of such factors as track record, the subsequent business performance of their graduates, the reputation of individual faculty members, relevance of their course content, how much press coverage they get, the strength and level of their links with business and industry, the quality of their research and for what clients it is being undertaken. A recent article in *The Guardian* also offers the sensible advice that it is worth checking which companies maintain active sponsorship programmes at any school you may be considering.

Research

A ranking of business schools in terms of their status as research centres has been issued by the Universities Funding Committee (UFC): see Part 2 pages 175–6, for a list which, it should be noted, includes almost all the UK MBA Schools, including many not currently accredited by AMBA.

Research is sometimes thought of as an abstract, academic activity, but in the context of business schools, largely dependent on client funding, it generally has to have practical applications and often very direct ones. The value of such research is then that it feeds back into teaching programmes and learning activities.

Fees

Information on fees is readily available from the schools, but a simple rule of thumb is that the best-known ones also charge the most. But take into account that fees, though more than the tip of the iceberg, are not the whole of it. In the case of full-time courses, accommodation and subsistence may cost as much as the fees themselves. Opportunity costs in lost earnings for full-timers, or being handicapped in the short career term by study requirements for part-timers and distance learners are also a factor. Then there are textbooks to consider and you may also be required to have a PC where this is not included in the tuition costs. According to a recent article in the *Times Higher Education Supplement*: 'The real cost of studying for a two-year MBA can be almost £70,000 or £40,000 for a one-year programme.'[7] But it seems that few people seriously interested in doing an MBA are put off by the cost factor.

Notes

1. op. cit
2. *The MBA Experience*, AMBA 1992
3. op. cit
4. It should be noted that this an *average*. Most cohorts have a sprinkling of forty pluses and even the occasional fifty plus
5. Carnell, C. *MBA Futures*, Macmillan 1992
6. ibid
7. 'Quality Assurances', *THES*, 11.9.92

4 Getting in

The best shows in town are always the hardest to get into, and so it is with MBA courses. All of them receive more applications than they can admit students, though the ratio between applications and admissions is not necessarily a decisive measure of how good the school is. A great many applications are rejected because they do not meet the basic criteria: generally a first degree or its equivalent, plus at least two years' work experience, or, in the absence of academic qualifications and in some fairly rare cases, at least five years' work experience at a significant level of achievement. The best schools – or at any rate the ones that rate highest in published rankings[1] or on the unofficial grapevine among leading employers and recruiters – tend to be the ones that have the toughest admission standards for those who are, prima facie, eligible. The ratio between those who meet admission criteria and those who are actually admitted therefore provides the clue to how choosy a school can afford to be.

Making your application

Irrespective of which school you are applying to and which mode of study you have decided on, there is one golden rule about applications: apply early. Application forms generally show a deadline. If the academic year begins, as in the case of full-time courses it generally does, in September/October,[2] the deadline is in April/May, but unofficially the advice is to apply at the beginning of the calendar year for the academic year in which you would like to start your course. In the case of part-time or distance learning programmes, which often begin in January, you should apply at least six months ahead.

That gives you a number of advantages. Firstly schools tend to fill up places on a first-come, first-served basis among those whose applications are accepted. Secondly scholarships, a list of which is given in the next chapter, are also allocated in this way. All other things being equal, the early bird gets the grant. Finally, since most schools operate a moving process of admission – applications are dealt with there and then, rather than procesessed after deadline day – if you are turned down by your first choice, you still have time to apply to other schools.

It is important to understand here that at postgraduate level there is no common applications procedure as there is for first degree courses through the Universities Central Council for Admissions (UCCA). You have to make the application yourself, direct to the school in question.

That raises the question of whether you should make multiple applications. Anecdotal evidence suggests that three is about the maximum. The 1992 EIU survey recommended that 'the wise applicant never restricts him or herself to applying to only one school', and this remains true despite the fact that there has been a drop in applications because of the recession. However, an increasing number of schools now charge an application fee of £25–£40, partly to discourage the 'just looking' brigade and partly to defray the costs of what, for most schools, is a selection process which is at least as sophisticated as that used in job applications. But it also seems to be the case that MBA students are in the main a very focused lot, who form a clear idea of what they want from a school, and who do a lot of homework on what is on offer before they send in their application.

That may range from a systematic evaluation of the criteria set out in the previous chapter to a gut feeling about the school and its culture. Thus a young UK doctor who chose the INSEAD MBA looked first at a number of blue chip American schools before deciding that INSEAD provided the most interesting and compatible mix of students. His initial intention had been to apply to Harvard, but he was deterred by its buttoned-down collar, Wall Street-related image. As we said in the previous chapter, compatibility between your own values and the culture of the school is as important as the hard facts of fees, course content, location, student:faculty ratio and so forth.

Incidentally, the example quoted above makes another point about admission policy – your experience does not have to have been in business for you to be considered for a place. On the contrary, schools rather like applicants with unusual backgrounds – provided they can demonstrate that they can both benefit from the course and bring an unusual and interesting perspective to it.

Application forms

One commentator has described the admission procedures to business schools as a two-way beauty contest: the school is as keen to find out about you as you are about it. One of its main instruments in the judging process is the application form. This is a very searching document – rather more so than most job application forms. Here are some of the things the school will want to know about you in addition to the usual personal details:

- details of current job, its level of responsibility and salary
- similar details of previous jobs
- subjects taken in secondary and higher education courses and results achieved in them – some schools, notably in the USA, may ask for certified copies of degrees, diplomas etc.
- non-curricular/extra professional activities and the role you took in them (e.g., as club treasurer, or whatever)

- international experience, either in a private or job-related context
- your financial resources – how your studies would be funded
- knowledge of languages – applicants to UK, US and many Continental schools whose first language is not English will have to show their score, either in the British Council's English Language Testing Service (ELTS) or in its USA equivalent: The Test of English Language As A Foreign Language
- Graduate Management Admission (GMAT) score

Some schools do not use GMAT as an admission criterion, but have devised tests of their own which are taken if the application proceeds. But these tests cover very similar areas of numeracy, literacy and verbal and numerical reasoning as GMAT.

The score on GMAT, or its equivalent, is generally seen as the cornerstone of your application – you will not be considered unless you achieve the score the school has set as its admission criterion – and we will deal with this in more detail shortly. But they stress that they are not interested in number crunchers and logic machines – in fact it is quite possible to achieve a high GMAT score and not be accepted, though by contrast a good GMAT score can offset a more modest academic record.

Schools are also interested in 'softer' attributes of motivation, character and personality. One school asks the following questions, which are fairly typical of what you might expect to find on an application form:

- what are the main factors which you believe account for your academic and professional development to date?
- what do you feel are your major strengths and weaknesses?
   Please provide examples to illustrate this.
- what do you feel you would contribute to the MBA at this school?

Some schools ask for such information in essay form. This also tests your ability to analyse your personal characteristics and actions and draw coherent conclusions from them in terms of your career aims. Some schools for instance, ask you to describe not only your main achievements – and why you regard them as such – but also to write about situations where you felt you failed to achieve your objectives. It asks you not only to consider how the MBA course would develop you as a manager, but what alternative means of pursuing your personal and professional goals you have seriously contemplated. American schools may ask questions which probe your views on business ethics. A major British school leaves a whole page in which it asks you to 'add any other information which you believe may influence our decision on your application.'

How honest should you be in giving your replies to application form questions? A number of books on how to handle job applications have given hints on what are allegedly favoured answers to questions about personal attributes; for instance, they recommend that you should say that your greatest weakness is to drive yourself too hard, or to expect the same high standards from others as you set yourself. Admissions administrators are, however, a pretty sophisticated and creep-resistant bunch. They can readily spot applications from those who are labouring to create the right impression, or those whose answers are inconsistent with other aspects of their application.

People who advise on job application procedures suggest that it is a good idea to make a photocopy of the document first and to draft your answers on that. These forms are very similar to business school admissions applications and the same advice applies to these. You may have second thoughts about some point or other, or find that you cannot fit the information you want to give into the available space – a problem that often arises if you type your reply, as some forms specify. (Look out, however, for those that specifically ask for your replies to be handwritten, a sign of graphologists at work.) An untidy document, or one thick with eraser fluid, creates a bad impression right away. 'Your application is an important part of the total package you present,' warns one writer. He goes on to add that attention to detail is very important. Before you send your completed form off, check that you have answered all the questions; and keep a copy – you may need to refer to it if you are called for an interview.

Another writer, John Byrne, who is responsible for one of the main ranking lists of US schools, advises particular care over essay questions. He suggests that applicants should look at the school's brochure to see what qualities it seems to emphasise and to orient their essay answers towards them. Thus, if a school places obvious value on internationalisation, you should focus either on your international experience or your desire to acquire it.

Indeed the general opinion of commentators on the admissions process is that evidence of an intelligent awareness of the way an MBA could add value to your present job and your future career as a manager is one of the points that admissions administrators look for. They also look for evidence of what you have done about self-development so far. The MBA course calls for a very high level of commitment and sheer hard work, so anything you can bring in to show that you are prepared to do more than your job in the personal pursuit of excellence is favourably noted.

References

As with job applications, business schools do not go on your version of your career and record alone. References are a very important part of the process and some schools call for specific information from referees. Usually they will ask for two sets of references, one from an academic source concerning your intellectual ability and at least one other focusing on your performance at work.

The latter can be a problem if you are intending to leave your job to do the course on your own. If that is the case, you should explain the circumstances to the admissions administrator, who may well be prepared to make your acceptance subject to receiving a satisfactory employer's reference, rather than requiring it in advance.

Some reference forms specify what information they want. Others leave it more open, though in the latter case what the admissions office is

looking for will be similar to the information sought in the former. (Bear in mind that we are using 'he' in its unisex sense!)

- how long the referee has known you and in what capacity
- how he rates your intellectual ability in areas such as analytical and communication skills, often in a range of 1 to 5 between poor and excellent
- how he rates your competence in the job you are now doing or in the job areas in which he has known you
- how he rates your personal attributes such as social skills, perseverance and emotional maturity
- what he considers to be your principal strengths and weaknesses
- how good your written and spoken English is, if this is not your first language. In the case of a non-English school, this question would apply to your ability in the language of the country concerned
- whether and how he thinks you will benefit from an MBA.

If these questions are not asked in the form provided for referees, it would be a good idea to brief the people you have nominated that the above is the kind of information the school will want to have. Character references as such are of little use, nor are vague statements about performance, even if they are complimentary. As far as possible they should be backed by facts. That makes giving a reference a modestly time-consuming experience for the referee. You should warn the people you are intending to nominate that you are going to do so – and make sure that they will return the reference form quickly.

The Graduate Management Admissions Test (GMAT)

The geometrical proof of Pythagoras's Theorem used to be called the 'pons asinorum' by schoolmasters of an older generation: the bridge of asses, or rather the bridge which asses fail to cross.

The role of GMAT is somewhat similar. Failing to achieve a respectable GMAT score does not make you an ass, but it does cast considerable doubt on your ability to complete an MBA. It does not, however, test specific subject areas which would be related to the actual contents of the course. Rather, it is a test of verbal and quantitative skills which, in the words of the GMAT Bulletin of Information, 'are associated with success in the first year of study at a graduate school of management.'

The mention of a 'first year' of study assumes a two-year course which is the usual length of the MBA in the USA and indeed GMAT is a US-based test, sponsored by an American body, The Graduate Management Admissions Council. It is administered by:

Educational Testing Service
PO Box 6103
Princeton NJ 08541–6103, USA

GMAT is used as an entry requirement by all but one US business school and has spread its net throughout the world. Even schools who have an admission test of their own will exempt applicants from it if they have taken GMAT and achieved a good score. Schools who do use GMAT will generally send you its current Bulletin of Information with your admissions pack. Otherwise, and if you intend to study in the USA, you can obtain a GMAT Bulletin by sending an A4 self-addressed envelope, stamped for 80 grams, to your nearest Fulbright Commission. The UK address is:

Educational Advisory Service
Fulbright Commission
62 Doughty Street
London WC1N 2LS
Tel 071 404 6880 Fax 071 404 6834

If you intend to study outside the USA, you can get a copy of the GMAT Bulletin by contacting the MBA and GMAT Advice Centre – see address later in this chapter.

The fee for doing the test is payable in US$ ($49 at present) but the test itself can be taken at various centres throughout the world at simultaneous dates in January, March, June and

October of each year. GMAT will advise you of the various UK locations and you can nominate which one you prefer. In view of the advice given about the importance of making early applications for entrance to business schools, it is obviously important to take GMAT well in advance of your application. Registration forms should be returned to the USA at least six weeks before the test date you have chosen – the absolute deadline for receipt of registration forms in the US is 43 days prior to the test date.

Sitting GMAT

The GMAT Bulletin includes a lot of detailed, useful information on the Test which lasts three and a half hours and measures the ability to read, understand and reason logically in both verbal and quantitative terms. It is divided up into sections, each of which contains 20–25 questions, to be taken in 30 minute units.

Since reasoning and analytical ability are the skills which are mainly being tested in both the quantitative and verbal elements of GMAT, each question needs careful thought. The sheer time pressure is therefore considerable, but the writers of the Bulletin say that accuracy is more important than speed. They advise that you should first tackle the questions you think you can answer and come back to the others when you have done so. Some people have suggested that the questions are ranked in order of difficulty, but this is denied by GMAT. They maintain that the later ones only seem more difficult because you get more tired as you go along.

The questions are multiple choice, which might be a temptation to guess answers if you do not understand or know enough about the question. This is a bad idea, because one quarter of the wrong answers are deducted from your score, whereas questions that are omitted are merely scored with a zero. When the test is marked, a separate score is attached to your numerical and your verbal skills, though a total score is also given out of a possible maximum of 800. A very small number of people do reach that, but anything over 700 is considered as excellent.

The results are sent to you and whoever else

you nominate, such as the school to which you are applying, within about six weeks. The more demanding ones look for a score of 580–650. The average of students at London Business School is reported to be 620. In percentage terms a score of 600 is equivalent to around 67%, which puts you in the top 15–20% of those taking the test.

500 is generally regarded as the absolute minimum you need to get to be able to tackle the course with any confidence. All schools would echo the words of Cranfield's Professor Colin New: 'We try not to pick people who may fail.' He says that he seldom considers applicants with scores much below 580. He adds that as well as looking at the total score, schools take into account the balance between numerical and verbal results. There should be a reasonable balance between them, though by all accounts if there is a bias, it would preferably be slanted towards the numerical end. You do not have to have A level maths to succeed in the GMAT – and by extension in the MBA programme – but an arts graduate with weak O level maths would undoubtedly struggle to get through the course.

Someone whose written and spoken English was poor would also have a problem in a school where English was the main medium of instruction. Those who are in this position would probably be required to take a preliminary proficiency test – usually the Test of English As A Foreign Language, also administered by the Educational Testing Service, whose address has been given above.

Preparation for GMAT

There are a number of ways in which you can get yourself in shape to take GMAT and to get a foretaste of the kind of questions you will encounter. This is advisable, even if you are thoroughly confident of your reasoning skills, because quite a lot of question material is taken from US reports and publications, the terminology of which you need to get used to. It is a bit like the driving test where, even if you think you can drive, it is advisable to take some lessons from a qualified instructor who knows what the examiner will be looking for.

It is not generally considered a good idea to take the test itself as a dress rehearsal, because when you make your application for admission to a business school, the three most recent previous GMAT results are reported along with your present score. According to the GMAT Bulletin, if your scores vary between the tests you have taken: 'Management schools are advised that . . . the average of an individual scores is probably the best estimate of his or her ability.'

Taking the test itself also does not give you enough feedback on what you need to do to improve your answering techniques or your weaker areas. There are a number of books and courses that can help you in this respect, often advertised in *The Economist*. Such sources include:

The MBA & GMAT	**GTAC Associates**
Advice Centre	**55 Gunnersbury Avenue**
PasTest	**London W5 4LP**
Rankin House	Tel 081 993 3983
Parkgate Estate	
Knutsford	
Cheshire WA16 8DX	
Tel 0565 755226	
Fax 0565 650264	

The most widely used book is the *Official Guide For GMAT Review*, produced by Educational Testing Services itself. This is available in the UK from PasTest. PasTest also publishes its own book, called the *GMAT Practice Examinations*, which reflect the content, difficulty and style of the official tests. Answers with explanations are provided, as well as a free marking service where the completed answers sheets are marked and the results returned to the sender, with feedback on areas of weakness and guidance on how to improve. PasTest also runs one-day courses on GMAT techniques. GTAC Associates conduct longer ones on the same theme.

Other admission criteria

A good GMAT score proves you can do the work. Language tests, where these apply, show you can understand what is going on in lectures and seminars. But these are not the only criteria which schools use in their admission procedures. Work experience and personality are equally important, because the teaching methods the schools use put considerable emphasis on student learning from each other, most notably in group work. Presented with a significant record of academic and work achievement schools will, within reason, accept that a GMAT score below their normal expectations reflects the fact that you may have had an off-day.

In that case they would probably call you for an interview, but that is not as universal a condition of acceptance as it is for a job. As with jobs, interviews for business school places are built around your application form, so it is a good idea to study what you have said in that before you go along; as we said earlier – make a copy before you send off your application.

Normally, as we have stated earlier, you need to make your application well in advance of the deadline and to line up all your preliminaries, like taking GMAT and contacting referees, with that in mind. But if you are turned down because you are slightly too late there is always a chance of last-minute admission if someone who had been promised a place drops out because they have changed their mind or because they have applied to several schools and had an offer elsewhere which they would prefer to take up. If you are in either position, do let the school know. Confirm your acceptance to the school of your choice if you have had more than one offer and let the others know that you are not coming.

Notes

1. European schools are sometimes ranked in business magazines, though there is no officially authorised ranking, except for research programmes
2. Not universally, though. For instance, the Ashridge programme runs from January to December

5 Financing your MBA

A January 1992 announcement from the Open Business School stated that over half the 4000 students on its MBA programme were 'sponsored or supported by their employer'. A year later the position remains much the same. It is not clear what is meant by 'support' in a financial sense, because it can cover anything from a modest contribution to payment of all the fees, but it fits in with anecdotal evidence on the funding of distance learning and part-time MBA students. That could be a misleading percentage for those thinking about doing a full-time course. Of these, the vast majority of students are self-funded, according to the CNAA Report on MBAs.[1] The reason is that few employers want to pay to lose the services of a high-flyer for one, or possibly two years – especially when there is no guarantee that they will return to them at the end.

The joys (and griefs) of being sponsored

The MBA is not a cheap course, wherever it is taken, or by whatever mode. The tuition fees for a full-time course in the UK range from around £4000 at the lower end of the scale up to as much as £18,500, while a part-time or distance learning programme at a major school costs around £6000 in total. (Fees are generally higher for non-EC nationals. Under EC rules, citizens of other member countries cannot be charged more than locals.)

A one-year residential MBA at a leading UK school may work out at as much as £30,000, taking living expenses into account – more in the USA and on the Continent. So does that indicate that, wherever possible, you should try and get your employer to pay?

If you are intending to make your career with him for a foreseeable spell – these days that is for about five years, realistically – it is worth doing. There is, however, a catch with consortium MBAs, a lot of the contents of which will be company-specific. Indeed even in other kinds of part-time programmes where employers have sponsored students they may have quite a lot of influence on the contents of what is taught. The risk with such programmes is that they might then become a kind of academic golden handcuff. Where this is not the case, it leaves you with at least a moral obligation to stay with the employer who has paid for your course for a reasonable period after graduating, and possibly on his financial terms.

On the plus side, the employer also has a moral obligation, which is to deploy the skills of MBAs properly. If he fails to do so, the unwritten, psychological contract can reasonably be regarded as broken. 'If the graduate MBA does not obtain recognition and change he is unlikely to put in 100% for the firm,' comments Barry Tuckwood, a recent graduate.

Financing your own studies

Taking the figures for Europe, according to the most recent EIU Survey 42% of those who financed their own MBA did so from savings, 33% from private or bank loans, and 14% from a variety of means, which included borrowing money from employers, redundancy payments and sending their spouses out to work. Scholarships, listed at the end of this chapter, were another source.

For the majority of students from the UK, bank loans through the Association of MBAs Business

School Loan Scheme would be the most cost-effective method. Another possibility would be through a Department of Employment-backed Career Development Loan.

Career development loans

If you are not accepted for a loan under the AMBA scheme, or if the school to which you are applying is not approved by AMBA, this is the route you can go. Provided you (a) live or intend to train in the UK, (b) that you intend to use that training for work in the UK or elsewhere in the EC and (c) that your course takes no more than a year, you can apply for a Career Development Loan (CDL) to the Clydesdale Bank, Barclays or the Co-operative Bank. Under a scheme they operate with the Department of Employment, you can borrow up to 80% of your course fees (subject to a limit of £5000), plus the cost of books, materials and other course expenses.

The participating banks all produce their own leaflet on the CDL scheme. The one put out by Barclays has a note of the things the bank wants to know. They probably apply to the Clydesdale and Co-operative schemes as well, though their leaflets do not explicitly state them:

- the amount you wish to borrow
- the date on which first payment of course fees is due
- if you wish to draw the loan in instalments, the amount and date of each instalment
- the length of the course
- the repayment period you are proposing.

The Department of Employment says that in spite of the one-year limit, students on distance learning or part-time MBAs are eligible to borrow for one year of their course. It suggests that in this case, application should be made for the final year, because you have to start repaying the loan three months after the study period is completed. Obviously one would not want to be burdened with repayments in the middle of one's course and the banks might not be willing to lend in such circumstances anyway.

The Government will pay all the interest on the loan while you are studying and for three months thereafter. During this time you need not make any capital repayments either. Figures supplied by the Clydesdale Bank show that, assuming an annual percentage rate of interest of 11.3%, the full cost of a £5000 loan repaid over 36 months would be £6725.

For further details on CDLs see a pamphlet available from: Career Development Loans, Freepost, Newcastle upon Tyne X, NE85 1BR.

Repayment

Loans have one big snag – they have to be repaid, whereas with sponsorship the only obligation, at present, is a moral one. Furthermore, as the table below shows, though the terms of the Business School Loan scheme are soft during the period of study, and for some months afterwards, they do harden up later.

At present the terms then are 2.5% above base rate. Though this is below the normal lending rate, you should recognise that the need to repay the capital and interest may have some impact on the remuneration you will need to be looking for on completing the course. That may inhibit your freedom of choice in the job market when you qualify.

Scholarships and grants

Holders of the MBA degree generally enjoy excellent career prospects in well paid jobs and incentives in the form of scholarships are not required to fill available places on MBA programmes. It is not surprising, therefore, that scholarships and grants are very hard to find.

Details of organisations offering scholarships and awards are included in this chapter. Scholarship and grants will normally cover part of the costs involved but it is unlikely that they would cover the full cost of study. Bursaries, usually covering partial tuition costs, are sometimes available from Business Schools and you should ask about these when making general enquiries at individual schools. In the case of US

TUITION FEES AT A SAMPLE NUMBER OF SCHOOLS

The tuition fees are valid for EC students and cover the entire course of study (unless stated otherwise). Some of these schools have not actually fixed their 1993/94 fees and the figures below may be subject to some slight adjustment. All the schools below offer at least one AMBA accredited course.

University/College	Full-time	Part-time	Distance Learning or Open Learning
Ashridge Management College	£18950	£19200	–
Aston University	£7000	£7500	£8000
Bath University	£7250	£6000	–
Bradford University	£7150	£6000	–
Bristol (West of England University)	–	£5200	–
City University	£7500	£13000	–
Cranfield School of Management	£10000	£ 8000 *	–
Durham University	£6000	£7000	£5150
Edinburgh University	£4950	£4195	–
Glasgow University	£6900	£6900	–
Henley Management College	£8500	£7950	£6250
Heriot-Watt University	£4250	£4000	£4230
Imperial College	£8000	£9000	–
Kingston University	–	£7500	£6500
Lancaster University	£6500	£9650	–
Leicester (De Montfort University)	£5800	£ 5400	–
London Business School	£9500 *	£21500	–
Loughborough University	–	£1750 *	–
Manchester Business School	£7500 *	£5000 *	–
Middlesex University	£5800	£3800	–
Newcastle University	£5720	£2035 *	–
Nottingham University	£6500	£6500	
Sheffield Hallam University	£6200	£1500 *	–
Sheffield University	£5800	£9500	–
Stirling University	£4750	–	–
Strathclyde University	£7500	£2250 *	£2250 *
Warwick University	£8300	£10365	£6130
Westminster University	–	£4125	–
ESC Lyon	FF90000	–	–
Massachusetts Institute of Tech. (Sloan)	$19,500 *	–	–

* first year tuitiion fee only

schools you may enquire about the possibility of 'Financial Aid'. However, if available at all, this will probably be in the form of a Research or Teaching Assistantship.

A comprehensive listing of sources of funding is included in the Grants Register (published by Macmillan) which is available in the reference section of academic and the larger public libraries. The addresses of scholarship and grant-making organisations are to be found in the 'Useful Contacts' section of this book.

Sponsorship

Full-time study

AMBA is often asked for a list of companies which sponsor full-time MBA study. This immediately signals to us that we are speaking to someone with unrealistic expectations. Sponsorship of UK students for full-time study is rare and restricted to funding for current employees of exceptional calibre. Such sponsorship is most typically found in a handful of the large consultancies, usually for study in the USA, and in the UK via consortium MBA programmes for one-year study.

Part-time, open-learning & distance learning

Recognition of the value of the new skills acquired by MBAs is clearly supported by the number of students who receive sponsorship. However, such sponsorship is heavily concentrated on those undertaking part-time or distance and open-learning courses. Over 60% of students in these categories receive a degree of sponsorship and at some institutions the percentage of sponsored students is significantly higher.

If you are looking for sponsorship you should first ascertain whether this is available within your own company. If it is then there should exist normal channels through which to pursue your enquiries. For those working for a company not currently sponsoring students, all is not lost. Places on many MBA courses are filled by students who are the sole representative from their company. In many instances they will have taken the initiative in persuading their employer of the advantages of sponsoring them.

The advantages of sponsorship are mutually beneficial. For their investment, the employer will gain the employee's goodwill, profit from the acquisition of additional skills and commit a key member of the team to the company for three or more years. Company-specific dissertations and projects also offer significant rewards. On the obverse of the coin, an employee refused sponsorship could decide to look for a more responsive employer. The ensuing cost to the company in finding a replacement could amount to more than that of offering sponsorship.

Finding a Sponsor

If you wish to know who sponsors MBA study in your area, this information should be available via the part-time MBA admissions officer at local Business Schools. For information on distance learning course sponsors contact the individual school.

Cold calling by prospective students on companies in search of sponsorship is usually unrealistic. Unless they have a sound business proposal to offer they are wasting their time and effort. We have met with very few successful examples of this technique.

The Association of MBAs Loan Scheme

A Loan Scheme providing loans at preferential rates for MBA study was established in 1969 by the Business Graduates Association, as the Association of MBAs was then known, in conjunction with Citibank. The scheme enabled individuals with relevant experience to return to full-time graduate study in business management.

As more UK schools introduced Master's courses in Business Administration the scheme's potential for encouraging business professionalism to the benefit of the UK economy. It aimed to achieve this by ensuring that no qualified British resident was prevented from studying for an MBA because of lack of finance. Two banks, Barclays and NatWest, currently participate in the scheme.

Eligibility

The Loan Scheme is aimed at encouraging those who already have relevant work experience to improve their business professionalism. The Scheme does not extend to those wishing to study for an MBA directly or soon after completing an undergraduate degree as the MBA is a post-experience in addition to being a postgraduate degree.

You are eligible under this scheme if you meet the following criteria:

a You must be a permanent resident of the United Kingdom. Five years' residence is generally looked for, although consideration is given to those with a clear commitment to the UK (e.g., expatriates, those with property or a business in the UK, etc.). The banks will not normally lend to people over 40 years of age.

b (i) You must hold a bachelor's degree and have a minimum of two years' relevant work experience at an appropriate level of responsibility on commencement of study; or, (ii) you must hold an equivalent professional qualification and two year's relevant work experience; or,

(iii) you must you have a minimum of five years' relevant work experience if without the qualifications outlined in (i) and (ii) above.

c You must have a place on either a full- or part-time Master's degree course included on the Association's approved list. (The Scheme does not extend to distance learning courses).

The Association approves courses and NOT business schools. These include full- and part-time study. Certain courses at the following institutions qualify under this scheme.

United Kingdom

Ashridge Management School	Lancaster University
Aston University Business School	Leicester Business School
Bath University	Loughborough University
Bradford University	London Business School
Bristol Business School	Manchester Business School
City University Business School	Middlesex University Business School
Cranfield Management School	Newcastle University
Durham University Business School	Nottingham University
EAP	Sheffield University
Edinburgh University	Sheffield Hallam University
Glasgow University	Stirling University
Henley, The Management College	Strathclyde Graduate School of Business
Heriot-Watt University	Warwick University Business School
Imperial College	Westminster University
Kingston University Business School	(London Management Centre)

United States of America

All courses accredited by the American Assembly of Collegiate Schools of Business (AACSB) will be considered. The AACSB accredits almost all leading US business schools.

Continental Europe

Belgium:	Leuven
France:	ESC Lyon, EAP, HEC-ISA, INSEAD
Italy:	SDA Bocconi
Netherlands:	Rotterdam
Spain:	IESE, ESADE
Switzerland:	IMD

Applications to other schools outside Europe will be considered but do not automatically qualify under the Scheme.

Individual business schools may offer more than one MBA degree course (e.g., full-time, part-time, distance learning, International etc.). Only the full- and/or part-time MBA programmes are likely to be on the Association's approved list. Refer to individual banks for further information or, if in doubt, you may check with the Association.

The Association's strict selectivity of the courses it approves is aimed at maintaining standards so that the value and credibility of the MBA qualification remains undiluted. This, in turn, enhances the employment potential of these courses' graduates. It is in recognition of the excellent employment prospects and future potentials of MBA graduates that the participating banks are willing to offer such advantageous rates.

When to apply

You should apply as soon as you have been offered, and have accepted, a place for the forthcoming academic year. The earlier you apply the more likely you are to receive a prompt decision. July and August are the two busiest months for the processing of applications.

How much can I borrow?

For full-time study you can apply for up to a maximum of two-thirds of your present, or last, salary for each year of study plus tuition fees. Any income received over the period of study must be deducted from the total and this may include a spouse's income, at the discretion of the individual lending manager.

For part-time study you may normally apply for course fees only. In the case of full-time study in particular, a projected cash flow, included with the application, will often enable the bank to make a speedier decision. For those unsure of their eligibility due a minimum of work experience, a detailed cv should be provided.

How to apply

Loan Scheme application forms are not available from the Association but may be obtained from certain business schools and from branches of the banks participating the Scheme. Enquiries about loans for MBA study are not everyday occurrences at most bank branches, although information will be always available in their 'working manuals'.

Completed applications for study in the UK should be forwarded to your business school. The admissions office there will confirm your place by endorsing the form. They will then send it on to the Association, which administers the Scheme. For overseas schools the application should be forwarded directly to the Association together with proof of placement and acceptance. Approved applications are then sent on by the Association of MBAs to the relevant office at the bank of your choice. There is some variation in the processing of applications from bank to bank.

- Barclays: have a number of 'designated branches' located near listed business schools. These are listed on their application form.
- NatWest: employ a system of regional offices which review applications and then pass them on to the customer's branch, or an appropriate branch for non-customers, with recommendations.

Applications arriving at the Association's office are dealt with on the day of receipt. In general, loan applications are processed promptly by the banks. However, delays can occur at the busier times of the year, mid-June to the end of August. Loan managers will usually wish to interview the customer before agreeing the loan. At this meeting they will not only decide whether or not to offer the loan, but also discuss the period of repayment and any security that may be required. Should the applicant be unhappy with the service being offered by the bank of their choice, they are free to apply to one of the other participating banks. The Association will not accept simultaneous applications to both banks and will ensure that not more than one loan is taken up by any one applicant.

If you already have an account with one of the

Bank	Rate of interest charged during course	Period after completion of course when interest charged remains at rate in 2nd column	Commencement of repayment on completion of course	Repayment period
Full-time study				
Barclays	6% below base rate	3 months	After 3 months	Max 7 years
NatWest	6% pa fixed	3 months	After 3 months	Max 7 years[*]
*10 years if you borrow £20,000 or more.				
Part-time study				
Barclays	6% below base rate Minimum 6%	3 months	After 3 months	Max 7 years
NatWest	6% pa fixed	3 months	After 3 months	Max 7 years

Repayment
Barclays Bank: 2.5% above base rate
NatWest Bank: 9.75% (managed rate)

participating banks you may find that they are able to make the quickest decision on any loan application. A 'one off' administration charge of 1% of any loan is added to all loans and is made payable to the Association of MBAs.

Those failing to complete the course of study will have their loans transferred to the normal lending section of the bank and will be subject to normal terms and prevailing interest rates.

Finally, free introductory membership of the Association is offered to all Loan Scheme students.

Awards/funding for MBA study

Unless otherwise stated the awards below are restricted to holders of first degrees. Only organisations which offer a significant level of

funding are included. A comprehensive listing of awards is to be found in *The Grants Register*.

Contact addresses are listed on pages 173–4 of this book.

British Universities North America Club

For students who already have funding BUNAC offer 10 'topping up' awards to recent British graduates. Tenable in USA and Canada only. Deadline – end March. Contact: BUNAC.

Business school loan scheme

By far the largesty source of funding for MBA study in the United Kingdom and overseas. The Association of MBAs administers the scheme on behalf of Barclays and NatWest banks. Preferential loans are available to permanent UK residents enrolled on full- and part-time courses only. Must hold degree or equivalent professional qualification and have a minimum of two years' relevant work experience. Five years' relevant work experience required if without a degree. Apply at any time. Contact: Association of MBAs or individual banks.

Career development loans

Barclays Bank, Clydesdale Bank and the Co-operative Bank offer loans of between £300 and £5000 for vocational study. Also available to non-graduates. Restricted to one year of study only. Contact: Individual banks or Career Development Loans.

Charles R E Bell Fund Scholarships

Awards for UK domiciles engaged in Commerce and for teachers in commercial education. Also available for non-graduates. Tenable for one year and not to exceed £1500 in the first instance but with possibility of additional £1500. Deadline – 31 December. Details from: London Chamber of Commerce.

Frank Knox Fellowships

Four awards for UK citizens who are graduates of a UK university or polytechnic for study at Harvard. Tenable for one year with possible renewal for a second. Includes a stipend plus health and tuition fees. Persons already in the USA are ineligible. Deadline – mid-October. Details from: Frank Knox Fellowships.

Fulbright awards

20 or more awards covering round-trip travel and maintenance for one academic year. Also a separate competition for travel-only awards for those gaining full funding. Eligibility: at least a 2:1 degree. Must be UK citizen. Recipients must return to the UK for at least two years upon completion of degree. Application forms available from July. Deadline October 30th. Send s.a. A4

envelope with 36p stamp to Fulbright Commission.

Fulbright Commission, Educational Advisory Service

Provides comprehensive list of awards for postgraduate (and undergraduate) study in the USA. Same organisation but separate office to that which administers Fulbright Awards. Details from: Educational Advisory Service, Fulbright Commission.

Kennedy scholarships

Up to 12 scholarships annually for study at MIT or Harvard. Open to individuals who are in the final year at university or who have graduated not earlier than three years prior to applying. Stipend plus travel and tuition fees. Deadline – 11 November. Details from Kennedy Memorial Trust.

Rotary Foundation Ambassadorial scholarships

For one year's expenses, with top limit, including round-trip transportation, on-campus board, tuition fees and limited expenses. Must be sponsored by a local Rotary Club. Deadline – April. Further details from Rotary Foundation.

Marion and Samuel T Pendleton Fellowship

Award covering tuition, fees, cost of living stipend and travel expenses for MBA study at University of Virginia. Must be under 26 years of age. Deadline – 15 January. Further details: Colgate Darden Graduate School, University of Virginia.

Thouron Awards of the University of Pennsylvania

Twelve awards tenable at the University of Pennsylvania. Covers tuition and fees plus monthly allowance of $860. Candidates must contact the university directly for course information and application forms. Deadline –

8 November. Award information from Thouron Awards.

In addition to these, some business schools award bursaries – you should request details when making your application. There are also minor awards, such as an award offered by *Cosmopolitan* magazine for the purpose of study at INSEAD.

PETER CALLADINE
ADMINISTRATOR, AMBA

Notes

1. op. cit

6 Business school profiles

The best way of giving readers a feel for what it is actually like doing an MBA is to present profiles of a number of different schools, showing a variety of modes of delivery of the course. The choice is by no means intended to indicate rankings. It is merely a representative sample – which we intend to rotate in future editions – to give readers some idea of what they might expect to find at a variety of characteristic, AMBA-accredited business schools. But in the words of a recent Financial Times survey of business schools, 'the best course is to visit the institution – and wade through the literature, not just for the course descriptions but basic facts about duration, cost, placement sucess and so on . . . word of mouth, surveys and consultants go so far, but there is no substitute for meeting deans and directors face to face';[1] to which list we would also add students and recent alumni.

Warwick Business School

The geographic connotation of Warwickshire suggests a setting somewhere in rural England, but the Warwick Business School is actually on the outskirts of Coventry, one of the main industrial centres of the West Midlands. The Warwick MBA has a 25-year pedigree, developing into five separate MBA programmes in a portfolio which, as at other business schools, includes a variety of management development courses. It was initially known as the School of Industrial and Business Studies when it was established by the University of Warwick in 1967 and despite its change of name, it remains an integral part of the University.

Warwick has a reputation for being somewhat oriented towards numerical methods in its teaching and for a strong emphasis on industrial relations. The latter was probably due to the prominence of Warwick's Professor Hugh Clegg, the leading British IR guru in the seventies and early eighties when industrial relations were at the heart of British industry's problems. Though the School still has an important research unit in this sphere, the teaching emphasis is more towards internationalisation. 'We're strong in certain fields of research, but we teach a generalist MBA,' explains Robin Wensley, Chairman of the School.

He adds that Warwick came out joint top in University Funding Council's assessment of the quality of business school research programmes by international criteria.

As for its reputation of being a tough place for the non-mathematically minded, the faculty say this is much exaggerated. Quantitative methods certainly are a core subject in the MBA programme, but they claim that the standards are no tougher than at any other good business school. Warwick's association with the numbers end of business probably has to do with an emphasis, now less pronounced, on operations research. That in turn was driven by the School's close associations with local industry, which up to the eighties was primarily in the manufacturing sector.

Relocation of head offices from the south-east to the Midlands, the drift from manufacturing into services and the privatisation of public sector organisations have all contributed to changing the pattern of what used to be the mainstay of the School's support for both its teaching and its research activities. That is now enormously wide and varied, covering virtually the whole spectrum of private and public sector organisations. If it is true that 'by their clients, ye shall know them', the roll call at Warwick supports the School's claim to be in the European first division.

The course directors at Warwick admit though that the recession of the last three years has taken its toll. Clients are being more careful with their cash, both as far as commissioning research and funding students for distance learning and part-time programmes – full-timers are mostly self-funded these days. As a result, the School has introduced a good deal of flexibility into allowing students to move between part-time and distance learning modes in mid-course. There is even flexibility of delivery within them. Some distance learning modules can, for instance, be taken as a residential course. 'Students' circumstances can change over the three years of the part-time programme,' explains Professor Brian Houlden. 'They can be promoted, moved around, or even lose their jobs within that time.'

In the latter case, a number of former part-time and distance learning students have used some of their severance package to complete the MBA on a full-time basis. Normally this is a 12-month programme, but since all core courses and same-title electives have the similar contents and standards, it is easy to award credits for work already done and to shorten the course accordingly in individual cases. A more common switch, though, is between part-time and distance learning, when people move jobs either beyond or into the 50-mile radius that is thought to be practicable for part-time study.

There is also a wide menu of choice at the outset in the various ways of doing a Warwick MBA: full-time over 12 months, part-time over three years, distance learning over three to four years, as a member of a consortium programme (called the Integrated MBA by the School) over 15 months, and starting next year, through a modular programme over three years – essentially a work and full-time residential study sandwich course.

The programmes start at different times of the year but their structure is similar. They consist of four parts, of which the first covers core management disciplines. The remaining courses, with the nine electives, come in the second and third parts, with the choice of electives widening in the latter. The third part also includes a language, optional for the part-time and distance learners, though the majority of them take it up.

The fourth part, which in the case of the full-time programme runs from July–September, takes the form of a consultancy-like project, carried out in an organisation or a company under the supervision of one of its senior managers and a member of the Warwick faculty. A typical example, says Bill Manuel, Administrator of the full-time programme, would be a detailed, quantified report on whether the host company should invest in new technology or to upgrade an existing plant. The degree, in the end, is awarded on an assessment based on individual work, group participation, examinations and the project.

There are also similarities in the underlying approach of the various programmes. Chairman Robin Wensley is sceptical about the trend to teach management solely by themes rather than subjects – he says that themes are no more found in isolation of disciplines in real life than disciplines exist in isolation of each other, and he is very keen on the connection with real life. For instance, guest speakers, for whom there is an unusually big programme, are working business people, not (or only incidentally) celebrities. And though there is a certain amount of competition among students to be among the top 10% who graduate with distinction, he is very much in favour of a participative, team-based learning culture. Thus all the programmes begin with a 'getting to know you' residential weekend and much of the work is carried out in syndicates of six to nine students, chosen by the faculty because they represent a good mix of skills and backgrounds.

Students find this approach invaluable through a tough course that characteristically takes a full-timer 60–70 hours work a week. That is also true of part-time and distance learning, incidentally. The extra time taken by studying for the MBA, people on these programmes report, amounts to an average of at least 14 hours a week. 'We help each other through the tough bits,' reports Albrecht Lange, a German who has chosen to do the full-time MBA at Warwick. 'There's always somebody in the group who knows quite a bit about a topic.' Those who do know 'quite a bit', on the other hand, find that the wide ranging and practical nature of the course is a lifeline in career terms from being stuck in the 'expert in' syndrome. Self-development through learning from others is as important an aspect of the course as the taught programmes, which is why previous work experience is one of the criteria of acceptance for the Warwick MBA, by whichever mode it is taken.

The School works hard to foster the same spirit during the 24 residential days of its three-year distance learning course, difficult though that is in the nature of things in that case. It recommends distance learning for those who live more than an hour away from the campus, but students are encouraged to form their own study groups among those living near each other. The faculty also tends to make up syndicates of distance learning students on that basis.

The School makes no bones about the fact that its MBA is a tough one, by whichever mode it is taken. That is why there is a good deal of emphasis, right from the outset, upon the fact that participants need to strike a proper balance between home, study, family and, in the case of part-timers, their job. Everyone is assigned a tutor who they can talk to if they run into difficulty on any of these fronts. Where students have families or partners, they are encouraged to consider themselves part of the community and to use the facilities of the Warwick University.

Not all management schools attached to universities have a harmonious relationship with them, but in Warwick's case the Business School features the connection, rather than playing down its existence. Computer and IT links with a major university are a key advantage. From the point of view of full-timers, another is that there is an infrastructure of fairly inexpensive student accommodation within easy reach of the campus as well as some actually on it. Overseas students, who make up about 40% of the student body, and handicapped students are guaranteed places there.

The University link is also proving valuable in another sphere that is becoming increasingly important. Though the vast majority of self-funded MBAs do find jobs within a short time of graduating – often in the companies where they have undertaken their projects – career management is an issue, even for students who are company sponsored. Being on the campus means that MBA students are in the frame for the milk round and the university's careers advisory service, but that is backed up by a good deal of more specific career counselling and testing. 'I would be very upset if collectively we didn't know every one of our students by name,' says administrator Bill Manuel. With 1800 students on the distance learning programme alone that is a tough mission statement, but it is one that business schools will have to aim at if they want to stay beautiful while growing big.

The Management School, Lancaster University

When the School was founded in 1965, its location might have counted against it in the eyes of students from abroad who make up around 50% of the full-time cohort. Improvements in transport since then now put it only three hours from London, and within an hour's drive from Manchester's growing international airport. At the same time, motorways place it within easy reach of the Lake District and the Yorkshire Dales.

However, the MBA does not leave a lot of time for leisure, so it is as well that students will find virtually everything they need either on the campus itself or in nearby Lancaster. In fact one of

the advantages the School has over some of its rivals in bigger towns is that accommodation is not a problem. Unusually for today's universities, a very high proportion of students live on campus, but rents in the surrounding areas are also very reasonable.

That is one of the School's attractions. The other is that though some sectors of the business community have yet to recognise its status, the Universities Funding Committee has in fact ranked it among the top business schools in the UK, with accounting and finance picked out as particular strengths. The 1992 Times 'Good Universities

Guide', while admittedly having no official standing, gave Lancaster first equal billing out of 100 UK universities for the quality of its teaching.

The Management School has some unusual features. It does not run a distance learning programme but it is one of the few top business schools to offer a single company MBA in the shape of a part-time course for employees of British Airways. VSEL (Vickers Ship Building And Engineering), another big north-west of England employer who also had a single company programme, have recently joined Lancaster's 24-month Consortial MBA. Six companies are core members of that, but some others also send people on it. Their numbers could grow since the Consortium is open to corporate members who are compatible with the existing group.

Their orientation is somewhat towards science and engineering; and finance, accountancy and operations management are a strong suit in all the programmes. But teaching on the consortial MBA is pioneering a trend that a number of other schools are considering: teaching themes, rather than traditional subject breakdowns. For instance, operations management is linked to marketing and strategic management is studied in the light of an internationally competitive business environment.

Companies in the Consortium are consulted on what they hope it will deliver to the students they nominate to go on it. They tend to be young executives (women are around 20% of the intake) on a fast track, marked out as future senior management. They include an occasional non-graduate but at an average age of around 30, the 65 current participants on the programme will have their undergraduate years well behind them. In any case graduate studies are a somewhat different proposition, so the course starts with a three-day residential workshop, covering everything from a 'getting to know you' exercise which involves students, staff and a visit by line managers from participating companies, to team-building events and tests.

Students are also given an overview of how the programme is structured. For the consortium the first year is built around a series of five-day residential modules, which are interspersed with assignments and two one-day tutorials arising out of them. In the second year, which includes a week's intensive study visit to Groupe ESC Lyon and its associated French companies, there is one further module, but the main emphasis is on a major company-based project. Exams taken in the first year are 'open-book' and are constructed around case studies rather than the retention of a body of learning. As in other business schools, assessment is on a mix of group and individual work, and the quality of the project. However, marks are only given for individually submitted pieces.

One of its criteria is whether it adds value to the companies where it is carried out. According to Pilkington director Derek Norman, projects are often consultancy-type commissions which are assigned to MBA students 'instead of expensive consultants.' From the point of view of individuals, the project often opens up paths to new directions in career development. For Bill Denison, for instance, a plant manager with BNFL, a project which involved looking at the possibilities of marketing fluorine eventually resulted in his becoming managing director of a new division in his company: BNFL Fluorochemicals.

The 12-month full-time MBA has a somewhat more conventional structure. It consists of first-term foundation of core courses in the basic management disciplines, which is accompanied by a support programme putting them into a wider context of business issues. In the second term, there are three more core subjects, but the emphasis starts to shift to the electives. Some of these are variants of fairly widespread and generally accepted themes in management education: internationalisation, management information systems and so forth, but there are number which look in more detail at aspects of marketing and there is also one on small business and entrepreneurship. One of the distinguishing features between the consortial and the full-time MBA is that the latter offers a much wider range of electives. That, of course, is a reflection of the fact that the consortial MBA is to some extent tailored for the companies that pay for their people to come on it.

There are two unusual elements in the full-time course. In the first place students who are considered to be not quite up to strength can do a nine-month pre-MBA course. Another feature answers an objection to the MBA that is sometimes voiced by those who come on programmes with a good deal of management experience under their belt. What happens if the foundation course of core subjects covers a good deal of ground they already know? At Lancaster there is an opportunity for such students to take the first term at either the Rotterdam or Copenhagen School of Management. They still cover the same subjects, and in English, but in the context of a different business environment.

The European and international dimensions are also prominent in the electives. Apart from those that deal directly with business issues, there are two which offer French and German for management. The international theme can then be carried on into the project that comes in the final period of the programme. An increasing number of students choose to do this through one of the several mainland European universities or the University of British Columbia which have links with Lancaster. The project, incidentally, is carried out by a small group under supervision by a staff member, rather than by individuals. That too reflects the reality of management in the flatter, leaner organisation of the nineties.

Durham University Business School

Though the campus is a mile from the town centre, Durham has what is probably the most spectacular arrival point of any university in Britain – a view across the old town to Durham's 11th-Century cathedral, in its day northern Europe's largest building and breathtakingly massive even by today's standards.

Durham University was founded only in 1832, but it has the collegiate atmosphere of a northern Oxbridge. Among the managerial public, the Business School is probably best known for its association with small- and medium-sized enterprises, a field in which it has a number of well-publicised research and development projects. 20% of the 180 or so participants in the part-time MBA are drawn from mostly local firms in this sector, attracted by, among other features, the structure of the programme. Starting each January, it runs over two years of 24 two-day weekends, plus two week-long workshops. To that, one has to add 12–15 hours a week of private study.

A notable feature of the part-time programme is the contract it has with the Northern Regional Health Authority, which is sending about 200 managers on it over the next five years. That may account for the unusually high proportion of women on the part-time programme overall: 43%.

The participants from the health authority do the same foundation courses as everyone else, but of the eight electives on the MBA, they do four on health administration-related topics.

The large choice of electives – there are 24 altogether, of which part-time students have to offer eight in the second stage – is one of the unusual features of all the Durham MBA. That is followed by a project which runs from September to December in the second year. It is presented as a dissertation of about 20,000 words, usually focusing on a live issue in their own organisation. Since most part-time students are sponsored by their employer, the project has a potential consultancy-related benefit for the sponsor, particularly as students have a faculty member to act as project tutor.

They also have a personal tutor and in fact the part-time MBA has quite a strong emphasis on personal development aspects. There is an introductory course and outdoor weekend which identify individual learning needs and management styles. There is also a three-day self-development workshop in the second year.

The part-time MBA has only been going since 1991. The open distance learning programme – so called because a residential element is included with the distance learning delivery – was started in

1988 and already has some 900 students on it, of which 40% are from outside the EC. Where possible they are backed by facilities in universities local to them with which Durham Business School has established alliances.

The ODL programme runs over three to four years, starting each June. It has four stages, which combine a syllabus of core subjects (plus electives in the third phase) with a generally thematic approach: from individual/corporate concerns in the first phase, to industry and international perspectives in stages 2 and 3. The final stage consists of a dissertation or, alternatively, two specialist electives. In September or October there is a residential module which students are strongly urged to attend, though the School recognises that there has to be an elment of flexibility in this. Flexibility also extends to people shifting between programmes. Most part-timers come from areas within an hour's drive from Durham, which is on the major road and rail networks. But promotion or relocation can mean a need to transfer from part-time to distance learning – or vice versa.

Assessment is on a mixture of examinations on assigned work, which obviously puts a considerable strain on the logistics of getting material to and from students who are not near any centre of population. In one case, a ship's officer had to write his examination locked in a cabin, with the papers posted from the vessel's next port of call! Normally, though, the faculty claim a quick turnround of assessed material, despite the fact that electronic media, apart from fax, have not made a big impact on distance learning as yet. The problem is the sheer weight of material – about 9000 pages go back and forth between student and faculty in the course of the programme.

The ODL course is estimated to take up 1350 hours of study time and as in all such programmes there is a fairly high (about 20%) drop-out rate. There is, however a consolation prize for those who successfully complete Stages 1 and 2. They are awarded the Diploma In Business Administration.

Numbers on Durham's full-time programme are smaller – around 50. It runs over 12 months, beginning in October, but it has one unusual feature. You can do it over two years on a block release basis. That may make it more attractive to older students, because the age profile is slightly higher than normal for an MBA course: 40% of students are over 30.

Essentially the full-time course follows the same subject matter as the part-time one, and is examined by the same external examiners. But there is one big difference – a wider range of electives: 25, out of which students have to choose 10. There is also a project, carried out in a firm in the last phase of study between June and September. Accompanied by a dissertation, it is as elsewhere, considered to be a vital part of the learning process.

Students at Durham speak highly of its various programmes. To sum up their opinions, they teach you where to look for the key issues in a business, which subjects you are good at and how to develop the interpersonal skills you need. They also expose you to topics which you might not otherwise come across – because of pressure of work at work, for instance. They also speak highly of the accessibility of the faculty and the way they are prepared to put in extra teaching hours. Yet Durham has a rather lowly research rating. Could that be because the faculty are too busy teaching?

University of Bradford Management Centre

Like all northern industrial cities, Bradford is branded by its association with dark, satanic mills, but their chimneys have long since stopped smoking and in fact have mostly ceased to exist. Today little remains of the town's industrial past, except a notable heritage of buildings from the

heyday of Victorian architecture.

The Management Centre is based round one of them, a rather grand quasi-ecclesiastical building in parkland a mile or two out of town, surrounded by what would once have been the houses of mill-owners. The change in the population structure of the town – it has a high percentage of Asian immigrants – makes accommodation fairly inexpensive. At the same time, communications are good. It is only 20 minutes by train from Leeds and the UK's main road/rail network.

While the organisation of the Bradford MBA – a core programme, electives and a project – is the usual one, it has a number of features which are peculiar to it:

- its partnership with the Netherlands Institute for MBA Studies (NIMBAS) under which the Bradford MBA is also offered in the Netherlands. Discussions are under way to extend this concept to Essen, in the nearby Ruhr.
- the extent of its commitment to the in-company MBA. Under the heading of the executive MBA, it offers its courses to employees of companies like Bass, Allied-Lyons and to several building societies and banks.
- an unusually high proportion of women on its full-time programme: 30% of the current cohort of 125.
- the fact that its full-time MBA can actually be taken over three years, at the rate of a term a year.

There are also some unusual aspects in the structure of the programme – the part-time, three-year version is very similar to the full-time one, though the choice of electives is more limited. Students are asked to declare, at the time they apply for admission, which of a number of options (e.g., International Business, TQM, Corporate and Economic Planning) they intend to focus on after the first foundation stage, which in the case of the full-time MBA runs from October-December. The electives they take in Stages 2 and 3 are largely, though not exclusively, grouped around these options which are followed up in more detail after the foundation stage. Since students are expected to have some work experience at the time they apply, the assumption is also that at this point in their careers they will have developed some idea of the interests they want to follow. The project in the final stage – a dissertation based on a specific management-related problem – is also usually based on the choice of option.

There is an unusually wide range of electives. Equally unusual, and potentially very useful to those with entrepreneurial ambitions, is the orientation of the course towards venture capital projects. That already begins in the second stage and runs through to the third stage. Professor David Weir, Director of Bradford Management Centre, stresses that this is not an academic exercise. They are undertaken by groups of five or six students and have the quality of at least 'virtual reality'; in fact there have been cases where they have been taken to the point of being offered funding from 3i, the sponsors of this part of the course. But they are all real in the sense that they have to be taken from inception to notional flotation and to pass the scrutiny of 3i's assessors. The object of the venture capital project is also to develop teamwork. That is a strong feature of the Bradford MBA, though there are also prizes for top individual performers.

Students have the option to do the third term at NIMBAS. Courses there are in English, but Bradford also has a strong commitment to languages. It has an unusually well-equipped language laboratory which offers Japanese as well as the main European languages. This is a voluntary programme at present, but it is planned for languages to be taken as a formally assessed elective in the future.

The high quality of the technical and other facilities at the Centre is coupled with fairly low fees – a combination which owes much to Bradford's high research rating with the University Funding Committee. This brings in substantial funding. It also leads, if indirectly, to the sponsorship of chairs by industry, such as the Heinz Professorship in Brand Management (the Heinz chairman and noted industrialist, Tony O'Reilly, got his PhD at Bradford) and a new Professorship in Credit Management. Bradford's research rating also attracts students from abroad. Brazilian Alex Alencar, a product engineer chose the school for that reason, plus a range of electives which, he said, would expand his horizons in international business. For Liz Feinstein, an investment banker, Bradford's electives offer a chance to integrate her financial knowledge with a wider business view which might provide a springboard for a change of career direction.

Bradford does not offer a distance learning MBA, but in addition to the executive MBA, there is a part-time programme running over about three years. The students on it must live within a 30-mile radius of the Centre and are put into working groups of five to six people who live near each other. The part-time course, which is essentially the same as the full-time one, though with fewer electives, takes place on Wednesdays after work. There is also a residential week and a project workshop.

The part-time MBA makes considerable demands on students' private and work life and there is a good deal of guidance, both formal and informal, on how to handle this. Faculty members have found that students from a background like accountancy, where part-time study is already the norm, find it easiest to handle the pressures of the part-time MBA. But bringing together students from a wide variety of sectors itself provides the holistic context necessary for business in the 1990s.

Groupe ESC Lyon: The CESMA MBA

The two acronyms throw light on the culture and content of this French management school: ESC – Ecole Superieure de Commerce; and CESMA – Centre d'Etudes Superieure du Management.

In other words, CESMA's one year full-time MBA – the only one it offers – is a product of the intellectually demanding but highly respected French grandes écoles system. In this sense it is more 'French' than the internationally better known INSEAD at Fontainebleau. Like INSEAD, Groupe ESC Lyon is a top European school, but whereas at the former most courses are given in English, and it is said that you can get by with only a good working knowledge of French, on the CESMA MBA over half the 20 hours of classes a week are in French. The proportion of French nationals is also much higher than at INSEAD – 85% for the 1992 cohort, though the number of students from abroad is rising.

That is also a reflection of Groupe ESC Lyon's commitment to an international view of business. It is not only that the non-French part of the student body comes from about 15 different countries and that 20% of the full-time faculty come from outside France. It is also that the case studies are international and that analyses of the way different problems are handled in different countries are a regular part both of the classroom and the group work.

Even more significant are the formal links with other business schools. The CESMA MBA has a partnership agreement with Cranfield School of Management, under which students from either School can carry out a period of study in the other during the third and/or fourth term. At the end of this programme they will get both the CESMA and the Cranfield MBA. This programme began in 1990, and whereas in 1992 it only attracted six students from Cranfield, this year there are 17. ESC Lyon also has an exchange programme with one of the leading Spanish schools, ESADE and with HEC Montreal as well as a range of co-operative agreements with major schools in most of the world's industrialised countries. Eventually it aims to send all its students abroad for a part of their course.

Though the structure of the CESMA MBA is broadly similar to that of the UK Schools described in this section, there are some differences. One is that the core course runs over two stages, beginning in September and January respectively. The electives form the third stage and are grouped round central themes, such as marketing or finance. It is possible to take all the electives in a particular discipline, but CESMA also stresses the integrated nature of management. For instance, scattered throughout the course there a number of seminars which involve faculty from a variety of disciplines; for instance on environmental challenges, crisis management, on the relationship between decision making and company analysis, or that between personal development and management.

The final stage offers a number of options: a project in a company, either in France or abroad, a research assignment or a more detailed study of particular topic, such as strategic management, competitive advantage or the analysis of management styles. In other words a practical project is not mandatory though it is strongly encouraged, certainly for those who intend to pursue a business career – students come from a wide variety of backgrounds, not all of them commercial (a minority, also, are not post-experience) – since it is often the first introduction to a potential employer or an industry sector in which students have a particular interest.

Teaching is carried out in the classroom and through the works of groups of six or seven, using case studies and business games. British students may find a cultural difference in the way classroom work is conducted. Though French students are sharply analytical and do not hesitate to challenge faculty when the occasion arises, their attitude is more formal than is the case in the UK. French faculty members also tend to be more distant in their relationships with students. Learning, perhaps, carries more status than it does in the UK, though that does not mean that the faculty are 'academics' in the traditional sense. Indeed they are mostly on three and a half or four day a week contracts and spend about one day a week on their own consultancy and research projects.

Lyon is an excellent centre for that, as the principal city of the Rhône-Alpes region, France's second biggest aggregation of commerce and industry. Indeed the Groupe ESC Lyon is affiliated to the Lyon Chamber of Commerce and Industry which is represented on the School's board of directors. For students the virtue of this relationship is the contacts the School has with the many major business in the area, as well as in

France as a whole. Its placement service is very active and the whole theme of career management is seen as an integral part of the MBA programme. Each member of the staff acts as adviser to a group of students and those whose personal style is identified as being likely to lead to problems in getting a job are given appropriate counselling. However, the French are not much enamoured of outdoor exercises as a way of identifying and diagnosing personal management styles. Intellectual rigour rather than British pragmatism is the order of the day in France.

According to a faculty spokesman, French companies expanding abroad or with existing foreign operations are showing strong signs of interest in CESMA MBAs. About 100 companies attend the School's bi-annual careers fair and the placement office receives several thousand approaches from employers each year which are notified to students through a fortnightly bulletin. He attributes this to the strongly international orientation of the course, which is nevertheless rooted in French culture, management style and general outlook. It bridges the potential gaps in this respect that sometimes appear in the case of Euro-manager jobs.

Employers want MBAs who are operational right away, so the CESMA MBA strikes a mix between theory and application. That means that there is a lot to cram into the one-year course. There is not much time to enjoy the amenities of Lyon itself, but it is in fact a city of great charm in its own right as well as being reasonably close both to the French Alps and the Mediterranean. It is a city to which students return for pleasure when there is more time to get to know it better.

Imperial College Management School

Imperial College is to the UK what MIT is to the United States: the country's undisputed leader in science and technology and the centre of its biggest concentration of Nobel Prize winners and Fellows of the Royal Society. It follows that its MBA programmes – a one-year full-time course starting in October and a three-year one, called the

Executive MBA, starting in January – have a scientific and technical orientation. Most participants have a science or engineering first degree.

Unusually, work experience is not a pre-requisite, but because of the nature and content of the course, a considerable degree of numeracy and computer literacy is regarded as essential. Another slightly unusual feature is that on the full-time course students are expected to do some pre-course preparation, which would include maths in the case of those whose knowledge is not up to the standard expected.

The reason for this becomes clear when you look more closely at the programme. The course itself follows a traditional structure in that it is built round a core of basic management functions. But these also cover information technology skills at a level that assumes a fair degree of prior expertise. At the beginning of the third term, by which time the ten core topics have been covered, there is a tough examination – ten 90 minute papers – in each of them.

In the third and fourth terms the accent moves away from the classroom and more to project and group work, for which the introduction of business games in the first two terms have given some preparation. The options which follow at this point are built round six 'specialisations' which reflect the link with Imperial College. They include the management of innovation, aspects of the management of technology, and project management. The finance option too has a strong computing and modelling content. However, there is also an option on the management of new ventures, designed to appeal to potential entrepreneurs, while the ones in management science and strategic management provide preparation for possible careers in consultancy. Through its placement service – rightly regarded as a very important aspect of the programme – the School keeps a close eye on career opportunities for its alumni. Most full-timers, it claims, get job offers before the end of their course. These are generally the students considering a job or career change. Those on the executive programme are usually sponsored by their employers and go back to them with, it is hoped, enhanced career prospects.

The final stage of the MBA consists of a research project, often one with a practical outcome carried on in a company, and a dissertation. Students have to pass all parts of the programme and the commitment in terms of time is fairly high – something of the order of 60 hours a week of private study, group work and classroom teaching time.

The failure rate on the full-time MBA is relatively high at around 7%–8%. On the Executive MBA it is more in line with the normal 3% though that programme is no less demanding. It follows a very similar pattern to that of the full-time course and requires a commitment from the employer as well as from the participants, because it runs all day (0900–1900) on alternate Fridays during term time. In addition there are three full week blocks in each of the first two years and a one week block in the third year. On top of that, there is a Saturday course on 'soft' skills – not mandatory, but students are encouraged to take it because these skills are sometimes a problem with technologists accustomed to seeing things in terms of right or wrong answers. The pace and time demands of the programme does make it difficult for part-time participants who have to meet work commitments as well. The faculty say that they are prepared to give students who temporarily have to give priority to their jobs the chance to catch up if they miss out on a part of the course, but they emphasise that it is not one that you can drop in and out of at will.

Group exercises on both the full-time and the executive MBA are done in syndicates of five or six. In the latter case the faculty put together people who live or work near each other and normally the syndicates are expected to stay together for a year. In the full-time MBA, syndicate groups are nominated on the basis of a complementary mix of age and experience. Both modes try to create a mix of co-operation and competition: distinctions are awarded very selectively and there are a few prizes, eg for the top students in some specialisations.

The close proximity to Imperial College, just across the road from the Management School, means that the facilities available to students are exceptional. Its more than 40 computers are linked to Imperial College's large mainframe systems and there are, of course, excellent library and language laboratory facilities; but it has to be said that the international aspect is stressed less here than in some MBA programmes. The School has a student exchange with its French counterpart, the École des Ponts et Chaussées and the part-time programme is developing a link with Darden Business School in Virginia, one of the top US business schools. There are also visits to European companies in the third and fourth terms, but on the whole the Imperial College MBA seems to be clearly aimed at a niche in the market – that of the scientist or technologist who wants to expand his or her skills into their application to business. There is, incidentally, a somewhat higher proportion of women than usual on the programmes: 25% on the full-time and 33% on the executive MBA.

In addition to working facilities, the School is also well resourced for leisure ones, though the reader will appreciate that the intensive nature of the programmes leaves little time for relaxation. Indeed one faculty spokesman says that the MBA should really be awarded jointly to the participants and their partners or spouses. With this consideration in mind a lot of effort is made to involve the latter in various social occasions that do occur during the course.

Participants in the Executive MBA are generally based in the Greater London area, but many of those on the full-time course come from further afield – there is a particularly strong presence from the Pacific rim. Accommodation, on a first-come, first-served basis, is available for both single and married students in the various University of London halls of residence – Imperial College is a constituent of London University – but students who are moving to London to do their MBA should make sure they have suitable accommodation lined up before they start their course. London is not an easy place to find reasonable and convenient places to live and the last thing anyone should be doing while studying for an MBA is to combine this with flat hunting!

Manchester Business School

As business schools have grown in size and financial muscle in recent years, so the relationship between them and the universities of which they were often originally departments, has at times come under strain. Manchester Business School has been the most highly publicised example of this, possibly because of the status of the School itself. Along with London Business School, it started in the sixties and, like LBS, it has a two-year full-time programme. But unlike LBS which, because of the federal nature of London University, was able to remain autonomous, MBS was more firmly linked to Manchester University.

The nature of that link has now been clarified, as has the sometimes confusing connection between MBS and the Manchester School of Management at the University of Manchester Institute of Science and Technology (UMIST). From next autumn, the University's Department of Accounting and Finance, UMIST and MBS will emerge in a new shape, that of the proposed Manchester Federal School of Business. It will provide an extensive research programme, management consultancy, undergraduate courses carried out at UMIST, and full-time and part-time MBA programmes at MBS.

This step consolidates a number of separate, though related, activities that up to now have come under these various institutions. At the same time, the two-year structure of the full-time programme is under scrutiny. This was really based on the US model and reflected the unevenness between some American first degrees which makes it necessary to bring students up to a uniform standard. Most European schools since then have gone on to a one-year full-time course.

MBS is now heading in the same direction, with a fast track entry for students with good qualifications and sound experience. They will be able to skip some of the foundation courses, while at the same time the content level of the core programmes is being raised. However, the part-time programme, which runs over two and a half to three years on two evenings a week will retain its existing structure. Another rationalisation will be that the Master's degree in Business Management – essentially a two-year sandwich course – will become an Executive MBA. Its programme will remain largely the same: a combination of residential work with a project in the sponsoring company of the individual in question.

In spite of these various rationalisations and re-organisations, the essence of the MBA on which MBS's reputation as a top school is based, is being preserved. One of its features is the strong similarity in style and substance between the part-time and the full-time programmes. A characteristic of the latter is that applicants are required to produce a 1500 word essay, thus underlining the importance of communication skills on the course – both traditional and IT based ones. In fact there are some optional introductory courses for those who need extra tuition in computer usage.

The programme proper follows a theme approach in the core stages – the usual MBA topics are built around analysis of decision and control (quantitative methods), analysis of the business environment (covering economics, marketing and labour relations) and strategies and techniques for change (e.g., strategic management and international business). What is unusual about the MBS MBA, however, is that right away after the completion of the core stage theory is put into the context of application through practical projects linking students with client companies. These are carried out in groups of four to six, under the supervision of faculty members, and the groups are asked to report their findings in both oral and written form – hence the importance attached to the essay in the admission application.

The structure is that once the core programme is completed, students are first given a number of subject areas from which to chose a specific project: for instance merger and acquisition or some aspect of public policy. The second project is really a short exercise which looks at and develops individual management skills. That is followed by a longer third project in the field of entrepreneurship, dealing with a new venture. The fourth project has an international business theme and involves syndicates spending time abroad, usually on behalf of a company which is trying to expand in some international market and under the supervision of a faculty member with relevant experience. In addition to the project, participants also choose a couple of individual options for further study. Finally, they complete a dissertation, which in the case of part-timers is generally based on a subject chosen by their own company.

What MBS calls 'the Manchester Method' is the integration of theory and practice; as the course progresses there is a growing emphasis on consultancy-type assignments and their implementation. The faculty is composed of people who are strong in both the academic and the practical sphere and several of them are recognised authorities on their subject.

They are resourced and backed up by the considerable facilities of Manchester University, itself one of the UK's major universities and a world leader in many fields, particularly in several aspects of science and technology. The link with UMIST will strengthen this still further. However, MBS has its own dedicated building, extensive computer facilities and language laboratories.

Languages, including Japanese, feature in the electives. Japan has an historic link with Manchester, through the cotton industry in the 19th century and this has been maintained in The Greater Manchester Centre for Japanese Studies, set up in 1989. Through it, MBA students taking a diploma in Japanese can get a placement with a company in Japan during their course. In fact, exchanges with other schools are a generally strong feature of MBS. Two-thirds of its students undertake some kind of exchange programme while they are there. There is also a marked presence of overseas students on the MBA course. 45% of those on the full-time programme come from outside the EC.

Though, as we said in the opening sentences, the connection with the University has been the source of some strain over the last couple of years – culminating in the resignation of the last Director – it is potentially a source of competitive advantage which the incoming Head of the School, Professor Cockerill, is determined to exploit. For instance, its overall status makes Manchester University a focal point for recruiters. At the same time its research reputation in many fields has forged both formal and informal links with business and industry which are as strong as those of any academic institution in the country and which also open potential career doors. It is probably not generally known that 28 foreign banks are based in Manchester and that 80 out of the FT top 100 companies have offices or headquarters there.

This combination of contacts, furthered by the emphasis on project work, makes MBS a good choice for those looking for a change of career direction – something which is often hampered by lack of access to the right people and by the dread Catch-22: lack of experience in the right sector. It affects the careers of people at all levels, but constant exposure to projects in a chosen field of activity can be a way of overcoming that problem.

Manchester, though it is a city of 800,000 people, is not expensive to live in and you generally get reasonable accommodation within half an hour's journey of the School. But there is also a further financial attraction: the availability of up to 30 assistantships each year. In return for 200 hours work, students can get their fees reduced by £2000. Everyone accepted by the School is invited to apply and the decision is then made on the basis of ability and need. The question is how much work is required in the 200 hours, bearing in mind the onerous nature of the MBA programme. But it is certainly a fact to keep in mind for those for whom £4000 is a material sum. As far as the 55% UK students are concerned, that might be quite a few.

Edinburgh University Management School

Edinburgh is one of the UK's oldest and most prestigious universities, so it is somewhat surprising that its management school seldom figures in the unofficial rankings or the gossip circuit about business schools – itself a sign of recognition of some kind. That is not a matter of Sassenach parochialism in reverse, because both Strathclyde and Stirling Business Schools are fairly well known south of the Border. It is probably a reflection of the fact that to some extent the reputation of a school is not a matter of size or academic excellence. It simply depends on how long it has been around and though Edinburgh University has been awarding MBAs since 1984, the Management School itself only started in 1990.

Its stated aim is unabashed: to be 'the quality Management School in Scotland' and its attachment to Edinburgh University could give it a big competitive advantage in this ambition. It has focused its publicity on Scotland, which is maybe why it is not as well known as some other schools of similar calibre. As it is, the Edinburgh MBA has something of the quality of a well-kept secret, though the number of those on it is growing rapidly; currently there are about 100 students on the full time course and a total of around 320 enrolled as part-time MBAs.

Those on the programme are enthusiastic about it, but Stephen Halvorson, a Canadian banker taking a year out to do a full-time course, may be typical of at least some foreign students when he says it might not have been his first choice had it not been that his wife had elected to do a PhD in nursing at Edinburgh's renowned medical school.

Having made his choice, though, he says that he feels it was the right one, both on academic and amenity grounds. The University is superbly resourced and its reputation has attracted, Michael Porter-style, a number of satellite bodies and institutions such as the Europa Institute and the Artificial Intelligence Applications Institute. Apart from that, Edinburgh is also a good place to live in: small enough to be easy to get about in, but large enough to provide consumer choice in accommodation and other matters. And while culturally the 'Athens Of The North' may be past its glory days, Edinburgh still has something of the air of a European capital, if a provincial one.

The other attraction of the Edinburgh MBA, from Halvorson's point of view, is its strong financial orientation. That reflects the Scottish capital's status as a major European financial centre. But as a banker with several years experience is he not going over a lot of ground with which he is already familiar? No, says Halvorson. 'A lot of the techniques have changed since I was an undergraduate and I'm re-examining a lot of what I learned earlier in the light of experience – not just my own but that of the other participants on the course.'

An unusual feature of the Edinburgh MBA is

that whereas in most schools the number of electives offered to part-time students is smaller than that available to full-timers, here the reverse is true. Part-timers have a choice of 37 options, from which they have to choose nine. Full-timers choose four courses from 19 options, but in both cases the idea is that to some extent students can tailor their own MBA towards a preferred specialisation, though all students have to take a minimum number of each of two quantitative and non-quantitative subjects. The unusually wide range of options, say the teaching staff, is possible because they can draw on specialists from other parts of the university, for instance in the elective on business law. Students also have access to the university's language teaching facilities, though languages are regarded as an extra, not covered by the course fee. Rates to students are very reasonable, but it has to be said that 'internationalisation' is not as explicit a feature of the programme as at some schools. The School has established strong ties with Poland, but the faculty has doubts how strong the demand for student exchanges really is. 'We have 60 students from abroad on our full-time programme, which in itself introduces an international flavour, but not so many from here who want to go abroad,' says the School's Director, Professor Coke. He points out that exchange visits create particular problems for non-EC nationals.

The first term, or, in the case of part-timers the first two terms, are taken up by core courses. Thereafter comes a mix of required subjects and electives. In the final term of the full-time course or the final year of the part-time one students have to produce a dissertation. This is based either on something going on in their own organisation or in one of many different enterprises based in and around Edinburgh. On the full-time programme participants undertake a consultancy project in the Spring vacation channelled to the School through the Local Enterprise Agencies.

The workload is tough for both the full and the part-timers. In the latter case it involves attendance at two evening teaching sessions per week over a 30-week year; plus, says a faculty spokesman, two further nights a week for private or group study and up to a day at weekends. There is an equivalent workload for the full-timers, again with an emphasis on both group and individual work. Results are assessed on the basis of both types, and the dissertation, and you have to have a 50% overall pass mark in the core subjects, 55% in the non-core ones. No re-sits are allowed, but the averaging of pass marks does mean that a weak result in one subject can be set off against a good one in another.

Edinburgh is also unusual in that Professor Simon Coke has argued cogently against awarding prizes and distinctions. He feels that this would encourage students to focus on what they are best at – most likely the subjects they already know – rather than to add to and expand their knowledge and personal development.

Another slightly unusual feature is that you do not necessarily need to have a first degree to gain admission, though in that case you would need to go through a tough interviewing process. The School is also concerned with making sure that foreign students know enough English to benefit from the course. Edinburgh University has a highly regarded language teaching institute at which non-English speakers can be brought up to strength.

The mix of nationalities, educational backgrounds and experience generates a stimulus in itself. Contrast on the part-time programme, for instance, Jack Aitken, a 50-year-old building society executive without a degree but with a wealth of practical experience in the world of financial services, and Joy Duncan, a highly-qualified consultant pediatrician who herself teaches some courses in her own field in another part of the university, and who is doing an MBA in order to better understand the management requirement of practice in the context of NHS Trusts; or on the full-time course Stephen Halvorson, a mid-career banker broadening his business skills, and Hugh Fulton, a former army officer doing a financially-oriented MBA to enhance his chances of making a change of career direction. Each of them has a different set of career aims, but each brings a different perspective to the course work that colleagues find as valuable as the formal teaching content.

Henley Management College

Henley has what may be the most beguiling site of all UK business schools. Its core, now extended and also surrounded by a growing number of new buildings, is an elegant late 18th-century manor house set in a meadow overlooking a peaceful stretch of the upper Thames. It was the family home of the owners of W H Smith and as such it assumes that visitors arrive by private transport. There is a good bus service, but otherwise getting there involves a complicated mix of rail and taxi travel.

However, MBA students will need to make this journey only occasionally. Both the full-time and the part-time courses are conducted on the Uxbridge Campus of Brunel University. In fact Henley is not in itself a university at all. It conducts a range of postgraduate management courses, but its degrees are awarded by Brunel University, with which Henley has a relationship going back to 1972. In the course of that time, Henley and Brunel have developed a wide range of methods for delivering the MBA: as well as part- and full-time courses, there are single and inter-company (i.e., consortium) programmes, a Hybrid Manager MBA which has been developed to relate IT and general management skills, what is termed an 'Active MBA' – essentially a sandwich course combining residential learning and in-company activity, and an MBA in project management.

However, the Henley MBA which is best known to the general public is the distance learning programme, started in the mid-80s. Its enormous success – it currently has some 5000 students, about 50% of them in the UK – has spurred several other schools to launch their own distance learning MBAs and indeed this may be the fastest growing sector in the whole MBA market.

Henley's most direct competitor, however, is the Open Business School, which next year is expected to graduate around 1000 MBAs. Asked why someone should choose Henley rather than OBS, School spokesperson Jill Ford points out the flexibility of the Henley programme: 'we take account of the realities of a working manager's life,' she says.

For this reason, Henley receives steady stream of applications from those who want to transfer to its distance learning courses because they need to build more flexibility into their learning process – for instance because their working circumstances have changed. 'We review them on a case by case basis and give credit for up to 50% of work already completed, if it is up to our standard,' explains Ms Ford. Unusually, Henley recognises a Diploma of Management Studies (DMS) in its acceptance criteria; it is regarded as equivalent to Stage 1 of the Henley MBA. Equally, students who successfully complete Stage 1 but are unable to finish the Henley course are granted a DMS.

More often, though, applications come from those who want to start from scratch. Here, previous experience is a pre-requisite and a first degree is preferred, though not essential. Those who do not have one may be required to take a GMAT test, in which a score of 550 is regarded as acceptable.

One aspect of the theme of flexibility is that admission to the three stages of the programme is a moving staircase on which one can step four times a year; indeed admission to the preliminary foundation course can occur at any time. Thereafter students proceed to Stage 1, which covers the basic functional skills of management and assigns work in them. That is followed by an exam. Stage 2 focuses on management strategy, again reinforcing learning points with assignments. In Stage 3 there is a single elective (from a choice of six) and a company-based project and dissertation. One of the electives is explicitly in International Business Management, but internationalism is implicit in a good proportion of the case studies.

Continuing the theme of flexibility, the Henley distance learning course requires fewer residential elements than several of its competitors; indeed it prefers to call them workshops. They are normally one-day events, though not all students may be able to get home at the end of them. Furthermore, the School has established links with associates in some 16 countries, so that the workshops –

regarded as an important way of establishing contacts with other students and tutors, though they are not mandatory – can be attended nearer to the student's location.

However, one reason why Henley puts less emphasis on physical attendances than some of its competitors is that the School prides itself on the excellence of its communication techniques and logistics. Jill Ford points particularly to its computer communications system HELP (Henley Extended Learning Programme) which puts all its members on a global learning network, enabling them to access data and tutors, exchange information and take part in electronic conferencing. Information systems naturally feature in both the first and second stages of the MBA.

The other feature to which Henley draws attention is the School's sheer experience in the design and delivery of distance learning. The learning modules come in a boxed set made up of audio and video tapes, dedicated and user-tested written materials, and textbooks. No more than two boxes, each containing an estimated 100 hours' worth of study time, are sent out at a time so that students do not get swamped. With each module there is an assignment that, when completed, is turned round by the school within a maximum of 28 days. At the same time, the computer and voice links that are integral to the distance learning course enables students to call for assistance on a 24-hour helpline if they run into difficulties with any of the material.

Appropriate parts of some of the other part-time courses are also taught through distance

learning. A case in point is the Active MBA, an 18-month programme which uses a mix of three mandatory residential modules of between four and six weeks, home study and company-based applications. It and the other Henley MBA courses cover a lot of ground which is common to all, but there are some significant differences. One is that a foreign language is a compulsory topic, both because Professor Mills, Director of the Active Programme judges it as important in itself, but also because he regards it as a good way to get people to 'open up'. The Active MBA is aimed at more senior managers – the average age on the course is 35 – and at this stage of one's career personal development is as important as honing functional skills. The final part of the Active MBA, as in other programmes, is a dissertation, based on a project done either in the student's own company, or with one of the many bodies with whom Henley has active working relationships.

Henley's aim is primarily to give specialists a broader view of management skills, while also giving generalists some insight into the main functional specialisms of management. Given the fact that career development is the main motive for most people doing an MBA, Jill Ford emphasises that it will not, for instance, turn an HR specialist into a marketing wizard. But it will equip students with enough in-depth information to understand what other functional specialists on a team are getting at and enough confidence to argue a point outside their sphere. That in itself will give them the edge on colleagues who do not have an MBA.

The 9th edition of the Guide included profiles of the following courses:

CRANFIELD	ONE-YEAR MBA
STRATHCLYDE	ONE-YEAR MBA
LONDON BUSINESS	
SCHOOL	21 MONTH MBA
INSEAD	ONE-YEAR MBA
HENLEY	DISTANCE LEARNING MBA
ASHRIDGE	ONE-YEAR, PART-TIME/
	FULL-TIME MBA
CITY UNIVERSITY	EVENING MBA

Photocopies of the above are available from the Association of MBAs (address in index section). Please state course you are interested in and forward a stamped, self-addressed envelope plus three loose first class stamps.

Notes

1. *Financial Times*, 29.4.93

7 Where does it all get you?
The MBA and your career

In the 1980s, the MBA was often described by the less well-informed sections of the press as the 'yuppies degree'. High salaries were said to be the reward and, by implication, often the main reason for taking an MBA.

Whatever the truth of the matter was then, the situation has certainly changed in the more sober 1990s. The survey of 4700 graduate members of AMBA to which we have previously referred[1] says that while 'increasing salary' was stated by 1980s graduates to be a motive for doing an MBA, more recent students put forward a variety of mainly career-related objectives.

That this is more than a desire not to offend the susceptibilities of researchers in the softer, gentler nineties is confirmed by the increase in numbers on part-time courses. In 1992, more than two-thirds of MBA students remained in employment while studying. As we have shown

earlier, part-time students are generally supported to a greater or lesser extent by their employers, and therefore tend to stay with them at least for some time after completing their degree. Their motives are more likely to be concerned with career development within their existing organisations than with re-launching themselves on the job market as a new and pricier product.

The switch of emphasis to the career, rather than the immediate financial advantages of doing an MBA also reflects anxiety about jobs. Recession has affected virtually all the world's economies but many commentators feel that it has merely accelerated a process that was happening anyway, in which the jobs of those whose skills and knowledge were not up to scratch would be at risk. Even today's highly-regarded experts and specialists can find that their knowledge reaches its 'sell by' date in a much shorter time than used

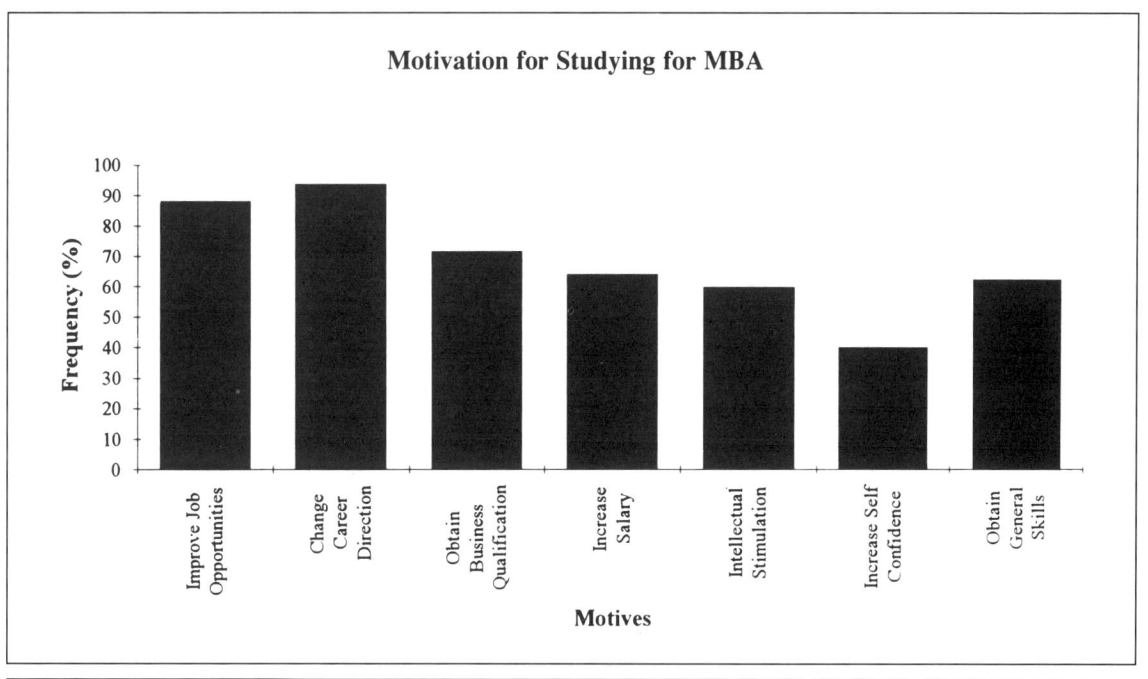

to be the case. In Tom Peters' phrase, the champ-to-chump cycle is getting ever shorter.

Taking an MBA is a way of remaining a champ. For specialists, its attraction is that it extends their competencies beyond the limited life of their specific, technical expertise and into that of general management. In the case of those who are already generalists, its value is that it broadens their understanding of business and business issues. The AMBA 25th Anniversary survey confirms that the vast majority of students believe that 'the main benefit to be gained will be the development of good, all round generalist (rather than specialist) skills. For them developing personal effectiveness by acquiring a wide range of management skills and competencies was the most important outcome.'

A further benefit they hoped for was gaining a good working knowledge of all the main functional disciplines of business. Many young managers who feel that colleagues in areas of which their own knowledge is limited – finance is a typical example for those without a financial

training – can pull the wool over their eyes. They hope the MBA will give them enough insight into every aspect of their job to enable them at least to know what is going on.

To what extent does the MBA programme deliver these expectations? Apparently satisfaction is very high. According to the AMBA survey of salaries and careers,[2] over 62% of those who had taken an MBA said they found the content of their course 'relevant or very relevant' to their eventual jobs. In informal discussions between the writer and current MBA students, the fact that they were acquiring enough understanding of the basic management discipline to understand what was going on in every key function was a theme that emerged again and again.

That is good news for employers who have sponsored managers to come on part-time courses. But how do those who finance their own studies in the hope of making a change in career direction, convince employers who may have been influenced by some of the negative talk about MBAs? What are the generic virtues of an MBA,

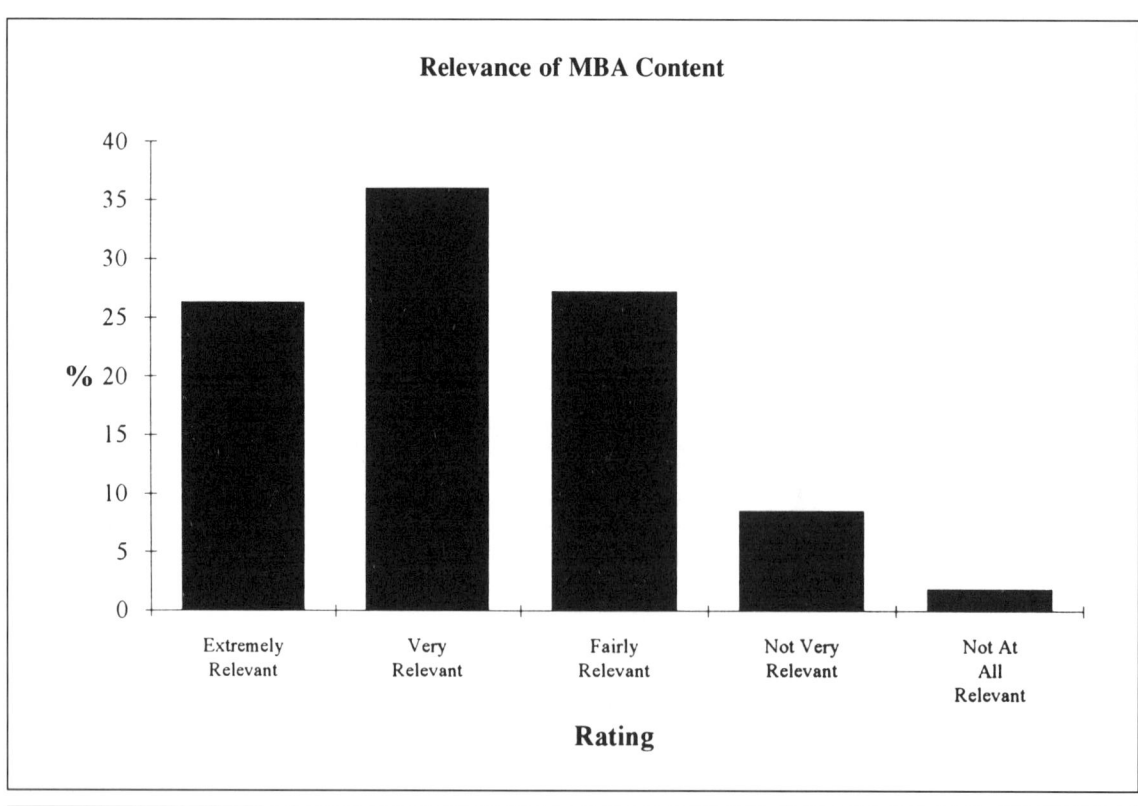

divorced from the relevance of its content to a particular organisation? Here are some ideas.

• *Evidence Of Dedication And Commitment*. As previous chapters have shown, the MBA requires a willingness to invest time and often money in acquiring a wider range of management skills – and a readiness to forego what might be more pleasurable things in the short term. Not everybody would put it that way, but an Ashridge graduate summed up a variation on an underlying theme when he said that he was faced with the choice of a Porsche or spending money on self-development, and chose the latter.

Commitment to the task in hand is a quality that employers are increasingly looking for. A number of commentators have pointed out that the relationship between employers and employees has changed from the feudal deal of protection by the former in return for loyalty by the latter.[3] Employers are no longer able to offer protection and no longer expect, or even particularly welcome, the prospect of loyal retainers. The relationship between knowledge workers and their employers has become much more like that between a football club and its players, which is one of full commitment on the field and in training, rather than to the individual player as such on the one hand, or to the club, as such, on the other. Being able to demonstrate a capacity for commitment is more important than being able to demonstrate loyalty. Employers look for a variety of experience, plus training (preferably paid for by someone else!) rather than years of loyal service.

• *Training Across A Broad Range Of 'Hard' Business Skills*. MBAs are sometimes criticised because they are short of experience 'at the sharp end'. But they can show that they have gone through an intensive training course across a variety of the hard disciplines of management, embodied in the core subjects of finance, marketing, information systems, operations organisational behaviour, economics and human resource management. At good schools, as we have shown earlier, the interconnection between these topics is the underlying theme of all teaching, just as it is in business practice. MBA graduates, in conversation with the writer, agree that this does not make you a great manager in itself. But it certainly enables you to understand what is going on around you, whereas many general managers, even good ones, have very little understanding of what functional specialists in these areas are talking about.

• *Development of 'Soft' Management Skills*. The way courses are taught, certainly in the part-time and full-time mode, with a great emphasis on group work, develops the soft skills that are becoming increasingly important in the context of flat-hierarchy, knowledge organisations: motivation, teamwork, presentation and negotiating skills.

That also enables MBAs to understand much more about themselves. Knowing one's own strengths and weaknesses is an essential part of learning to function as a team player. The EIU Guide quotes placement officers as wisely advising that students should not start targeting jobs until they have been through the self-assessment phase of the programme. That is not, of course, a specific set of units, but a realisation that begins to gell about half-way through the course.

• *An International Orientation*. 'Talk to the head of a business school today and the word internationalism will probably enter the conversation at some point,' London Business School Director, George Bain wrote in the *Times Higher Education Supplement* recently. The trend towards internationalism is taking two forms. Some courses are called 'International', or 'European' MBAs and involve students taking the elective part of the programme in different countries; that, for instance, is the arrangement between Strathclyde Graduate Business School, Groupe ESC Nantes and the Universidad Commercial de Deusto in Bilbao to which we have referred earlier.

Others view this trend with a certain amount of scepticism. In a world of global trading and transnational relationships, they argue, it is impossible to isolate internationalism as a separate strand of business. In practice MBA courses almost everywhere are now increasingly international in the content of teaching – for instance in extending the use of case studies from international business, in encouraging foreign students, recruiting foreign members of faculty and visiting speakers from abroad, in focusing on projects with an international content, in running language courses and in exchange and collaboration arrangements with business schools in other countries.

It is noteworthy that the same thing is happening in the USA, where the MBA has in the past taken little account of the world scene. Following a report by the Graduate Management Admission Council which urged US business schools to be less parochial in their teaching, a 'global view' is now one of the criteria used in the American *Business Week*'s influential ratings. Its surveys of the top 20 US executive MBAs show that many schools offered their international programme as their 'highlights'.[4] A background in international business is what most of the current generation of managers lacks. It is not the same thing as making business trips abroad.

- *The Ability To Work Under Pressure.* By whichever mode the MBA is taken, it involves working under pressure. That is not just a question of having to learn to turn out quality work with little time in which to do it. It means acquiring time management skills and the ability to prioritise tasks. Many graduates mentioned that at first they felt they were given a greater workload than they could possibly handle, until they realised that being able to focus on essentials was part of the training.

The Anti-Climax Effect

All the MBAs the writer talked to mentioned 'greater confidence' as one of the gains of the course. But in career terms that has a downside. MBAs on sponsored courses come away with a feeling summed up by one who said: 'You feel you've changed, but the organisation hasn't.'

Many people on sponsored MBAs move on after a decent interval because, although their salary has gone up, they feel their experience and hard-won skills are not being used properly by their employers. Even at Ashridge, whose course consists of a mix of in-company and residential modules, 40% of company-sponsored students reported that few of the recommendations arising out of their main project had been accepted. For non-sponsored ones the situation was worse.

Perhaps the lesson for part-time and distance learning programmes is that the whole thing, not just the project, needs to be integrated with your normal work. In fact many part-timers talk of the thrill of finding that what they are learning on their MBA programme has an immediate bearing on their day to day tasks.

But that does not always happen on its own. MBAs need to be proactive in seeing that what they do presents opportunities for the practical application of learning, even though the pressures of simply doing the course make it hard to focus on longer-term objectives.

Another way that MBAs can hit the ground running when they return to their employers or re-enter the job market is to link the project which forms part of the elective to their career aims. One woman on a business course – not an MBA in this case – chose as her project opening up a small, specialist, luxury food retail operation in London's Kings Road. She got an enormous amount of what would otherwise have been very expensive consultancy support from the faculty at her college as well as doing all the feasibility studies as her elective. When she graduated, she put her idea into practice, with great success.

Impact On Salary

What about salary prospects, though? While MBAs may not be looking for a direct reward simply because they have the degree, the idea of an eventual pay-off must linger in most of their minds somewhere. Even those who have been sponsored by their employer will have made a considerable sacrifice in terms of time, while self-funded MBAs will have made a direct and substantial financial investment, often funded through the AMBA loan scheme. There are also opportunity costs to consider. Full-timers will have lost a year's income and even part-timers might have had to put a promotion on hold because of the additional pressure of work that it might have entailed.

AMBA's research into the salaries of its members does show that having an MBA is worthwhile from a financial point of view – though not as much as it was in the 1980s. Those who graduated in 1991 and changed employers were being paid 34% above their previous base salary. Allowing for salary inflation, this represented a real increase of 16.5% over and above what they might have expected to earn anyway had they not taken the MBA. However, during the period 1980–85, those figures were much higher: 65% and 40% respectively.

The decline in the rate of pay increases to MBAs reflects the laws of supply and demand coming from two different directions. One is the decline in the executive job market. The other is the increase in the number of MBA graduates. The latter gives added point to the consideration being given by recruiters as to where the degree was obtained.

The good news, however, is that the salaries earned by MBAs are relatively high. The AMBA survey shows that 30% of the respondents were earning base salaries of between £30,000 and £40,000 pa. Only 7% were getting less than £20,000 and at the other end of the scale 8% reported salaries greater than £70,000. 3% earned more than £100,000.

Changing Places

Another aspect of the difficulty of making anything other than broad comparisons between salaries is the variation between sectors, functions and regions. The highest rewards are reported by MBAs currently working in the financial and consultancy sectors. The lowest, unsurprisingly, are in the public sector.

Looking at the picture from a further point of view – that of function – general management,

finance and, this time surprisingly, personnel, come out best, whereas MBAs in production and administration do least well. There are also geographic variations. Salaries are highest in inner London, which is probably also a reflection of the concentration of consultancy and finance-related jobs there. They are significantly lower in the North-East and East Anglia.

This raises an important question: to what extent can having an MBA facilitate a change of career direction in search of more money or better prospects? Reports indicate that this can be very difficult, except in the case of those who want to move into consultancy or some of the more analytical areas of financial services. 'The MBA gives a sound grounding in strategic thinking, aside from providing a theoretical framework from which to operate and provides exposure to ideas and situations which would not be confronted by someone other than working at senior management/CEO level,' says Elaine Golding, a recent MBA. In other words, it adds value to experience by giving it an intellectual framework, a strategic view of the business you are in. But it is of limited, immediately bankable value without that experience, which is another reason why many organisations prefer consortium MBAs to more general programmes and why moves into a totally diferent sector are hard to make.

Where these do occur, research confirms that they are mostly into finance and consultancy and out of construction and some branches of engineering.

Another significant trend is for MBAs to move from larger to smaller organisations which perhaps indicates that new and more dynamic companies value them more highly than the established ones. But there are hopeful signs among the latter too. There has been much criticism of the way MBAs were used by large employers – often subjected to trial by some kind of management ordeal rather than being put into roles where they could best apply what they had learned. The suggestion was that this might best be in internal consultancy-related roles. The four-fold increase in the number of MBAs going into the corporate strategy and planning function indicates that this might actually be happening.

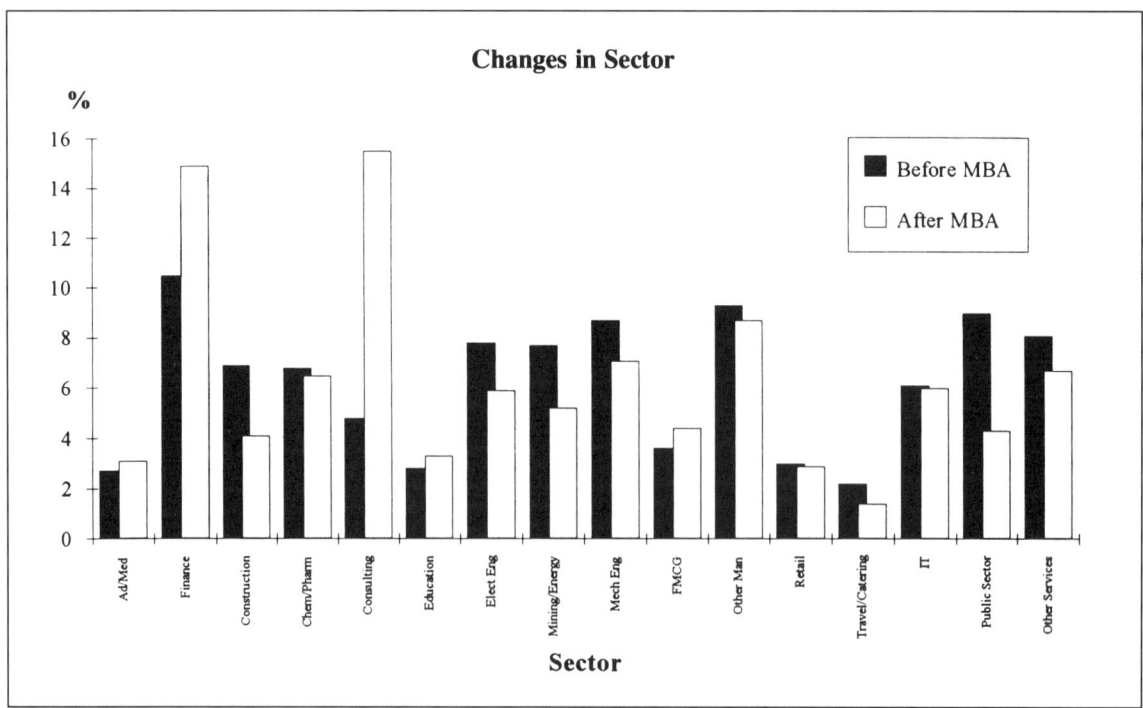

Changes in Sector

%

Before MBA
After MBA

Sector

In spite of the disclaimers about a financial motive for doing an MBA, the conflict many face on graduating is between short-term financial gains, driven possibly by the need to repay a loan, and long-term career development. The former can push you in the direction of the highest bidder, rather than the best career move. That is why it is important to have a career strategy, as the writer has advocated in *Smart Moves*,[5] a book targeted towards the career path of MBAs. For instance, going for an increase of £10,000 on your previous salary when you graduate may push you along a career path in consultancy and a plateau at partnership level. If your sights are set on a chief executive role in industry, consultancy is generally thought to be the wrong road to take – the skills are different from those of line management. But a firm of consultants or financial analysts will generally pay a significantly higher starting salary to an MBA than one in, say, a manufacturing company.

An even greater danger is that of making a false first move for financial reasons. It has happened, and executive search and selection consultants say that an MBA who has suffered a career crash in his or her first postgraduate job is in a worse position than someone without an MBA. Employers will think they should have known better! Fortunately career management strategies, as well as 'how to get job' basics, are beginning to be recognised by schools as a significant adjunct to MBA programmes.

Follow your passion

A stimulating article by Tom Peters, unpublished in the UK, is entitled 'Hey MBAs, Follow Your Passion. 'It offers some of the best career advice to MBAs that the writer has seen. Peters writes: 'MBAs often ask me how to assess companies that recruit at their schools. My response: If the interviewer turns you on, move ahead. If he or she is a stiff you wouldn't be caught dead hanging out with, forget it. Don't assume that he's the rare jerk in a company of gems.'

Basing his words on his own experience, Peters advises his readers to go for the person, not the assignment. 'A lousy boss can make the best assignment hell. A super boss can make the dullest assignment sparkle.'

Above all he advises MBAs to follow their

'passion' – the things they're really interested in. 'If necessary, apprentice yourself for bread and board to someone who can teach you to excel at doing something you already love,' he writes and adds. 'Tough advice for top-school MBAs, I admit. Many have borrowed $50,000 or more to finance their education. No wonder they're suckers for big, dull companies who overpay entry-level MBAs . . . In smaller firms talented people have a good chance of making a huge difference, fast.' Some people, of course, feel happier in large companies, dull or otherwise. The whole business of career management is all about aligning your own skills and values with the appropriate tasks and organisational culture – the core message of 'Smart Moves'. Getting to know about yourself and where you fit into the corporate world may not be something the MBA expressely teaches you, but it emerges by implication from your studies, the work you do with fellow students and the company-related project you undertake. That is one of the most valuable things, in career terms, that the MBA provides.

PART TWO

School directory

This section of the Guide provides brief profiles on individual schools. It is designed to enable the intending student to draw up a short list of schools to contact for more detailed information. Included are: contact addresses, telephone numbers, details of courses available, information on student intake, the school's faculty, facilities, affiliations and special features. The schools are listed in alphabetical order.

No attempt is made to rank courses and each school has been allocated the same space irrespective as to size or reputation. Although many of these schools offer PhD programmes, specialist masters degress or diploma courses, only MBAs or near equivalent degrees are outlined in this section. The information provided was submitted by individual schools in February/March 1993.

Which schools are included

All UK schools offering a UK university accredited MBA course were invited to complete a questionnaire so as to be included in this section. Questionnaires were sent to all 92 individual institutions in the United Kingdom which qualified under this criterion. Overseas schools were included on the basis of offering Association of MBA's approved courses and, additionally, on sufficient interest having been noted in the school at the Association's general enquiry desk.

Schools not included here have either failed to meet the criteria specified above or they failed to return their questionnaires.

Schools by geographical area

The schools in this section are listed in alphabetical order and according to three geographical areas: United Kingdom, Rest of Europe and North America.

For those contemplating part-time study, in particular, a school's location is of great importance. When checking UK schools by geographical location you should remember that most cities of any size have not one, but often two or even more schools.

Eligibility for MBA study

The MBA is a post-experience as well as a prostgraduate degree. An MBA is, therefore, only as valid and useful as the cv that supports it. You should note hat the average full-time MBA candidate is 27 years of age on commencement of study and the average part-time student is six or seven years older.

A recent graduate may feel it expedient to study for an MBA immediately or shortly after graduation. This would be an ill-advised course of action as employers of MBAs are looking to recruit people with proven business acumen who can utilise newly-acquired MBA skills in a general management role. Such highly-paid key jobs are not offered to unknown quantities. Employers will not give the benefit of doubt when there is no shortage of well-qualified MBAs who do meet their expectations.

If you will not have a minimum of two, and preferably more than three, years' relevant work experience at the commencement of a course you will be well advised to postpone your plans to study for the MBA until a later date. Places at the better schools are seldom offered to candidates without significant relevant work experience.

AMBA accreditation

Reasons for accreditation

The Association of MBAs was established in 1967 to encourage management education at postgraduate level in order to create professional managers. Part of its mission was to ensure that any expansion in business school numbers was matched by an equal concern for the quality of the product. The machinery established to secure this was one of accreditation: assessing the characteristics of the business school against specific criteria. The criteria initially established by the Association have been progressively refined over the years. Both employers and business schools have made major contributions to this process.

With over 90 business schools in the UK, and an increasing number of schools in continental Europe, ever more requests are being received for accreditation. Sir Graham Day, Chairman of AMBA's Advisory Council, states of this growth that: 'Welcome though this expansion is, it calls for corresponding vigilance to ensure that the standards of quality are maintained. The Association of MBAs sees the criteria as a major tool in developing this objective. It seeks to do so with the support, not only of its members, but of employers and of the leading business schools.'

Membership of the Association of MBAs is open only to students at, or graduates of, accredited courses, and only students on such courses can take advantage of the AMBA Business School Loan Scheme (see chapter on Financing Your MBA).

Process of accreditation

As a first step AMBA welcomes an initial discussion with a business school seeking first-time accreditation, in order to establish whether there is a reasonable consistency of outlook and the likelihood that, if undertaken, an accreditation visit would have a successful outcome. The school will then be asked to complete a self-audit of the salient points of AMBA criteria. This ensures that any subsequent team visit uses its time in the most productive way possible. The assessment team, which is commissioned by AMBA, normally comprises four individuals and the visits take a full day, following a pre-specified schedule. The team prepares a report for the business school and for the National Committee of the Association. This highlights those areas where criteria are, or are not, met and if appropriate offers suggestions for improvements at the school. The business school is invited to respond to the report. After a response from the school the final report to the National Committee recommends: a) accreditation; b) accreditation subject to qualification; or c) non-accreditation.

Aspects considered in accreditation

An accreditation includes a thorough review of: the business school as an entity, the faculty, the research base, the student body, the MBA curriculum (particularly the course content), admission criteria, assessment, facilities, and services to students.

Re-accreditation

A number of recent developments has led the Association to review the operation of its procedures. The increase in the number of business schools offering the MBA has placed acute demands on the process. The need for accreditation has, therefore, become increasingly important.

AMBA has responded by strengthening the accreditation team and by re-assessing its criteria and procedures. The previous process by which accreditation, once agreed, was of permanent validity has been discontinued. The new approach, introduced in 1992, reassesses schools every seven years. In January 1993 Aston Business School became the first school to be successfully re-accredited in this way.

Distance learning MBAs

It is important to note that AMBA accredits individual courses, and not schools. Under current rules only full- and part-time MBA courses are eligible for accreditation. However, a significant development over recent years has been the growth in the number of universities offering the MBA by distance learning and in the numbers of students enroling in these courses.

As 'distance learning' has substantially changed in style and approach over recent years, AMBA is now investigating ways and means by which the 'quality' of these courses might be assessed.

Schools offering Courses approved by AMBA

United Kingdom

Ashridge Management School
Aston University Business School
Bath University
Bradford University
Bristol Business School
City University Business School
Cranfield Management School
Durham University Business School
EAP
Edinburgh University
Glasgow University
Henley, The Management College
Heriot-Watt University
Imperial College

Kingston University Business School
Lancaster University
Leicester Business School
Loughborough University
London Business School
Manchester Business School
Middlesex University Business School
Newcastle University
Nottingham University
Sheffield University
Sheffield Hallam University
Stirling University
Strathclyde Graduate School of Business
Warwick University Business School
Westminster University (London Management Centre)

Continental Europe

Belgium: Leuven
France: ESC Lyon, EAP, HEC-ISA, INSEAD
Italy: SDA Bocconi
Netherlands: Rotterdam
Spain: IESE, ESADE
Switzerland: IMD

In the United States the professional accreditation body for the MBA is the American Assembly of Collegiate Schools of Business (AACSB). In most countries there is no equivalent accrediting organisation to the AMBA or the AACSB.

ABERDEEN MBA PROGRAMME

Location and Contact Details:

Address	27-29 King Street
	Aberdeen
	AB2 3AA
	UK
Telephone Number	0224 620223
Facsimile Number	0224 620252
Contact Name	Ailsa Forbes

School Description:

The Aberdeen MBA programme is a joint course involving The Robert Gordon University and the University of Aberdeen. It is a modular course with flexibility to fast track over 2½ years or extend over a longer period.

School Details:

MBA Courses	*Part-time*
Duration	2½ years
Class Contact	2 eves/week + some weekends
Dissertation or Project	dissertation
Assessment	exam/course

Final date for applications:
before end April advised

Estimated Fees 1993/1994 Academic Year:
£2,025 year 1   £2,375 year 2

1992 Student Intake:

Intake	45
UK	45
Women	13%

ANGLIA BUSINESS SCHOOL

Location and Contact Details:

Address	Danbury Park Conference Centre
	Main Road, Danbury
	Essex CM3 4AT
	UK
Telephone Number	0245 225511
Facsimile Number	0245 224331
Contact Name	Mrs Rita Abernethy

School Description:

Anglia University is regional. The MBA is offered at Chelmsford, Cambridge, Norwich and Berlin. The fees include an overseas visit.

School Details:

MBA Courses	*Full-time*	*Part-time*
Duration	1 year	2 years
Class Contact	400 hours	400 hours
Dissertation or Project	dissertation	dissertation
Assessment	course	course

Final date for applications:

	1st September	30th September

Estimated Fees 1993/1994 Academic Year:

	£9,325	£3,125

1992 Student Intake:

Intake	starts 1993	186
UK		166
Other EC		19
Non-EC		2
Women		20%

Faculty Details:

Dedicated MBA programme teaching staff	16
Full professors	1
Visiting lecturers/professors	4
With Master's degree	10
With PhD	6

Facilities:

Library hours	09.00-20.00 Mon-Fri; Sat am
IT availability	Lap-tops and 100 fixed terminals
Cultural opportunities	Very wide range as in all UK Universities

International Affiliations:

Fachhochschule für Wirtschaft, Berlin; HEAD, Limburg; Grenoble II, Grenoble

---

Individual courses approved by AMBA are indicated by a 'tick'.

PART TWO   69

ASHRIDGE MANAGEMENT COLLEGE

Location and Contact Details:
Address   Berkhamsted
             Herts HP4 1NS
             UK
Telephone Number   044 0442 84 3491
Facsimile Number   044 0442 84 2259
Contact Name   Mrs Doris Boyle

School Description:
Features include: Practical approach to learning via major strategic project; leadership development; most topics are covered within the context of a general management programme; languages are offered as electives.

School Details:
MBA Courses	Full-time ✓	Part-time
Duration	1 year	2 years
Class Contact	modular/	modular/
	750+ hours	750+ hours
Dissertation		
or Project	project	
Assessment	exam/course	

Final date for applications:
          throughout year   September
Estimated Fees 1993/1994 Academic Year:
          £18,950 + VAT   £9,475 + VAT

1992 Student Intake:
Intake	19
UK	8
Other EC	2
Non-EC	9
Women	20%

Faculty Details:
Dedicated MBA programme teaching staff	60
Full professors	n/a
Visiting lecturers/professors	6
With Master's degree	43
With PhD	10

Facilities:
Library hours	08.00-22.00
IT availability	1 per candidate, fully equipped Learning Resource Centre, library, Information Service, Media and Video facilities

International Affiliations:
City University

ASTON BUSINESS SCHOOL

Location and Contact Details:
Address   Aston University
             Aston Triangle
             Birmingham B4 7ET
             UK
Telephone Number   021 359 3011
Facsimile Number   021 333 4731
Contact Name   Dr Mark Oakley
                        Director of Postgraduate Studies

School Description:
Unlike most MBA courses, we take the trouble to cater for younger managers stream. Nature of international links: 1) spend part of course on overseas study; 2) specially designed short study visits. The school has an active Graduate Network, a support group comprising Chief Executives and Senior Directors, provides career support and guidance and has high quality bespoke teaching facilities. Features include: academic strengths in problem solving and innovation; Active Professional Development Programme, providing support in topics as diverse as Business Ethics, Legal Environment of Business, and Self Marketing; recently launched MBA in Public Sector Management.

School Details:
MBA Courses	Full-time ✓	Part-time ✓	Distance Learning
Duration	12 months	33-36 months	33-36 months
Class Contact	450 hours	450 hours	450 video hours
Dissertation			
or Project	project	project	project
Assessment	exam/ course	exam/ course	

Final date for applications:
          August   August   August
Estimated Fees 1993/1994 Academic Year:
          £7,000   £2,500   £8,000

1992 Student Intake:
Intake	71	60	35

   Schools offering an AMBA-approved course are indicated in this section by the AMBA 'roundel'.

O ver 2500 Aston MBA graduates worldwide are leading businesses towards the 21st Century. Equip yourself to join them through our On-Campus Full-time and Part-time programmes (now including an exciting new Public Sector Management MBA) or the **unique and highly innovative** ABS Real-time Video Distance Learning MBA. With an emphasis on problem solving and innovation, the Aston MBA course offers options in:

- *Marketing*
- *Finance and Information*
- *Operations*
- *Human Resources*
- *Public Sector Management*
- *International Business (including the opportunity for study abroad)*

The academic programme is supported by a range of services covering languages and interpersonal skills training, career development and the international Aston MBA Graduate Network.

For further details contact:
The Postgraduate Office, Aston Business School
Birmingham. B4 7ET
TEL: 021-359 3011 extension 5014
(24 hour ansaphone)

ASTON UNIVERSITY

CELEBRATING 25 YEARS
25 years
ASTON BUSINESS PROGRAMMES

UK	43	58	32
Other EC	15	1	3
Non-EC	13	1	0
Women	35%	25%	25%

Faculty Details:

Dedicated MBA programme teaching staff	30
Full professors	7
Visiting lecturers/professors	10
With Master's degree	20
With PhD	18

Facilities:

Library hours	09.00-22.00 Mon-Fri/ 10.00-17.00 Sat
IT availability	Bespoke MBA syndicate rooms (10) with computers; 2 micro workshops totalling 60 computers. Access to Mac lab with 40 computers. Access to on-line business data sources.

International Affiliations:
Exchange agreements with: Maastricht, Mannheim, Lille, Marseille

BANGOR INSTITUTE FOR FINANCIAL MANAGEMENT

Location and Contact Details:

Address	MBA Office, University of Wales Bangor Gwynedd LL57 2DG UK
Telephone Number	0248 382162
Facsimile Number	0248 370769
Contact Name	Mr Robert Henry

School Description:

The course is designed as an accelerated, 18-month programme building on professional qualifications for managers in banking, finance, insurance and administration. The school is a member of the Lombard Scheme. Strengths include Accounting, Economics, Finance, International Business, Marketing, Operations Management, Organisational Behaviour.

School Details:

MBA Courses	*Part-time, Distance Learning & Company/Consortium*
Duration	18 months accelerated course; 30 months full.
Class Contact	workshops – 2 x 3 days every 6 months
Dissertation or Project	project
Assessment	exam/course

Final date for applications:
Intakes Jan/July. Distance learning: open.

Estimated Fees 1993/1994 Academic Year:
£4,290 (18 months);
£6,490 (30 months)

1992 Student Intake:

Intake	215
UK	102
Other EC	6
Non-EC	107
Women	10%

Faculty Details:

Dedicated MBA programme teaching staff	23
Full professors	4
With PhD	4

Facilities:

Other facilities	Overseas Study Support Centres in Hong Kong, Singapore, Malaysia, Jamaica and Jordan. More centres proposed for July 1993 intake.

International Affiliations:
Manchester Business School

Schools offering an AMBA-approved course are indicated in this section by the AMBA 'roundel'.

MBAth

The Bath MBA programmes give you an intensive management education designed to release you from your current functional box so that you are involved in, and influence, all areas of your company's business.

These long-standing programmes are designed and run by highly qualified management experts in the University's Centre for Executive Development. All of the tutors have wide experience of industry and commerce.

Executive MBA
Are you a middle manager able to spend the Friday and Saturday of alternate weekends at the University of Bath? If so, get the Executive MBA brochure by ringing Lorraine Chard on 0225 826211.

Full-time MBA
Are you aged between 27 and 35, with relevant management or professional experience, and looking for the next step forward in your career? If so, get the full-time MBA brochure by ringing Frances Free on 0225 826152.

CENTRE · FOR · EXECUTIVE · DEVELOPMENT
University of Bath, Claverton Down, Bath, BA2 7AY.
Please quote ref. 93/04

UNIVERSITY OF BATH

UNIVERSITY OF BATH, SCHOOL OF MANAGEMENT

Location and Contact Details:

Address	University of Bath	
	Claverton Down	
	Bath BA2 7AY	
	UK	
Telephone Number	FT: 0225 826152	
	PT: 0225 826211	
Facsimile Number	0225 826210	
Contact Name	FT: Ken Clark	
	PT: Anthony Birts	

School Description:

School offers full- and part-time MBAs. There is also a Malaysian MBA with the Malaysian Institute of Management. Both MBAs offer a strong core course structure with an integrative international perspective. FT: summer options include Environment, Gender Issues, Ethics, Managing in Europe. We foster and encourage a nutually supportive and cohesive working environment for students. Courses form part of the Centre for Executive Development within the School of Management. The majority of PT students are from our Sponsoring and Founding Companies – approx. 60%. All students on both courses must have some work experience on a managerial level. For FT: TOEFL is required for those whose native tongue is not English. Average GMAT score is 550.

School Details:

MBA Courses	Full-time ✓	Part-time
Duration	1 year	2 years
Class Contact	459 hours	432 hours
		(36 days/year)
Dissertation		
or Project	project	project
Assessment	exams/course	exams/course

Estimated Fees 1993/1994 Academic Year:

	£7,250	£6,000

1992 Student Intake:

Intake	41	21
UK	27	21
Other EC	2	
Non-EC	12	
Women	17%	

Faculty Details:

Dedicated MBA programme teaching staff	41
Full professors	7
Visiting lecturers/professors	3
With Master's degree	25
With PhD	25

Facilities:

Library hours	09.00-24.00 Mon-Fri/10.00-20.00 weekends (term-time)
IT availability	25 pcs all with Windows and Micro-office, Microsoft Word 5 and Lotus 123, all linked to Sun Server
Cultural opportunities	Bath is U.N. World Heritage City, with music, theatre, ballet etc. University has many cultural facilities
Other facilities	new MBA teaching facilities, dedicated lecture theatres (fully equipped with all audi-visual and video equipment) and syndicate rooms for small group work

International Affiliations:
None

THE BIRMINGHAM BUSINESS SCHOOL

Location and Contact Details:

Address	The Graduate Centre for Business Administration
	University of Birmingham
	Priorsfield, 46 Edgbaston Park Road
	Birmingham B15 2RU
	UK
Telephone Number	021 414 6693
Facsimile Number	021 414 3553
Contact Name	David Perman

School Description:

The School offers 3 full-time MBA programmes in International Business, European Business and International Banking and Finance, underpinned by a 9 month diploma programme in Business Administration. A Sectoral Modular MBA is also offered in Biotechnology Management. There is also a Masters Degree in Development Finance and Accounting. School strengths are in Industry Regulation, International Banking and Finance, Trade and International Finance, Consumer Behaviour and Marketing, and Development Finance.

Schools offering an AMBA-approved course are indicated in this section by the AMBA 'roundel'.

**THE UNIVERSITY
OF BIRMINGHAM**

THE BIRMINGHAM BUSINESS SCHOOL

The MBA & Diploma Programmes

FULL-TIME PROGRAMMES of 12, 18 OR 24 months duration

*MBA International Business   *MBA European Business
*MBA International Banking and Finance
*Diploma in Business Administration

PART-TIME PROGRAMMES of 24 to 48 months
duration taken by Evening or Modular Study

*MBA International Business   *Modular Executive MBA
*Modular Biotechnology Management MBA
*Diploma in Business Administration

THE PROGRAMMES FEATURE:

* Flexible entry points depending on qualifications, age and experience
* International student body and faculty
*Substantial extracurricular agenda

The Birmingham Business School has been providing international
management education for almost a century. The research expertise of the
school, especially in International Finance, Trade and Industrial Strategy,
Marketing and Consumer Behaviour, is assimilated in to the taught programmes,
and complements the practical bias, to give an in-depth knowledge of the
operational and strategic aspects of managing organizations.

The Birmingham Business School
The University of Birmingham
Priorsfield
46 Edgbaston Park Road
Birmingham, B15 2RU
ENGLAND
Tel: 021 414 6693/4   Fax: 021 414 3553

School Details:

MBA Courses	Full-time	Part-time	Modular
Duration	12-24 months	24-36 months	21-42 months
Class Contact	497	308	514
Dissertation or Project	either	either	either
Assessment	exam/ course	exam/ course	exam/ course

Final date for applications:

	May	September	continual

Estimated Fees 1993/1994 Academic Year:

EC	£4,500	£2,300	£5,750 or £900/ module
Overseas	£6,300		

1992 Student Intake:

Intake	188	29	20
UK	28	28	19
Other EC	29	1	
Non-EC	131		1
Women	31.8%	24.3%	40%

Faculty Details:

Dedicated MBA programme teaching staff	33
Full professors	6
Visiting lecturers/professors	7
With Master's degree	17
With PhD	12

Facilities:

Library hours	08.00-20.00
IT availability	2 labs with over 120 pcs available, datastream, high speed network spans 5 continents
Cultural opportunities	Students from over 42 different countries in 1992/3.
Other facilities	Visits to Ironbridge, Longbridge, York, Lake District & Oxford arranged for students

International Affiliations:

Brest, Montpelier, Sorbonne, South Carolina, Memphis, Wuppertal, Florence, Hitotsubashi, Keio, Madrid, Antwerp, Besançon, Bordeau, Clermont-Ferrano, Le Havre, Mannheim, Regensberg, Verona, Lisbon

UNIVERSITY OF BRADFORD MANAGEMENT CENTRE

Location and Contact Details:

Address	Emm Lane Heaton Bradford West Yorkshire BD9 4JL UK
Telephone Number	0274 384373
Facsimile Number	0274 546866
Contact Names	Gail Barbour (MBA Sec.) Dr Chris Parkinson (Dir.)

School Description:

Excellent language teaching facilities; additional vocational skills courses available; very attractive environment; emphasis on group/team work alongside opportunities for personal development. Subject specialisations in: Finance; Marketing; Human Resource Management; Economics & Corporate Planning; Production Operations Management; Business Policy; International Business; General Management.

School Details:

MBA Courses	Full-time ✓	Part-time ✓	Modular	Company/ Consortium
Duration	12 months	2/3 years	varies	varies
Class Contact	350 hours	350 hours		
Dissertation or Project	either	either		
Assessment	exam/ course	exam/ course	exam/ course	exam/ course

Final date for applications:

	July	July/ August	July	by agree- ment

Estimated Fees 1993/1994 Academic Year:

EC	£7,150	£3,000	Yrs½ then £0	£7,150 over period of course
Non-EC	£6,500			

1992 Student Intake:

Intake	128	45
UK	68	45

Schools offering an AMBA-approved course are indicated in this section by the AMBA 'roundel'.

Other EC	15	
Non-EC	45	
Women	30.5%	15%

Faculty Details:

Dedicated MBA programme teaching staff	60
Full professors	12
Visiting lecturers/professors	80 (not simultaneous)
With Master's degree	20
With PhD	38

Facilities:

Library hours	08.45-14.00 Mon-Fri
IT availability	56 terminals available for students in centre + access to extensive facilities on main campus
Cultural opportunities	Exchanges possible in the Netherlands, Germany, France, USA, Canada, Australia

Other facilities	Links with most European countries and also in the Far East. MSc in Human Resource Management available in Singapore

International Affiliations:

Netherlands Institute for MBA studies, Utrecht and Essen; Carnegie-Mellon; Aarhus University; Carleton University, Toronto; University of Miskolc, Hungary; ESC Groupe-Lyon; Montpelier, France

Individual courses approved by AMBA are indicated by a 'tick'.

UNIVERSITY OF BRIGHTON BUSINESS SCHOOL

Location and Contact Details:

Address	EMBA Programme Office, Mithras House
Address	UBBS, Lewes Road,
	Brighton, East Sussex BN2 4AT
	UK
Telephone Number	0273 642197
Facsimile Number	0273 642153
Contact Name	Christina Pepper

School Description:

The designation University was established by an act of British Parliament, and its title approved by Her Majesty's Privy Council. The University is firmly committed to continuing professional education education – widening participation in higher education is fundamental to our work. CAT accepted for part-time and modular MBA. Specialist full-time MBA includes foreign language training and an optional term abroad thinking and working in your new foreign language. Specialist modular MBA in technology management. Further study opportiunities include D.Phil research programme. Consortium and in-company MBAs from 1993.

School Details:

MBA Courses	Full-time	Part-time	Modular	Company/ Consortium
Duration	12/16 months	24+ months	22-48 months	by arrange-ment
Class Contact	540 hours	480 hours	440 hours	470-500 hours
Dissertation or Project	dissertation	project	dissertation	dissertation
Assessment	course	exam/ course	course	course

Final date for applications:

	31st Aug	31st Aug	None	by arrange-ment

Estimated Fees 1993/1994 Academic Year:

UK 12 Month	£5,000	£2,100	£2,500
EC	£5,000 + £1,500 language training & term abroad		
Non-EC	£7,500		

1992 Student Intake:

Intake	25	45	15
UK	6	40	15
Other EC	13	3	0
Non-EC	6	3	0
Women	25%	30%	20%

Faculty Details:

Dedicated MBA programme teaching staff	38
Full professors	3
Visiting lecturers/professors	1
With Master's degree	38
With PhD	9

Facilities:

Library hours	09.00-21.00 Mon-Thurs
	09.00-19.00 Fri
	09.00-13.00 Sat
IT availability	3 pools of networked PC-AT compatibles (48 terminals); 8 pcs for MBA syndicate work. Access to Datastream, cd roms etc.
Cultural opportunities	Brighton has a unique blend of history, eccentricity and elegance. Attractions include Theatre Royal, Gardiner Arts Centre, Brighton International Festival and probably the best selection of restaurants, pubs, clubs and winebars outside London

International Affiliations:

SAA, University of Torino; IUAE, University Autónoma Madrid; FHW Pforzheim; ESC Graduate School of Business Grenoble

BRISTOL BUSINESS SCHOOL

Location and Contact Details:

Address	University of the West of England, Bristol Frenchay Campus, Coldharbour Lane, Bristol BS16 1QY UK
Telephone Number	0272 656261
Facsimile Number	0272 763851
Contact Name	Part 1: Geoff Heaven BSc
	Part 2: John Howdle

Schools offering an AMBA-approved course are indicated in this section by the AMBA 'roundel'.

School Description:

Holders of a DMS with distinction can enter Part 2 directly; emphasis on Financial Services, Public Sector, Management of Technology. The school is one of only seven English schools to receive 'outstanding quality' rating from PCFC in 1991. All schools company sponsored. There is a wide choice of electives, and a dedicate librarian for part-time students.

School Details:

MBA Courses	Part-time ✓
Duration	2 years 4 months
Class Contact	483 hours (incl. residentials)
Dissertation or Project	dissertation
Assessment	exams/course
Final date for applications:	
	July
Estimated Fees 1993/1994 Academic Year:	
pt 1	£2,750
pt 2	£2,450 (incl. residentials/core text books)

1992 Student Intake:

Intake	30
Women	20%

Faculty Details:

Dedicated MBA programme teaching staff	27
Full professors	3
With Master's degree	25
With PhD	8

Facilities:

Library hours	09.00-21.00 Mon-Thurs
	09.00-18.00 Fri
	09.30-13.00 Sat
IT availability	300+ pcs in University; 120 dedicated to Business School; networked; industry standard software; 24-hour access
Cultural opportunities	Sports Centre; Centre for Performing Arts

Individual courses approved by AMBA are indicated by a 'tick'.

UNIVERSITY OF BRISTOL

Location and Contact Details:

Address	MBA in International Business
	10, Woodland Road
	Bristol BS8 1UQ
	UK
Telephone Number	0272 737683
Facsimile Number	0272 737687
Contact Name	Lyn Hoffman

School Description:
Study in Bristol, Paris and Berkeley. Visiting Faculty from Universities and the business community around the world.

School Details:

MBA Courses	*Full-time*
Duration	13-15 months
Class Contact	9-4 or 9-8 term-time
Dissertation or Project	both
Assessment	exam/course

Final date for applications:
15th July
Estimated Fees 1993/1994 Academic Year:
£11,000

1992 Student Intake:

Intake	20
UK	4
Other EC	6
Non-EC	10
Women	30%

Faculty Details:

Dedicated MBA programme teaching staff	12
Full professors	2
Visiting lecturers/professors	18
With Master's degree	8
With PhD	14

Facilities:

Library hours	08.45-23.00 Mon-Thurs; 08.45-18.00 Fri-Sat; 14.00-22.00 Sun
IT availability	24-hour access to computing service; 50 terminals – 5 terminals available with EXTEL software in MBA building.

Other facilities   Languages as part of the programme: French, German, Spanish, Japanese, Russian

International Affiliations:
Ecole Nationale des Ponts et Chaussées (EPNC), Paris

Individual courses approved by AMBA are indicated by a 'tick'.

BUCKINGHAMSHIRE COLLEGE OF HIGHER EDUCATION

Location and Contact Details:

Address	The Business School
	Newland Park, Gorelands lane
	Chalfont St Giles, Bucks HP8 4AD
	UK
Telephone Number	0494 874441
Facsimile Number	0494 872380
Contact Name	Postgraduate Registrar

School Description:

The Business School has a marked European and international orientation; there are overseas visits and contacts withoverseas managers and academics. Enhanced entry for Students with DMS.

School Details:

MBA Courses	*Part-time*
Duration	2 years
Class Contact	360 hours
Dissertation	
or Project	dissertation
Assessment	exam/course
Final date for applications:	
	September
Estimated Fees 1993/1994 Academic Year:	
	£2,000

1992 Student Intake:

Intake	45
UK	45
Women	25%

Faculty Details:

Dedicated MBA	
programme teaching staff	12
Visiting lecturers/professors	varies from year to year
With Master's degree	9
With PhD	3

Facilities:

Library hours	Term: 09.00-21.00 Mon-Thurs; 09.00-5.30 Fri; 10.00-16.30 Sat. Holiday: 09.00-16.30
IT availability	100 terminals
Cultural opportunities	Contact with European and American students

International Affiliations:

Szamalk Open Business School, Budapest; Kutztown University, Pennsylvannia; Fachhochschule Osnabruck, Germany; University of Economics, Prague inter alia.

UNIVERSITY OF CAMBRIDGE: THE JUDGE INSTITUTE OF MANAGEMENT STUDIES

Location and Contact Details:

Address	Fitzwilliam House
	32 Trumpington Street
	Cambridge CB2 1QY
	UK
Telephone Number	0223 337051
Facsimile Number	0223 324009
Contact Name	Mrs Jean Teall

School Description:

The Cambridge MBA has a sandwich structure which links academic study with work-based learning and is both intellectually challenging and practical. Small classes and small group tuition support a uniquely creative and cooperative environment for learning. Features include Integrative Management, Interpersonal Skills, International Aspects of Business, Technology Management.

School Details:

MBA Courses	*Sandwich*
Duration	33 months
Class Contact	35 weeks ft
Dissertation	
or Project	both
Assessment	exam/course
Final date for applications:	
	end March
Estimated Fees 1993/1994 Academic Year:	
	£7,200

1992 Student Intake:

Intake	15
UK	7
Other EC	1
Non-EC	7
Women	13%

Schools offering an AMBA-approved course are indicated in this section by the AMBA 'roundel'.

Faculty Details:

Dedicated MBA programme teaching staff	23
Full professors	3
With Master's degree	32
With PhD	30

Facilities:

Library hours	09.00-19.15
IT availability	University Computing Laboratory plus dedicated terminals

Cultural Opportunities	All those associated with a world-class historic university city
Other facilities	Language learning facilities plus University Language Centre. All students will be members of one of the Cambridge Colleges.

CANTERBURY BUSINESS SCHOOL

Location and Contact Details:

Address	University of Kent Canterbury, Kent CT2 7PE UK
Telephone Number	0227 764000 Ext. 3451/7726
Facsimile Number	0227 761187
Contact Name	Mr Bernard J. Kemp

School Description:

A graduate only school, new purpose-designed building opened in 1992, with links between programmes and services to corporate clients. Strong emphasis on Europe; specialist programme in Health Service Management; dedicated options on Environmental Management.

School Details:

MBA Courses	Full-time	Part-time	Modular	Company/ Consortium
Duration	12 months	c.30 months	c.30 months	c.30 months
Class Contact	542 hours	542 hours	542 hours	600 hours
Dissertation or Project	dissertation	dissertation	dissertation	dissertation
Assessment	exam/ course	exam/ course	exam/ course	exam/ course

Final date for applications:

October start	1st September	1st September
January start	1st December	1st December
April start	n/a	15th March

Estimated Fees 1993/1994 Academic Year:

home/EC	£5,015	£195/module
(c.£1,770/year)	£195/module (c.£1,770/year)	
overseas	£7,525	

1992 Student Intake:

Intake	85	30	25
UK	22	30	25
Other EC	34		
Non-EC	29		
Women	45%	40%	50%

Faculty Details:

Dedicated MBA programme teaching staff	20
Full professors	5
Visiting lecturers/professors	14
With Master's degree	9
With PhD	14

Facilities:

Library hours	09.00-22.00 (term-time)
IT availability	20 terminals, 7 days a week
Cultural opportunities	Full University student sports and social facilities available and active Business School Social Programme

International Affiliations:

ESC, Reims; Northeastern, Boston; ESTE, San Sebastian, Spain; RWTH, Aachen, Germany; Ottowa

Individual courses approved by AMBA are indicated by a 'tick'.

CARDIFF BUSINESS SCHOOL

Location and Contact Details:

Address	Aberconway Building
	Colum Drive
	Cardiff CF1 3EU
	UK
Telephone Number	0222 874198
Facsimile Number	0222 874419
Contact Names	Ms S. Jarrett

School Description:

The school offers a wide range of electives, as well as HRM, Japanese Management Systems, and Motor Industry. No credit transfer. A 2-5 year module course is also offered – details are available on request.

School Details:

MBA Courses	Full-time	Part-time	Modular
Duration	12 months	27 months	2-5 years
Class Contact	360 hours	360 hours	400 hours
Dissertation or Project	dissertation	dissertation	dissertation
Assessment	exam/ course/ dissertation	exam/ course/ dissertation	exam/ course/ dissertation

Final date for applications:

	July	July	rolling programme

Estimated Fees 1992/1993 Academic Year:

UK residents	£5,400	£2,700	£740/ module

1992 Student Intake:

Intake	208	36	16
UK	62	36	16
Other EC	36		
Non-EC	110		
Women	32%	28%	13%

Faculty Details:

Dedicated MBA programme teaching staff	68
Full professors	16
Visiting lecturers/professors	4
With Master's degree	21
With PhD	36

Facilities:

Library hours	09.00-21.30
IT availability	103 pcs/terminals + 18 printers

UNIVERSITY OF CENTRAL ENGLAND BUSINESS SCHOOL

Location and Contact Details:

Address	Perry Barr
	Birmingham B42 2SU
	UK
Telephone Number	021 331 5200
Facsimile Number	021 331 6366
Contact Name	Course Support Unit
	(MBA programmes)

School Description:

The full-time MBA is based on practical problem-solving to develop implementation skills within an international environment. Globalisation is a key feature of the course. Applicants may be admitted with advanced standing. The part-time course is delivered through active participative learning approaches and facilitates work-based relationships with mentor support. Course customisation is possible to reflect student interests and/or organisational requirements. Applicants may be admitted with advanced standing.

School Details:

MBA Courses	Full-time	Part-time
Duration	1 year	2.75 years
Class Contact	650 hours	370 hours
Dissertation		
or Project	project	project
Assessment	exam/course	exam/course
Final date for applications:		
	mid-August	August and December

Estimated Fees 1992/1993 Academic Year:

UK/EC	£5,500	£1,390(Stages ½) £1,550 (Stage 3)
Non-EC	£7,500	

1992 Student Intake:

Intake	19	70
UK	9	70
Non-EC	10	
Women	26%	19%

Faculty Details:

Dedicated MBA programme teaching staff	22
Full professors	3
With Master's degree	22
With PhD	8

Facilities:

Library hours	08.30-20.00 Mon-Thurs/08.00-19.00 Fri/10.00-14.00 Sat
IT availability	150 terminals
Cultural opportunities	City of Birmingham has outstanding cultural artistic facilities
Other opportunities	Business School MBA programmes are designed to be smaller sized than other schools to encourage/enable close staff-student contact and relate the programme to student need.

CITY UNIVERSITY BUSINESS SCHOOL

Location and Contact Details:

Address	Frobisher Crescent, Barbican Centre
	London EC2Y 8HB
	UK
Telephone Number	071 477 8606
Facsimile Number	071 477 8898
Contact Name	Ms L Taylor

School Description:

The school was the pioneer of the consortium-based MBA. It has an international staff and student body; close links with 'city' institutions and practitioners and an excellent location. Full-time MBA specialises in one of the following: Finance, Human Resource Management, Information Technology and Management, International Business and Export Management, Marketing

School Details:

MBA Courses	Full-time ✓	Part-time ✓	Con-sortium
Duration	12 months	24 months	varies
Class Contact	c. 520 hours	c.250 hours	varies
Dissertation			
or Project	project	project	project
Assessment	exam/ course	exam/ course	course
Final date for applications:			
	31st May	continuous	continuous

Estimated Fees 1993/1994 Academic Year:

home/EC	£7,500	£6,500 (£13,000 the course)	on application
Overseas	£9,500		

Individual courses approved by AMBA are indicated by a 'tick'.

U·C·E

LETTERS of DISTINCTION

M·B·A

*T*he team at UCE Business School are experts in developing people. With our help, people from all backgrounds have discovered that they have got what it takes to gain an MBA. Here are just a few of the reasons for our success:

A practical approach

We fully appreciate that MBA study should not exist in an academic vacuum. Our 'real-life' case studies have been achieved through close links with businesses and an appreciation of the national and international challenges facing these companies in a competitive market.

European & Global Dimensions

In all areas of study, we seek to include an appreciation of International and European perspectives in decision making.

Relevant Assessment Methods

We recognise that business survival and success takes far more than an ability to regurgitate business theory. For this reason, the UCE team have lead the way in developing a variety of assessment methods including testing the performance of students in real-life business scenarios.

Close support all the way

We strive to maintain a healthy balance of skills, experience and background – both amongst our student teams and lecturing staff. This provides a first class supportive environment in which to develop new ideas, new skills and new horizons. Help and advice is always on hand, to identify and eliminate problems well before they become set backs.

Take the next easy step

Just complete and return the quick response coupon to Graham Walker, Course Director, Full-Time MBA at the address below and he will send you full details of the UCE MBA.

Alternatively, call him for an informal discussion on 021-331 5530.

UCE Business School, Room D436,
The University of Central England,
Perry Barr, Birmingham B42 2SU.

1992 Student Intake:

Intake	160	85
UK	54	77
Other EC	39	2
Non-EC	67	6
Women	32%	11%

Faculty Details:

Dedicated MBA programme teaching staff	51
Full professors	19
Visiting lecturers/professors	80
With Master's degree	44
With PhD	21

Facilities:

Library hours	until 21.00
IT availability	approximately 70 terminals.
Cultural opportunities	Located in the Barbican Centre
Other facilities	shared common room, mail delivered to pigeonholes, personal tutors appointed to postgraduates, University Sports Centre and clubs

International Affiliations:

ESCP, Paris; Solvay, Brussels; Luiss, Rome; TV, Berlin; Complutense, Madrid

CITY
University
BUSINESS SCHOOL

MBA Programmes

- **Full-Time MBA**
  An intensive 12-month programme, incorporating courses in general management and specialising in one of the following: Finance, Human Resource Management, Information Technology & Management, International Business & Export Management or Marketing.

- **Evening MBA**
  A 24-month programme designed particularly for those in the City and in finance, allowing participants to pursue their careers without interruption and to integrate course learning into their work experience.

- **Management MBA**
  A programme based on a consortium between City University Business School and several major companies, providing managers with a customised programme. Study is project-based and in the workplace.

- Please contact The Postgraduate Admissions Officer, City University Business School, Frobisher Crescent, Barbican Centre, LONDON EC2Y 8HB, England.

  Telephone: 071 477 8608 (national).
  +44 71 477 8608 (international).

  Fax: 071 477 8898 (national).
  +44 71 477 8898 (international).

Individual courses approved by AMBA are indicated by a 'tick'.

COVENTRY BUSINESS SCHOOL

Location and Contact Details:
Address   Coventry University
              Priory Street
              Coventry CV1 5FB
              UK
Telephone Number   0203 838738
Facsimile Number   0203 838251
Contact Name   Kaye Carding

School Details:
MBA Courses   *Part-time*
Duration   12 months taught + 2 years project
Class Contact   6 hrs/week
Dissertation
  or Project   project
Assessment   exam/course
Final date for applications:
              1st Septmber
Estimated Fees 1993/1994 Academic Year:
              £4,100 per course

1992 Student Intake:
Intake   25
UK   25

Faculty Details:
Dedicated MBA
  programme teaching staff   10
Full professors   1
Visiting lecturers/professors   15
With Master's degree   17
With PhD   7

Facilities:
Library hours   09.00-21.00 Mon-Fri; 09.00-17.00
              Sat-Sun
IT availability   60 terminals dedicated to Business
              School
Cultural   Various arts and cultural societies,
  opportunities   student activities
Other facilities   Civic amenities

CRANFIELD SCHOOL OF MANAGEMENT

Location and Contact Details:
Address   Cranfield
              Bedford MK43 0AL
              UK
Telephone Number   44 0234 751122
Facsimile Number   44 0234 752439
Contact Name   Mrs Pat Hayes

School Description:
Rural location with good availability of campus and local accommodation, career development and counselling and placements facilities regarded as very important. Graduate programmes constitute about 33% of School activities. In addition the school is involved in Management Research and offers a wide range of short courses for practising managers. Specialist option in project management. Exchange with the CESMA MBA of Groupe Lyon ESC enables French- speaking participants to study both in France and the UK and be awarded MBA degrees by both universities. 4 semester (40 weeks of classes) enables 2-year content to be studied in one year. Part two of the programme consists of a wide range of electives timetabled to meet student choice.

School Details:

MBA Courses	*Full-time* ✓	*Part-time* ✓
Duration	12 months	2 years
Class Contact	44 weeks	
Dissertation		
or Project		project
Assessment	exam/course	
Final date for applications:		
	none	none
Estimated Fees 1993/1994 Academic Year:		
UK/EC	£10,000	£8,000 pa
Non-EC	£14,500	

1992 Student Intake:

Intake	160	78
UK	120	76
Other EC	20	4
Non-EC	20	
Women	20%	20%

Faculty Details:
Dedicated MBA
  programme teaching staff   89
Full professors   14
Visising lecturers/professors   16 + 24 occasional
                        fellows
With Master's degree   61
With PhD   28

    Schools offering an AMBA-approved course are indicated in this section by the AMBA 'roundel'.

Facilities:

Library hours	08.30-21.00 Mon-Fri/09.30-18.00 Sat
IT availability	dedicated computer studio with 30 networked pcs with laser printers etc., DTP and scanning facilities, Microsoft Windows 3. Access to main university VAX computer facilities via studio. 08.00-22.00 daily.
Other facilities	fully equipped tv studio with VHS editing facilities available to students, satellite tv and recording facilities

International Affiliations:
Groupe ESC Lyon, University of Washington, Seattle, ESSEC, Koblenz, University of Aarhus, MacQuarie University

---

DERBYSHIRE BUSINESS SCHOOL

Location and Contact Details:

Address	University of Derbyshire Kedleston Road Derby DE3 1GB UK
Telephone Number	0332 47181 ext. 1421
Facsimile Number	0332 385991
Contact Name	Joe Marshall

School Description:
Both part-time and full- time modes of study are modular. Students can be considered for APL for prior qualifications and/or experience. Full- and part-time DMS is also available. There is a specialist MBA in European Marketing, based on MBA, but with specialist third stage.

School Details:

MBA Courses	Full-time	Part- time Modular
Duration	1 year	3 years
Class Contact	200	
Dissertation or Project		dissertation project
Assessment		exam/course

Final date for applications:
1st Sept   15th Sept   1st Sept

Estimated Fees 1993/1994 Academic Year:
£1,000 year 1, £1,300 year 2, £1,800 year 3

1992 Student Intake:

Intake	25	100
UK	15	100
Other EC	8	
Non-EC	2	
Women	30%	40%

Faculty Details:

Dedicated MBA programme teaching staff	12

Facilities:

Library hours	09.00-20.00 Mon-Fri; 10.00-13.00 Sat

DORSET BUSINESS SCHOOL

Location and Contact Details:

Address	Holland House Oxford Road, Bournemouth Dorset, BH8 8EZ UK
Telephone Number	0202 595451
Facsimile Number	0202 298321
Contact Name	Mr John Gatrell, Associate Dean

School Description:
Prestige location in central Bournemouth, strong European Corporate and Academic links, involved in European Community Initiatives. MBA (European Enterprise Management) subject to approval, based on the established postgraduate Diploma programme. Flexible entry to the programme including CAT.

School Details:

MBA Courses	Full-time	Part-time
	(subject to approval)	
Duration	18 months	3 years
Class Contact	16 hrs/week	8 hrs/week
Dissertation or Project	project	project
Assessment	exam/course	exam/course

Final date for applications:
August   September

Estimated Fees 1993/1994 Academic Year:
c. £5,000   av. £1,950

1992 Student Intake:

Intake	32	60
UK	8	55

Individual courses approved by AMBA are indicated by a 'tick'.

Other EC	21	1
Non-EC	3	4
Women	60%	36%

Faculty Details:

Dedicated MBA programme teaching staff	11
Full professors	1
Visiting lecturers/professors	2
With Master's degree	9
With PhD	4

Facilities:

Library hours   09.00-21.00 Mon-Thurs;
09.15-17.15 Fri; 09.30- 18.00 Sat;
10.00-17.00 Sun

IT availability   30 IBM PC, 30 Apple Mac; main campus (2 miles distant) has open learning centre, 24 hrs, 7 days/week.

Cultural opportunities   Main Campus Students Union, easy access to town centre, theatres, sailing, windsurfing, beaches, New Forest, Symphony Orchestra.

International Affiliations:

University of Barcelona; FHS, Fulda; TUT, Poitiers

DUNDEE INSTITUTE OF TECHNOLOGY

Location and Contact Details:

Address	Bell Street
	Dundee DD1 1HG
	UK
Telephone Number	0382 308471
Facsimile Number	0382 308877
Contact Name	Mr Graeme Martin

School Description:

The school offers a linked programme of Certificate in Management, Diploma in Management Studies, and MBA. Range of options in Marketing, IT and Public Sector specialisations

School Details:

MBA Courses	*Part-time*
Duration	3 years
Class Contact	7 hours/week
Project or Dissertation	yes
Assessment	coursework and exams
Final date for applications:	
	August

Estimated Fees 1993/1994 Academic Year:

EC	£1,325
non-EC	£3,950

1992 Student Intake:

Intake	20
UK	20
Women	8
Dedicated MBA programme teaching staff	10
Full professors	1
Visising lecturers/professors	2
With Master's degree	5
With PhD	4

Facilities:

Library hours	09.00-21.00
IT availability	16 terminals
Other opportunities	International residential weeks in Frasce, Germany

Schools offering an AMBA-approved course are indicated in this section by the AMBA 'roundel'.

UNIVERSITY OF DUNDEE

Location and Contact Details:

Address   MBA Office
University of Dundee
Scotland
DD1 4HN

Telephone Number	0382 23181 ext. 4737
Facsimile Number	0382 28890
Contact Name	Mr Michael J. Tooze

School Description:

The MBA is organised on a federal-type structure from within the Department of Economics and Management, and employs suitably qualified and experienced tutors from other university departments on its fully integrated executive programmes. Courses are interactive with a maximum number of students in each class. Entry qualification is either a degree or professional qualification and at least 3 years management experience. Specialist MBA programmes in Project Management, Construction Management, Financial Management, Oil and Gas Management and Mineral Resources Management.

School Details:

MBA Courses	Full-time	Part-time	Modular	Company/Consortium
Duration	1 year	2 years	up to 5 years	by negotiation
Class Contact	300 hours	300 hours	300 hours	300 hours
Dissertation or Project	dissertation			
Assessment	exam/course			
Final date for applications:	31st Aug	31st Aug	variable	variable
Estimated Fees 1993/1994 Academic Year:	£5,900	£1,650	£550 per module	

1992 Student Intake:

Intake	12	121	3
UK	2	120	3
Other EC	1		
Non-EC	9	1	
Women	25%	32%	100%

Faculty Details:

Dedicated MBA programme teaching staff	19
Full professors	3
With Master's degree	12
With PhD	4

Facilities:

Library hours	09.00-22.00 Mon-Fri; 09.00-12.00 Sat
IT availability	100+ terminals
Cultural opportunities	Dundee has a rich tradition in theatre, cinema and music.
Other facilities	Tayside contains a rich variety of scenery, with opportunities for sailing, golf, hillwalking, skiing and many other pursuits.

International Affiliations:

ESC Brest and Troyes; Universities of Paris-Sud, Grenoble, Valladolid, Burgos, Milan, Innsbruck, Graz, Oldenburg, Siegen, Växjö and Turku.

University Of Dundee

MASTER OF BUSINESS ADMINISTRATION

The University of Dundee offers the following full and part-time executive programs:

MBA IN CONSTRUCTION MANAGEMENT

MBA IN FINANCIAL MANAGEMENT

MBA IN MINERAL RESOURCES MANAGEMENT

MBA IN OIL AND GAS MANAGEMENT

MBA IN PROJECT MANAGEMENT

MBA (GENERAL)

Entry requirements are normally either a degree or equivalent professional qualification and at least three years management experience.

Further particulars can be obtained from Mr Mike Tooze, Course Director, MBA Office, University of Dundee, Dundee, Scotland DD1 4HN.
(Tel 0382 23181 ext 4737; Fax 0382 28890)

DURHAM UNIVERSITY BUSINESS SCHOOL

Location and Contact Details:

Address	Mill Hill Lane
	Durham DH1 3LB
	UK
Telephone Number	091 374 2233
Facsimile Number	091 374 3748
Contact Name	Dr David Stoker

School Description:

Durham University Business School is a well-established school and MBA programme. Students are given the opportunity for working with small businesses via the Small Business Centre. There is a mandatory foreign language course, and project and consultancy work with companies. There is an excellent staff/student ratio, a friendly atmosphere and refurbished facilities including a purpose-built MBA wing. Specialisations include Small Business and HEM; Outdoor/Personal Development and Communications Skills are emphasised. The school also offers open-learning and distance-learning MBAs – details are available on request.

School Details:

MBA Courses	Full-time ✓	Part-time ✓
Duration	1 year	2 years
Class Contact	600 hours	570 hours
Dissertation or Project	dissertation	dissertation
Assessment	exam/course	exam/course

Final date for applications:

	September	December

Estimated Fees 1993/1994 Academic Year:

	September	December
EC	£6,000	£3,500/year
Non-EC	£9,000	

1992 Student Intake:

Intake	44	85
UK	30	82
Other EC	3	2
Non-EC	11	1
Women	25%	43%

Faculty Details:

Dedicated MBA programme teaching staff	25
Full professors	3
Visiting lecturers/professors	8
With Master's degree	14
With PhD	5

Facilities:

Library hours	08.00-20.00
IT availability	20 terminals

International Affiliations:

None

EAP EUROPEAN SCHOOL OF MANAGEMENT

Location and Contact Details:

Address	12 Merton Street
	Oxford
	OX1 4JH
	UK
Telephone Number	0865 724545
Facsimile Number	0865 251960
Contact Name	Janet Turrell

School Description:

Owned by the Paris Chamber of Commerce and industry and partly funded by the Berlin Senate. Faculty from 10 countries, over 1,000 graduates working in 30 countries. Offers 2 × 3 year, 3 country full-time, European Masters in Management for recent graduates, drawn from every country of the EC. AMBA approved and with an annual entry of about 170. Concours in each EC country every spring for September entry. Good French or Spanish and English is essential. Also offers full range of executive programmes.

School Details:

MBA Courses	Full-time ✓	Part-time ✓
Duration	1 year	2 years
Class contact	360 hours	
Dissertation or Project	European Research Project	
Assessment	course	course

Final date for applications:

	Mid-June	30th October

Estimated Fees 1993/1994 Academic Year:

	Mid-June	30th October
	£12,000	£11,000 over 2 years

1992 Student Intake:

Intake	36	18
UK	14	16
Non-EC		1
Women		44%

Schools offering an AMBA-approved course are indicated in this section by the AMBA 'roundel'.

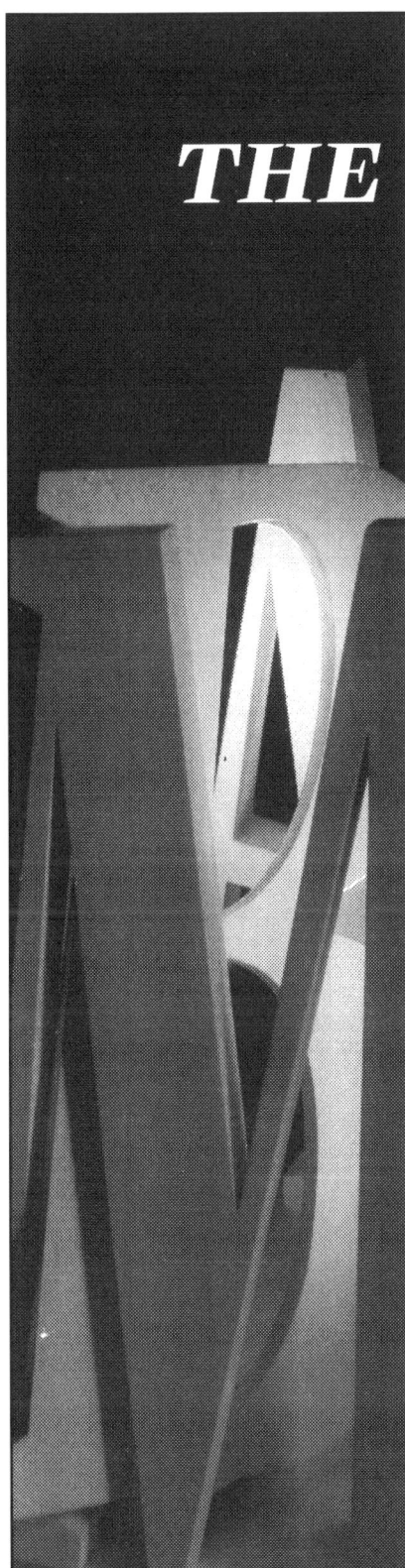

THE DURHAM MBA

Enhance your career opportunities by studying for an internationally recognised MBA with an organisation which, unashamedly, puts people and quality first.

At Durham University Business School we offfer three programmes to suit the varying needs of professionals and organisations, but our philosophy remains the same.

The Full-Time MBA

The Full-Time programme (one year in duration beginning each October) places emphasis on the needs of the individual: classes are kept deliberately small (about fifty participants enter the programme each year), ensuring an excellent staff/student ratio and regular access to personal and project tutors. About twenty five elective subjects are offered of which ten are followed by each participant. An extended individual project is an integral element of the programme.

For further information contact the Programme Administrator on 091 374 2233

The Part-Time MBA

Offering similar course content and emphasis as the Full-Time programme, the Part-Time programme is structured around twenty four Friday/Saturday workshops over a two year period.

For further information contact the Programme Administrator on 091 374 2233

The Open Distance Learning MBA

Learning is by home-based study using specially prepared material together with intensive residential sessions and an individual project. The programme will normally be completed in three to four years.

For further information contact the Programme Administrator on 091 374 2219

Durham University Business School, Mill Hill Lane, Durham City, DH1 3LB Tel: 091 374 2211 Fax: 091 374 3748

Individual courses approved by AMBA are indicated by a 'tick'.

Faculty Details:

Dedicated MBA programme teaching staff	35
Full professors	28
Visiting lecturers/professors	20
With Master's degree	35
With PhD	29

Facilities:

Library hours	09.00-19.00
IT availability	80 terminals (40 in Paris, 40 in Oxford) modem links

Cultural opportunities	MBA students have one-week visits to our other centres.
Other facilities	unlimited access to buildings, including weekends

International Affiliations:

EAP is one school in four countries – a Grande Ecole in Paris, a University in Berlin and a charitable trust/company in Madrid.

UNIVERSITY OF EAST ANGLIA

Location and Contact Details:

Address	Management Education Office
	The Registry
	Norwich NR4 7TJ
	UK
Telephone Number	0603 593209
Facsimile Number	0603 58553
Contact Name	Stephanie Jones

School Description:

The course is run in the evening in response to employer and student demand. The two compulsory main strands, Money & Systems and People & Motivation, are followed by a Management in Context optional topic (currently one of: Information Systems, Europe, Environment, Public Sector or Production and Operations Management) and a dissertation of about 15,000 words. Faculty from a wide range of disciplines and experience contribute to the MBA, allowing for a broad perspective and stimulating course. Lecturers are drawn from the Schools of Economic and Social Studies, Information Systems, Environmental Sciences, Education, Law, Social Work, and Modern Languages and European History.

School Details:

MBA Courses	Part-time
Duration	2 years
Class Contact	240 hours
Dissertation or Project	dissertation
Assessment	course assessment
Final date for applications:	
	30th April 1993

Estimated Fees 1993/1994 Academic Year:
£3,450

1992 Student Intake:

Intake	18
UK	18
Women	17%

Faculty Details:

Dedicated MBA programme teaching staff	14
Full professors	3
With Master's degree	2
With PhD	12

Facilities:

Library hours	Term: 09.00-22.00 Mon-Thurs; 09.00-20.00 Fri; 09.00-17.00 Sat; 14.00-19.00 Sun. Vac: 09.00-18.00 Mon-Fri.
IT availability	40 terminals; Computing Centre open Mon-Fri term: 09.00-21.45; vac: 09.00-17.45.
Cultural opportunities	Sainsbury Centre for visual art on campus, concerts are held in the Music Dept. and Student Union, Films and Plays are put on, programmes of open lectures on a wide variety of topics.
Other facilities	Sports facilities include a running track, gym, squash, badminton and tennis courts and a sauna.

Schools offering an AMBA-approved course are indicated in this section by the AMBA 'roundel'.

EAST LONDON BUSINESS SCHOOL

Location and Contact Details:

Address	The University of East London
	Duncan House, High Street
	Stratford, London E15
	UK
Telephone Number	081 590 7722 ext. 3364
Facsimile Number	081 534 4168
Contact Name	

School Description:

Our MBA focuses on a Strategic Management Orientation with opportunities for pathway specialisation at year 2 (pt) or the later semester of the full-time mode. Opportunities for research and consultancy work in Singapore have been seized and developed by staff and feed into an International Pathway and a proposed MSc in Comparative Management.

School Details:

MBA Courses	Full-time	Part-time	
	From Oct '93	In Singapore only	
Duration	1 year	2 years	
Class Contact	720 hours	216 hours + residentials	216 hours + residentials
Dissertation or Project	project	project	
Assessment	exam /course	exam/ course	exam/ course
Final date for applications:	July 1993	Aug 1993	Dec 1993 for Feb 1994 start

Estimated Fees 1993/1994 Academic Year:

home	£6,000	£2,000
overseas	£7,000	

1992 Student Intake:

Intake	n/a	75	25

Faculty Details:

Dedicated MBA programme teaching staff	All staff in School
Visiting lecturers/professors	policy of 15% practitioner input
With Master's degree	70%
With PhD	11%

Facilities:

Library hours	Across University 09.00-21.00 Mon-Fri; 10.00-5.00 Sat. Sites have different availability.
IT availability	Sites have different availability: c. 25 on one site, 175++ on another.
Cultural opportunities	Our Barking site is one of the key sites of UEL: our Stratford site is part of the other key sites. As such many opportunities are available.

International Affiliations:

Work in Singapore through the Management Development institute – now finalising links with French and German institutions.

EDINBURGH UNIVERSITY MANAGEMENT SCHOOL

Location and Contact Details:

Address	7 Bristo Square
	Edinburgh EH8 9AL
	UK
Telephone Number	031 650 8066/5
Facsimile Number	031 650 6501
Contact Name	Mr J Moyes (FTMBA)
	Mr J N Crook (PTMAS)

School Description:

EUMS is located in the heart of Edinburgh, the second financial centre of the UK, and as part of a large and historic university has access to a full range of academic and social facilities. The school offers a very extensive range of option courses.

School Details:

MBA Courses	Full-time ✓	Part-time ✓
Duration	12 months	30 months
Class Contact	257 hours	
Dissertation or Project	yes	yes
Assessment	various	various
Final date for applications:	15th September	30th September

Estimated Fees 1993/1994 Academic Year:

home/EC	£4,950	£1,400
overseas	£6,750	

1992 Student Intake:

Intake	104	111
UK	40	111
Other EC	22	
Non-EC	42	
Women	27	32

Faculty Details:

Dedicated MBA programme teaching staff	40
Full professors	7
Visiting lecturers/professors	7
With Master's degree	14
With PhD	17

Facilities:

Library hours	09.00-21.45 Mon-Fri 09.00-12.30 Sat
IT availability	48 terminals, 7 days a week, 24 hours a day
Other facilities	dedicated buildings; own lecture theatres, computer labs, syndicate rooms, marketing/placement officer

Schools offering an AMBA-approved course are indicated in this section by the AMBA 'roundel'.

UNIVERSITY OF ESSEX

Location and Contact Details:

Address   MBA Programme, Dept of A.F.M.
University of Essex, Wivenhoe Park
Colchester CO4 3SQ
UK

Telephone Number   0206 873376
Facsimile Number   0206 87
Contact Name   Denise Haines

School Description:

The School accepts credit accumulation & transfer of a suitable standard and integrates work on theory with work-based projects and dissertations. The learning programme utilises understanding of how adults learn best. The small numbers encourage social learning.

School Details:

MBA Courses	*Part-time*
Duration	2 years
Class Contact	240 hours
Dissertation or Project	both
Assessment	course assessment

Final date for applications:
    1st October
Estimated Fees 1993/1994 Academic Year:
    £2,750 stage 1   £4,000 stage 2

1992 Student Intake:

Intake	15
UK	15
Women	20%

Faculty Details:

Dedicated MBA programme teaching staff	12
Full professors	2
Visiting lecturers/professors	various
With Master's degree	11
With PhD	6

Facilities:

Library hours	09.00-22.00 7 days
IT availability	100+ terminals
Cultural opportunities	Various including Social Welfare (i.e. creche facilities); sport; cafeteria & restaurant; hotel; bookshop; banks – all on campus.

International Affiliations:

European Visit (1 week) to Brussels Euro Parliament + 400 businesses (compulsory).

UNIVERSITY OF EXETER CENTRE FOR MANAGEMENT STUDIES

Location and Contact Details:

Address   Thornlea
New North Road
Exeter, Devon EX4 4JZ
UK

Telephone Number   0392 263213/264517/264518
Facsimile Number   0392 494181
Contact Name   Dennis Norman

School Description:

Executive programmes run for Company Directors. For Managers and Administrators Diploma and Certificate courses available Courses run with & for European Universities. Special language support given. Industrial/commercial visits an integral part of studies.

School Details:

MBA Courses	*Full-time*	*Part-time*
Duration	1 year/16 months	2-5 year
years	16 months-5 years	
Class Contact	580 hours	580 hours
Dissertation or Project	project/either	either
Assessment	exam/course	course

Final date for applications:
    6 weeks before course begins
Estimated Fees 1992/1993 Academic Year:
    £6,500   £6,500

1992 Student Intake:

Intake	72	13
UK	4	10
Other EC	22	
Non-EC	46	3
Women	50%	25%

Faculty Details:

Dedicated MBA programme teaching staff	15
Visiting lecturers/professors	60
With Master's degree	6
With PhD	3

Facilities:

Library hours	09.00-22.15 Mon-Fri
	09.00-17.00 Sat
IT availability	management centre: 10 terminals; postgraduate centre: 10; others: 40 (all 24 hrs)

Cultural opportunities Full range of University clubs, societies, sports. Also theatre & cinema on campus.

International Affiliations:
Rennes, Universite de Haut Savoie, Chambery, Fachhochschule Reutlingen.

GLASGOW CALEDONIAN UNIVERSITY

Location and Contact Details:

Address	Cowcaddens Road (City Campus) Glasgow G4 0BA Scotland UK
Telephone Number	041 331 3625/3411/3408
Facsimile Number	041 331 3269
Contact Name	Mrs E. Vaughan
	Mr C. Chisholm (International MBA)
	Mrs J. McCallum (Admin.)

School Description:
The School offers individual development through group processes; action learning runs throughout the programme linked to research dissertation. Applicants for the full-time programme should be qualified to degree level in Business Studies. The Part-time programme has a common foundation year with the Diploma in Management studies.

School Details:

MBA Courses	Full-time international (from September 1993	Part-time
Duration	1 year	3 year 4 months
Class Contact		6 hours/week
Dissertation or Project	dissertation	dissertation
Assessment	exam/course	exam/course

Final date for applications:

	all year	all year

Estimated Fees 1993/1994 Academic Year:

	£7,400	£1,250 year 1; £1,550 year 2; £2,200 year 3

1992 Student Intake:

Intake	45
Women	33%

Facilities:

Library hours	Term: 08.30-21.00 Mon-Thurs; 08.30-18.00 Fri; 09.00-17.00 Sat. Vac: 09.00-17.00 Mon-Fri
IT availability	Extensive lab facilities equipped with IBM PCs.
Cultural opportunities	Overseas visit integral part of programme.

International Affiliations:
Links being developed within International MBA which will have cross-over effects for part-time MBA programme.

Schools offering an AMBA-approved course are indicated in this section by the AMBA 'roundel'.

GLASGOW UNIVERSITY BUSINESS SCHOOL

Location and Contact Details:

Address	55 Southpark Avenue
	Glasgow G12 8LF
	UK
Telephone Number	041 339 8855 ext.6302/6300
Facsimile Number	041 330 5669
Contact Name	Mrs Catherine Burgess

School Description:

In addition to the International and Executive MBAs, the school offers a jointly-taught Summer School with European and American partners; laptop pcs are an integral learning tool; and there is also an Outward Bound experience. Small intake numbers are emphasised on all programmes. A pilot competence programme is now in place.

School Details:

MBA Courses	Full-time	Part-time ✓
Duration	12 months	3 years
Class contact	480 hours	480 hours
Dissertation or Project	dissertation	dissertation
Assessment	exam/course	exam/course
Final date for applications:	1st August	15th September
Estimated Fees 1993/1994 Academic Year:	£6,900	£2,300

1992 Student Intake:

Intake	34	45
UK	3	45
Other EC	10	0
Non-EC	21	0
Women	8%	25%

Faculty Details:

Dedicated MBA programme teaching staff	None (39 contributors)
Full professors	15
Visiting lecturers/professors	5
With PhD	21

Facilities:

Library hours	09.00-21.00 Mon-Fri; 09.00-12.00 Sat
IT availability	35 IBM terminals plus Apple Network. (Part-time – laptop requirement)
Other facilities	European Summer School for Advanced Management (in 1993 – Lisbon)

International Affiliations:

Aarhus School of Business; Leeuwarden Business School; Catholica Portuguesa University; University College Dublin; ITESM (Mexico).

UNIVERSITY OF GREENWICH BUSINESS SCHOOL

Location and Contact Details:

Address	Riverside House, Beresford Street
	Woolwich, London SE18 6BU
	UK
Telephone Number	081 316 9032
Facsimile Number	081 316 9005
Contact Name	Mike Edmunds

School Description:

Formerly Thames Business School. Over 20 years' experience in running postgraduate management courses. Flexible modular credit based structure. The programme must be completed in five years. Own selection tests as part of the selection procedure. Integrative course, rather than functionally based.

School Details:

MBA Courses	Full-time	Part-time	Modular	Company/ Consortium
Duration	30 months			
Dissertation or Project	project			
Assessment	exam/course			
Final date for applications:	20th Sept	20th Sept	20th Sept	by arrangement
Estimated Fees 1993/1994 Academic Year:	£5,000	£2,000	£5,000	

THE GLASGOW UNIVERSITY BUSINESS SCHOOL

offers both full and part-time MBA programmes

UNIVERSITY
of
GLASGOW

The International MBA is offered on a 12 month full-time basis, and specialises in International Business. Cohorts are fully international: in 1992/93 there are 34 participants from 15 countries.

The Executive MBA is offered on a 3 year part-time basis. This is a post- experience course for practising managers and specialises in syndicate group teaching where management theory and relevant practices are explored.

GLASGOW UNIVERSITY
BUSINESS SCHOOL

Glasgow University Business School prides itself on providing a personalised MBA. The small cohort, syndicate group teaching fits an MBA niche based on high quality and high standards.

GLASGOW UNIVERSITY BUSINESS SCHOOL
Department of Management Studies 53-59 Southpark Avenue, Glasgow G12 8LF.
Tel: 041-339 8855 Fax: 041-330 5669

1992 Student Intake:

Intake	30
UK	30
Women	20%

Faculty Details:

Dedicated MBA programme teaching staff	30

Visiting lecturers/professors	6
With Master's degree	26
With PhD	4

Facilities:

Library hours	08.30-20.30 Mon-Fri + Sat am
IT availability	950 terminals – running mainly in Windows

Schools offering an AMBA-approved course are indicated in this section by the AMBA 'roundel'.

The University of Hull

MBA (Management)
at Greenwich College, London

MBA (Financial Management)
at the Institute of Directors, Pall Mall, London

- 12 month Full-time or 24 month Evening attendance

- January, June and September enrolment dates

- Diploma in Management Studies (Full-time and Evening) of Greenwich College also available

  (Successful completion of this course can lead to MBA programmes)

For further details, contact:

**Greenwich College
Meridian House, Royal Hill
Greenwich, London
SE10 8RT**

Tel: 081-853 4484
**(24 hour service)
Fax: 081-305 1782**

Greenwich College, London

Individual courses approved by AMBA are indicated by a 'tick'.

HENLEY MANAGEMENT COLLEGE

Location and Contact Details:

Address   Greenlands
Henley-on-Thames
Oxon RG9 3AU
UK

Telephone Number   0491 571454
Facsimile Number   0491 410184
Contact Name   Mrs Susan Saunders-Miller

School Description:

General Management founded on 40 years' experience. Credit accumulation and transfer. The school also offers a distance learning MBA and an Active (Modular) MBA – details are available on request.

School Details:

MBA Courses	Full-time ✓	Part-time ✓	Modular ✓	Distance Learning
Duration	1 year	2 years	3½ years	18 months
Class Contact	7 months	18 months		
Dissertation or project	Diss'n	Diss'n	Diss'n	Diss'n/ project
Assessment	exam/ course	exam/ course	exam/ course	exam/ course

Final date for applications:

No formal deadline application by Easter is advised	No formal deadline application by Easter is advised	No formal deadline application by Easter is advised	Can apply at any time

Estimated Fees 1993/1994 Academic Year:

Full Time

UK/EC	£8,500
Non-EC	£10,500
Part-time	£7, 950; Year 1 £3,750; Year 2 £3,750 £450 dissertation fee

Modular

UK/EC Non-residential	£9,750; Stage 1 £5,500; Stage 2 £4,200
Non EC Non-residential	£12,000; Stage 1 £6,500; Stage 2 £5,500

1992 Student Intake:

Intake	50	67	26	839
UK	15	67	17	409
Other EC	18		2	108
Non-EC	21		7	322
Women	24%	32%	20%	20%

Faculty Details:

Dedicated MBA programme teaching staff	30
Full professors	11
Visiting lecturers/professors	50
With Master's degree	19
With PhD	3

Facilities:

Library hours	Henley: 09.00-17.15 Brunel: 09.00-21.00 Mon-Thurs 09.00-18.00 Fri; 09.30-17.00 Sat; 14.00-19.00 Sun; 09.00-17.00 Hols
IT availability	Henley: computer terminals always available; Brunel: computer terminals available in library and also in computer centre, open 08.00-23.45 Mon-Fri (term-time), 09.00-17.00 Sat
Other facilities	Henley: computer mediated communications, contact list, evening get-togethers for distance learners, swimming pool, sports facility (racquet sports, snooker, trim trail), bar, occasional evening concerts, art exhibitions; sports centre

International Affiliations:

full-/part-time: Ecole Superieur de Commerce Grenoble; Active: LEME IMISP St Petersburg; Distance Learning: ABS Consulting, Africa, Australian Institute of Management, The Zagreb Business School, OAI A/S, Denmark, Oy Rastor AB, Finland, Gesellschaft für Foerderung der Weiterbildung gfw, Germany, Henley Management College, Hong Kong, Kassim Chan Management Training Sde Bhd, Malaysia, University of Malta Department of Management, Nederland/ICBA, The Centre for Executive Education, New Zealand, GIMT, South Africa, Singapore Institute of Management, Mgruppen, Sweden, School of Accounting and Management, Trinidad

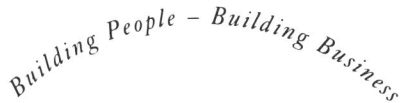

Building People – Building Business

Six ways to a Henley MBA

Henley, in conjunction with Brunel University, can offer you a choice of six routes to an MBA designed to meet your personal objectives.

The **MODULAR** Programme requires 16 weeks at Henley, spread over 12 months, and covers group work, project work and a range of optional subjects.

The **FULL-TIME MBA** is a one-year course based at Brunel and has an international focus.

PART-TIME is also based at Brunel in Uxbridge, and runs one day a week over two years.

PROJECT MANAGEMENT MBA combines periods of residence with Part-Time or Distance Learning Study.

DISTANCE LEARNING uses expertly designed study packages, video and audio material backed by tutorial workshops.

The **DIPLOMA IN MANAGEMENT**, when successfully completed gives its students entry at stage 2 of the Distance Learning MBA.

For full details of any of Henley's MBA courses please contact MBA Information on **0491 571454** (International code: 44 491) or **(0491) 410239** (Answerphone), Fax: (0491) 410184.

Henley Management College, Greenlands, Henley-on-Thames, Oxfordshire, RG9 3AU, England.

INCORPORATED 1945   ROYAL CHARTER 1991

HENLEY *Management College*

HERIOT WATT UNIVERSITY BUSINESS SCHOOL

Location and Contact Details:

Address	P.O. Box 807, Riccarton
	Edinburgh EH14 4AT
	UK
Telephone Number	031 449 5111
Facsimile Number	031 451 3190
Contact Name	Dr Howard Kahn (FT/PT)
	Mr Charles Ritchie (FT/PT)

School Description:

The school has strong links with eastern Europe, particularly Hungary and Russia. There are also strong links with industry, commerce and the public sector. There are unique software programs and credit for previous academic experience for the Distance Learning MBA – further details are available on request. More than 22 electives are available in the following groupings: General Management (4 electives), Manufacturing (2), International Business (2), Operations and Technical Management (5), Arts Management (4), Health Service (4). The distance learning course is written by an International Faculty, has no maximum intake, a variable start date and open access.

School Details:

MBA Courses	Full-time ✓	Part-time ✓	Distance learning
Duration	1 year	2-4 years	7 years max.
Class Contact	16-20 hrs/ week	8-10 hrs/ week	
Dissertation or Project	dissertation	dissertation	neither
Assessment	exam/ course	exam/ course	exam

Final date for applications:

	end June	end August, any time or earlier if course full

Estimated Fees 1993/1994 Academic Year:

home/EC	£4,500	£4,200	£315-515/ module
Overseas	£6,000		

1992 Student Intake:

Intake	26	74
UK	7	74
Other EC	15	
Non-EC	4	
Women	33%	33%

Faculty Details:

Dedicated MBA programme teaching staff	33
Full professors	6
Visiting lecturers/professors	6
With Master's degree	4
With PhD	6

Facilities:

Library hours	09.00-21.45 Mon-Fri 10.00-17.00 Sat-Sun term-time
IT availability	80+ terminals
Cultural opportunities	Edinburgh Festival, Opera, Ballet, Theatre, Jazz etc.

International Affiliations:

Technical University of Budapest, Hungary.

UNIVERSITY OF HERTFORDSHIRE BUSINESS SCHOOL

Location and Contact Details:

Address	Hertford Campus
	Mangrove Road
	Hertford, Herts SG13 8QF
	UK
Telephone Number	0707 285406/7
Facsimile Number	0707 285410
Contact Names	Ms Jenny Aitken

School Description:

Strong emphasis on strategic management; there is a Tavistock Conference on group dynamics; open book case study exams; flexible modular structure; small class sizes ensure full participation. Students may be able to join in January as well as September. Possibility of gaining a Diploma in Management Studies as an interim qualification.

School Details:

MBA Courses	Full-time	Part-time
Duration	12 months	24/36 months
Class Contact	570 hours	570 hours
Dissertation or Project	project	project
Assessment	exam/course/project	

Final date for applications:

July	July

Schools offering an AMBA-approved course are indicated in this section by the AMBA 'roundel'.

Estimated Fees 1993/1994 Academic Year:

£6,000	£3,000 (2 year),	
	£2,000 (3 year)	
	£350/module	

1992 Student Intake:

Intake	22	34
UK	14	24
Other EC[TAB	2	
Non-EC	8	8
Women	20%	25%

Faculty Details:

Full professors	2
Visiting lecturers/professors	5
With Master's degree	all
With PhD	7

Facilities:

Library hours	08.45-21.00 weekdays
	14.00-17.00 Sat
	14.00- 19.00 Sun (term-time);
	09.00-17.00 weekdays (vacation)
IT availability	20 mainframe connections, 21 Viglen 386s operating Windows, 35 Apple Macs, 40 Opus 2 pcs, DTP room, laser printers from all software; 09.00-22.00 weekdays, 10.00- 20.00 Sat/Sun (no evenings during vacation)
Cultural opportunities	Close to London with its varied cultural opportunities

International Affiliations:
Växjö University, Sweden (Hatfield MBA is franchised).

HUDDERSFIELD UNIVERSITY

Location and Contact Details:

Address	Department of Management, Queensgate Huddersfield West Yorks HD1 3DH UK
Telephone Number	0484 422288 ext.2026
Facsimile Number	0484 516151
Contact Name	Mrs Barbara Sherwood

School Description:
The school offers a modular system to facilitate credit accumulation and transfer. Some specialisation is possible in Stage 2. Particular strengths are Accounting, Business Strategy and Management Information Systems.

School Details:

MBA Courses	Full-time	Part-time
Duration	48 weeks	3 years
Class Contact	15 hours	2 evenings
Dissertation	yes	yes
Assessment	assignments/exams	
Final date for applications:		
	end June	mid-September

Estimated Fees 1993/1994 Academic Year:

UK/EC	£3,000	£1,300
Overseas		£5,500

1992 Student Intake:

Intake	30	24/30

Faculty Details:

Dedicated MBA programme teaching staff	20
Full professors	2
With Master's degree	11
With PhD	4

Facilities:

Library hours	08.45-21.15 + weekends
IT availability	60 IBM compatible pcs with appropriate business software

---

THE UNIVERSITY OF HUDDERSFIELD
QUEENSGATE, HUDDERSFIELD HD1 3DH
TEL: 0484 422288   FAX: 0484 516151

Division of Management

Master of Business Administration Full-time Modular Programme

The Huddersfield MBA recognises that the professional manager of the 1990s and beyond needs a clear international perspective and the highest level of appropriate management education and training. The programme places an emphasis on the development of practical and intellectual skills to fit the needs of the Manager in today's highly competitive environment.

For those participants wishing to specialise in Marketing or Information Systems, pathways are also available leading to MBA (Marketing) and MBA (Information Systems).

Contact: Mrs L Bennett, Division of Management, The University of Huddersfield, Queensgate, HUDDERSFIELD, HD1 3DH. Tel: (0484) 422288, Ext 2346

MBA
PROGRAMMES

The School of Management offers General, Information Management and Financial Management MBAs as well as the part time Executive MBA.

If you are interested in contemporary ideas in management then enquire about the University of Hull's innovative full and part time MBAs for thinking practitioners.

For further details contact:
        Masters Admissions, School of Management.
        The University of Hull,
        Hull HU6 7RX
        United Kingdom.
        Telephone 0482 857464 Fax: 0482 857518.

 THE
UNIVERSITY
OF HULL

IMPERIAL COLLEGE
UNIVERSITY OF LONDON

THE MANAGEMENT SCHOOL

MBA PROGRAMMES

If you are serious about a career in management, our full-time **One Year MBA Programme** will equip you with a comprehensive grounding in management skills. Or, if you are looking for promotion to senior management, then choose the three-year part-time **Executive MBA**. Both programmes offer a choice of specialised areas of expertise.

- **Management of New Ventures**
- **Strategic Management Consultancy**
- **Finance**
- **Management of Innovation**
- **Major Project Management**
- **Management Science**

For full details contact Kay Maguire (ext 7124, One-year MBA) or Siew Lim (ext 7027, Executive MBA).

The Management School, Imperial College, 53 Prince's Gate, London SW7 2PG. Tel: 071-589 5111 ext. 7124. Fax: 071-823 7685.

IMPERIAL COLLEGE, THE MANAGEMENT SCHOOL

Location and Contact Details:

Address	52 Prince's Gate
	London SW7 2PG
	UK
Telephone Number	071 589 5111
Facsimile Number	071 823 7685
Contact Name	Kay Maguire (f/t)
	Siew Lim (p/t)

School Description:

The school offers a choice of specialisation in one of the following: Management of Innovation, Management of New Ventures, Management Science, Strategic Management Consultancy, Project Management, Finance. Imperial College is one of the largest colleges of London University and is a leading centre for research and teaching in science and technology.

School Details:

MBA Courses	Full-time ✓	Part-time ✓
Duration	12 months	3 years
Class Contact	650 hours	290 hours
Dissertation		
or Project	project on which a report is written	project on which a report is written
UK/EC	£8,000	£5,000
Non-EC	£8,500	

1992 Student Intake:

Intake	125	30
UK	30	30
Other EC	32	
Non-EC	63	
Women	22%	20%

Faculty Details:

Dedicated MBA programme teaching staff	38
Full professors	5
Visiting lecturers/professors	13
With Master's degree	19
With PhD	16

Facilities:

Library hours	09.30-21.00 Mon-Fri
	09.30-17.30 Sat
IT availability	35 terminals + other equipment
Cultural opportunities	College sports complex. Humanities programme including classical music concerts. Close to Hyde Park and the major London museums.

International Affiliations:

Darden School of Business, Virginia, USA.

KEELE UNIVERSITY, SCHOOL OF MANAGEMENT AND ECONOMICS

Location and Contact Details:

Address	Keele
	Staffs ST5 5BG
	UK
Telephone Number	0782 3008
Facsimile Number	0782 715859
Contact Name	Ian F. Bird

School Description:

Special features of the MBA include courses in Industrial Relations, Education Management and Health Service Management. The school also offers a Distance Learning MBA and a Company MBA – details are available on request.

School Details:

	Full-time	Part-time
MBA Courses		
Duration	12 months	24/30 months
Class Contact	372 hours	280 hours
Dissertation or Project	dissertation	dissertation
Assessment	course/exams	course/exams

Health, population and nutrition in developing countries		
Duration	12 months	
Class Contact	372 hours	
Dissertation or Project	dissertation	
Assessment	course/exam	

Health Executive		
Duration		24/30 months
Class Contact		280 hours
Dissertation or project		dissertation
Assessment		course/exam

Individual courses approved by AMBA are indicated by a 'tick'.

Education Management
Duration 24/30 months
Class Contact 280 hours
Dissertation
 or Project
Assessment dissertation / course

Final date for applications:
MBA 1 July 1 December
Health, Pop'n 1 September
Health Executive 1 September
Education Management 1 December

Estimated Fees 1992/1993 Academic Year:
MBA
UK/EC £3,675 £2,800
Overseas £6,700
Health, Pop'n £5,040
Health Executive £2,520
Education Management £1,500

1992 Student Intake:
MBA
Intake 53 10
UK 17 10
Other EC 6
Non-EC 30
Women 30% 50%

Health, Pop'n
Intake 17
Non-EC 17
Women 29%
Health Executive
Intake 22
UK 22
Women 45%
Education Management
Intake 24
UK 24
Women 46%

Faculty Details:
Dedicated MBA
 programme teaching staff 21
Full professors 4
Visiting lecturers 6
With Masters 4
With PhD 15

Facilities:
Library hours 10.00-22.05 Mon-Sat
14.00-22.00 Sun (term-time)
IT availability 50 terminals

KINGSTON UNIVERSITY BUSINESS SCHOOL

Location and Contact Details:

Address	Kingston Hill
	Kingston-upon-Thames
	Surrey KT2 7LB
	UK
Telephone Number	081 547 2000
Facsimile Number	081 547 7026
Contact Name	David Browne

School Description:

This is a well-established programme from one of the UK's largest business education centres. With about three student intakes per year, Kingston offers particular flexibility of timing to candidates. Evening or weekend part-time study depending on choice of programme. Particular strengths include Marketing, Information Systems and Human Resources.

School Details:

MBA Courses	Part-time ✓	Open Learning ✓
Duration	2.5 years	2 years
Class Contact	530 hours	250 hours
Dissertation		
or Project	project	project
Assessment	exam/course	
Final date for applications:		
	December	February (March intake)

August (September intake)

Estimated Fees 1993/1994 Academic Year:

	£3,000	£3,250

1992 Student Intake:

Intake	80	240
UK	80	235
Other EC		5
Women	15%	15%

Faculty Details:

Dedicated MBA programme teaching staff	84
Full professors	6
Visiting lecturers/professors	15
With Master's degree	64
With PhD	12

Facilities:

Library hours	08.45-20.45 weekdays
	10.00-16.00 Sat
IT availability	5 laboratories of 30 networked 386 SXs. Open access 08.00-21.30 weekdays, 10.00-16.00 weekends
Other facilities	Town easily accessible by motorways

LANCASTER UNIVERSITY, THE MANAGEMENT SCHOOL

Location and Contact Details:

Address	Lancaster LA1 4YX
	UK
Telephone Number	0524 594068
Facsimile Number	0524 381454
Contact Name	Prof M Pidd

School Description:

The School has a first calss rating in business and management, having been placed in the top category for research for international excellent(UFC) and for teaching *(Times Good University Guide)*. In addition to full-time and consortial MBA programmes there are specialist masters in 7 management subjects and a doctorial programme. The School has a Graduate Division with over 350 post-graduate students. It has strong international links and its courses all emphasise applied project work and active learning. The full-time MBA has a set of core courses followed by a wide range of electives with particualr emphasis on

strategy, marketing, international business, human resources, finance, operationa management. A limited number of bursaries is available.

School Details:

MBA Courses	Full-time ✓	Company/ Consortium
Duration	12 months	24 months
Class Contact	470 hours + project supervision	550 hours
Dissertation		
or Project	project	project
Assessment	exam/course	exam/course
Final date for applications:		
	none	end July
Estimated Fees 1993/1994 Academic Year:		
UK/EC	£6,500	£9,650 (2-year course)
Non-EC	£7,500	

Individual courses approved by AMBA are indicated by a 'tick'.

KINGSTON MBA

The MBA is the essential qualification to develop your company's management potential. The Kingston MBA is a well-established and highly regarded programme.

Kingston is also highly flexible, offering two study modes, and three start dates per year.

OPEN LEARNING
This 2 year programme provides a combination of individual study and intensive weekend tuition modules. Programmes start in March and September each year.

EVENING
This 2½ year programme involves evening study and 2 full-time week modules. The programme starts in January.

Both programmes are designed specifically for professionals for whom time is a valuable resource, enabling candidates to remain at work while earning their MBA.

The employer benefits too, since a valuable colleague is retained. In addition, students can be used as internal consultants over the study period, to maximise benefits to the organisation.

For further details please contact the MBA office
on 081 547 7120 or fax 081 547 7029.

1992 Student Intake:

UK	40%	100%
Other EC	15%	
Non-EC	45%	
Women	20%	15%

Faculty Details:

Dedicated MBA programme teaching staff	32
Full professors	16
Visiting lecturers/professors	15
With Master's degree	54
With PhD	48

Facilities:

Library hours	73 hours per week
IT availability	open-access and bookable pc and Mac rooms, all connected to the university network; laser printers; technical support; currently 50+ terminals in the School, many more elsewhere on campus
Cultural opportunities	On campus there is a theatre and an art gallery; the music rooms host an international concert series.
Other facilities	language teaching for all major languages; study skills support

International Affiliations:

Wirtschaftsuniversität, Wien; Ecole Supérieure de Commerce de Lyon; Università Commerciale Luigi Bocconi, Milan, Erasmus Universität, Rotterdam; University of British Columbia.

LEEDS BUSINESS SCHOOL

Location and Contact Details:

Address	Leeds Metropolitan University
	4, Queen Square
	Leeds LS7 8AF
	UK
Telephone Number	0532 832600 ext. 4314
Facsimile Number	0532 833227
Contact Name	MBA Admissions Officer

School Description:

Modular programme. All modules are CATS rated.

School Details:

MBA Courses	*Part-time modular*
Duration	18 months
Class Contact	6 hours/week
Dissertation or Project	project
Assessment	exam/course
Final date for applications:	
	September 1993
Estimated Fees 1993/1994 Academic Year:	
	£1,850

1992 Student Intake:

Intake	20
UK	20
Women	40%

Faculty Details:

Full professors	1
With Master's degree	40%
With PhD	10%

Facilities:

Library hours	09.00-21.00 7 days
IT availability	Open access labs in Central Library and in Business School

International Affiliations:

We have general links with many European institutions.

Individual courses approved by AMBA are indicated by a 'tick'.

PART TWO   111

LEEDS UNIVERSITY MANAGEMENT SCHOOL

Location and Contact Details:

Address	University of Leeds
	Leeds LS2 9JT
	UK
Telephone Number	0532 334494
Facsimile Number	0532 332640
Contact Name	K.J. Woolmer

School Description:

All 3 MBAs are fully modularised on standard 120 credit basis – all can be credit accumulated and are fully portable/transferable. Full-time MBA offers major option of foreign language French, German, Spanish and Japanese at 3 levels including beginners.

School Details:

MBA Courses	Full-time	Part-time (eve)	Modular
Duration	1 year	2 years	2 years
Class Contact	432 min.	404	380
Dissertation or Project		project	dissertation
Assessment	exam/ course	exam/ course	exam/ course
Final date for applications:	July 31st	July 31st	open (3 start dates each year)

Estimated Fees 1993/1994 Academic Year:

UK/EC	£6,000	£2,500	£3,000
Non-EC	£6,500		

1992 Student Intake:

Intake	starts 1993	35	135
UK		35	135
Non-EC			1
Women		17%	35%

Faculty Details:

Dedicated MBA programme teaching staff	70
Full professors	9
With Master's degree	26
With PhD	26

Facilities:

Library hours	09.00-21.00 Mon-Fri; 09.00-13.00 Sat
IT availability	50 terminals in School; over 1,000 more in University
Cultural opportunities	Full range of cultural, recreational, sporting and other extra-curricular activities as befits a metropolitan city.

International Affiliations:
IEFSI, Lille.

LEICESTER BUSINESS SCHOOL

Location and Contact Details:

Address	De Montfort University
	The Gateway
	Leicester LE1 9BH
	UK
Telephone Number	0533 551551
Facsimile Number	0533 517548
Contact Name	Joan Beaver

School Description:

Part-time attendance either one day per week or two evenings per week. Strategic Management Options permit study selection. Wide range of electives on full-time programme including Strategic Management and Public Sector.

School Details:

MBA Courses	Full-time	Part-time ✓
Duration	1 year	2½ years
Class Contact	540 hours	500 hours
Dissertation or Project	both	project + thesis
Assessment	exam/course	
Final date for applications:	early application is recommended	

Estimated Fees 1993/1994 Academic Year:

	£5,800	£1,850

1992 Student Intake:

Intake	160
UK	156
Other EC	2
Non-EC	2
Women	20%

Faculty Details:

Dedicated MBA programme teaching staff	12
Full professors	3
With Master's degree	12
With PhD	6

The University of Leeds MBA Programmes

The University of Leeds has a top quality national and international reputation. The City of Leeds is a major UK centre for financial, legal and communications services together with good balance of thriving industries. This lively City and its University offer you ready access to a wide range of social, cultural and sporting facilities.

At the Leeds University Management School we recognise the needs of busy managers and executives in the 1990s. Our portfolio of MBA programmes offers a variety of routes to raise the effectiveness of managerial performance by developing skills in analysis, judgement and implementation.

The one-year Full-time MBA starts in October each year. It is aimed at both the UK and international market. We offer the option to study a foreign language, Japanese, French, German or Spanish, at levels from beginners to advanced.

The Executive MBA is organised around a series of three-day modules with a flexibility of timing and choice to suit busy management schedules. This two year part-time programme starts three times a year, in January, April and October.

The Evening MBA involves summer and autumn-school weeks as well as evening study. As with the Executive MBA this two year part-programme is for managers and professionals in both the private and public sectors. It starts in September each year.

For further information please contact the MBA Programme Secretary by telephone 0532 332638 or fax 0532 332640 or by writing to us at The Leeds University Management School, University of Leeds, 11, Blenheim Terrace, Leeds, LS2 9JT.

Facilities:

Library hours	until 21.00 weekdays
	until 16.00 weekends term-time
IT availability	6 IT labs;100 terminals

Cultural opportunities	Rich and varied leisure, recreation and sport

LEICESTER UNIVERSITY MANAGEMENT CENTRE

Location and Contact Details:

Address	University of Leicester
	Educational Management Development Unit,
	University Centre, Barrack Road,
	Northampton NN2 6AF
	UK
Telephone Number	0604 30180
Facsimile Number	0604 231136
Contact Name	Mrs Valerie Cocks

School Description:

Specialist unit for school and college management. CATS rated. Linked with Digital Equipment Company Ltd and Northamptonshire LEA.

School Details:

MBA Courses	Part-time	Modular	Distance Learning	Company/ Consortium
Duration	2 years			
Class Contact	150 hours			
Dissertation or project	dissertation			
Assessment	exam/course			

Final date for applications:

	Start of each term	Start of each term	Open	Open

Estimated Fees 1992/1993 Academic Year:

UK/EC	£750	£250 per module	£750

1992 Student Intake:

Intake	120
UK	120
Women	60%

Faculty Details:

Dedicated MBA programme teaching staff	5
Full professors	1
Visiting lecturers/professors	0
With Master's degree	4
With PhD	1

Facilities:

Library hours	09.00-21.00
IT availability	Many
Cultural opps.	Full range of university facilities.

LIVERPOOL BUSINESS SCHOOL

Location and Contact Details:

Address	98 Mount Pleasant Buildings
	Liverpool L3 5UZ
	UK
Telephone Number	051 231 3851
Facsimile Number	051 231 3836
Contact Name	Mr B Whorrall

School Description:

The school offers flexible learning contracts with an exit qualification at the end of each year – Cert. DIP Master's. All study is work-based; CATS accreditation of prior learning. The school also offers a Block MBA – details are available on request. A Distance Learning MBA will be offered from 1993.

School Details:

MBA Courses	Part-time
Duration	3 years
Class Contact	470 hours

Dissertation or Project	dissertation: 25,000 words
Assessment	course assessment

Final date for applications:

	3 intakes per year

Estimated Fees 1993/1994 Academic Year:

	£1,600

1992 Student Intake:

Intake	250

Faculty Details:

Full professors	7
With Master's degree	25
With PhD	10

Facilities:

Library hours	09.30-19.30
IT availability	20+ terminals

Individual courses approved by AMBA are indicated by a 'tick'.

THE UNIVERSITY OF LEICESTER

Master of Business Administration

The University of Leicester MBA programme emphasises the strategic dimension of management decisions. Participants on the MBA are introduced to the fundamental techniques of Management in the areas of Accountancy; Organisation Analysis and Control; Marketing; Operations Management; Financial Management; Human Resource Management; Decision and Information Sciences; Managerial Economics and Business Policy. These areas are integrated through specialist topics in strategic management using case studies. Evaluation is by continuous assessment and written examination. The programme lasts for 12 months and commences 1st October.

For further details please contact:

**The Admissions Office, University of Leicester Management Centre
Leicester LE1 7RH
Tel: Leicester (0533) 523952**

LONDON BUSINESS SCHOOL

Location and Contact Details:

Address	Sussex Place
	Regents Park
	London NW1 4SA
	UK
Telephone Number	071 262 5050
Facsimile Number	071 724 7875
Contact Name	Val Morgan/Penny Levinson

School Description:

New MBA curriculum places emphasis on 3 Is: Internationalisation, Implementation (i.e. strong emphasis on practical work such as projects, in international locations) and Integration across different disciplines as learnt in real-life situations. The programme is unique in that students are drawn equally from each of the main economic blocs of America, Europe and Asia/Pacific.

School Details:

MBA Courses	Full-time ✓	Part-time ✓
Duration	18-21 months	30 months
Project	yes	yes
Assessment	exam/course	

Final date for applications:

	1st May	1st November

Estimated Fees 1993/1994 Academic Year:

	£9,500	£7,100

1992 Student Intake:

Intake	180	70
UK	25%	80%
Other EC	21%	2%
Non-EC	54%	18%
Women	21%	23%

Faculty Details:

Dedicated MBA programme teaching staff	66 total staff
Full professors	28
Visiting lecturers/professors	13
With Master's degree	101
With PhD	72

Schools offering an AMBA-approved course are indicated in this section by the AMBA 'roundel'.

Facilities:

Library hours	09.00-21.00 Mon-Fri
	09.00-17.00 Sat
IT availability	6 terminals
Cultural opportunities	Full range of sports, cultural and business-related clubs

International Affiliations:

Exchange with 25 top business schools around the world

LONDON GUILDHALL UNIVERSITY, CENTRE FOR MANAGEMENT

Location and Contact Details:

Address	84 Moorgate
	London EC2M 6SQ
	UK
Telephone Number	071 320 1451
Facsimile Number	071 320 1585
Contact Name	Paul Tregenza

School Description:

An integrated management development programme of skills and knowledge enhancement aimed at employees of local financial services companies.

School Details:

MBA Courses	*Part-time*
Duration	2 years
Class Contact	250 hours
Dissertation or Project	project
Assessment	exam/course
Final date for applications:	
	mid-Sept
Estimated Fees 1993/1994 Academic Year:	
	£3,000

1992 Student Intake:

Intake	40
UK	36
Other EC	2
Non-EC	2
Women	28%

Faculty Details:

Dedicated MBA programme teaching staff	20
Full professors	1
Visiting lecturers/professors	12
With Master's degree	19
With PhD	3

Facilities:

Library hours	09.30-20.30 Mon-Fri; 10.00-16.00 Sat
IT availability	more than 100 terminals/pcs, hours as library

---

LONDON MANAGEMENT CENTRE, in UNIVERSITY OF WESTMINSTER

Location and Contact Details:

Address	University of Westminster
	35 Marylebone Road
	London NW1 5LS
	UK
Telephone Number	071 911 5000
Facsimile Number	071 911 5059
Contact Name	The Faculty Officer

School Description:

The University of Westminster is a recognised centre of excellence by the Institute of Personnel Management and is licensed as an accreditation centre by the Management Charter Initiative. The MBA is modularised and credit-based. Limited exemption for approved prior qualifications may be allowed. The MBA is designed as a General Management Programme. The first year provides coverage of the major functional areas, and development in organisational analysis and interpersonal skills. The second year focuses on strategic management, with supporting modules in marketing, design and operations strategy, financial strategy, strategic management of information and human resource strategy.

Individual courses approved by AMBA are indicated by a 'tick'.

PART TWO   117

School Details:

MBA Courses	*Part-time* ✓
Duration	22 months
Class Contact	average 6 hours/week
Dissertation	
or Project	major final project
Assessment	exams/assignments

Final date for applications:
August/January

Estimated Fees 1993/1994 Academic Year:
£2,800

1992 Student Intake:

Intake	61 Year 1
	50 Year 2
UK	all
Women	33% Year 1
	30% Year 2

Faculty Details:

Dedicated MBA programme teaching staff	16
Full professors	1
Visiting lecturers/professors	4
With Master's degree	16
With PhD	4

Facilities:

Library hours	09.15-21.00 Mon-Thurs
	09.15-17.00 Fri
	11.00- 16.00 Sat, Sun (term-time);
	09.15-17.00 Mon-Fri (vacation)
IT availability	Four 20-station Novell networks and one 20-station Macintosh network available for course member use

UNIVERSITY OF WESTMINSTER

Today's Decision, Tomorrow's Career

London Management Centre

The University of Westminster offers Masters or postgraduate Diploma programmes starting February and October, in the following areas:

- Human Resource Management

- Management Studies

- Marketing

- Diplomatic Studies

- Statistical Applications in Business and Government

We also offer the MBA for experienced managers and professionals by part-time study.

For further information see the entry in the directory section under the London Management Centre or contact the London Management Centre Faculty Office, University of Westminster, 35 Marylebone Road, London NW1 5LS **Telephone 071 911 5000**

LOUGHBOROUGH UNIVERSITY BUSINESS SCHOOL

Location and Contact Details:

Address	Ashby Road	
	Loughborough	
	Leicestershire LE11 3TU	
	UK	
Telephone Number	0509 223140	
Facsimile Number	0509 233313	
Contact Name	Mr Jim Saker	

School Details:

MBA Courses	Part-time ✓	Company/
		Consortium
Duration	3 years	3 years
Class Contact		500 hours
Dissertation		
or Project	dissertation	dissertation
Assessment	exam/course	

Estimated Fees 1993/1994 Academic Year:
£1,750

1992 Student Intake:

Intake	28

Faculty details:

Dedicated MBA	
programme teaching staff	45
Full professors	9
Visiting lecturers/professors	4
With Master's degree	23
With PhD	16

Facilities:

Library hours	09.00-22.00
IT availability	LAN of 25 PCs plus 5 stand alone PCs. Link to the University Mainframe

MANCHESTER BUSINESS SCHOOL

Location and Contact Details:

Address	Booth Street West
	Manchester M15 6PB
	UK
Telephone Number	061 275 6333
Facsimile Number	061 275 6489
Contact Name	Ms Alison Walker

School Description:

The school has one of the best business libraries in Europe, and the largest international exchange programme of any MBA. Over 100 days of live project work, which makes it a very practical programme. The school also offers a Master of Business Management (MBM) and a Company MBA – details are available on request. Language tuition is provided and the School offers up to 30 student assistantships worth £2,000 each.

School Details:

MBA Courses	Full-time ✓	Part-time ✓
Duration	21 months	33 months
Class Contact	1,350 hours	700 hours
Dissertation	15,000 words	15,000 words
Assessment	mixture	mixture
Final date for applications:		
	30th June	31st July
Estimated Fees 1992/1993 Academic Year:		
UK/EC	£7,500	£5,000
Overseas	£9,000	

1992 Student Intake:

Intake	100	46
UK	32	46
Other EC	15	
Non-EC	53	
Women	15%	25%

Faculty Details:

Dedicated MBA	
programme teaching staff	45
Full professors	12
Visiting lecturers/professors	40
With Master's degree	33
With PhD	29

Facilities:

Library hours	08.50-22.30
IT availability	65 dedicated MBA pcs, link with University mainframe, local area network for MBA students; available 24 hours per day
Cultural opportunities	Over 100 University clubs and societies
Other facilities	MBA Students have their own consulting club, finance club and marketing society

International Affiliations:

40 schools worldwide for exchange, including Kellogg, NYU, Chicago, Berkeley, Rotterdam, Melbourne.

Individual courses approved by AMBA are indicated by a 'tick'.

MANCHESTER METROPOLITAN UNIVERSITY

Location and Contact Details:

Address   Faculty of Management and Business
            Aytoun Buildings
            Aytoun Street
            Manchester M1 3GH
            UK
Telephone Number   061 247 3717
Facsimile Number   061 247 6319
Contact Name   Mr Stuart Horsburgh

School Description:

The school offers a modular programme, allowing a wide range of elective choices from a large staff resource base.

School Details:

MBA Courses	Part-time	Company/ Consortium
Duration	2½ years	2½ years
Class Contact	late aft, eve, 4 Fri/Sat each yr	late aft, eve, 4 Fri/Sat each yr
Dissertation or Project	dissertation	dissertation
Assessment	exams/course	exams/course

Final date for applications:
           December   April
Estimated Fees 1993/1994 Academic Year:
           £2,500

1992 Student Intake:

Intake	60
UK	100%
Women	30%

Faculty Details:

Dedicated MBA programme teaching staff	20
Full professors	3
Visiting lecturers/professors	varies
With Master's degree	15
With PhD	5

Facilities:

Library hours	09.00-21.00; open Saturdays
IT availability	300 workstations
Cultural opportunities	European or Central and East European module in second year

International Affiliations:

EADA, Barcelona; Prague International Business School.

the
MANCHESTER
METROPOLITAN
UNIVERSITY

Master of Business Administration
Part-Time Evening Study

The Manchester Metropolitan University is the UK's largest provider of business and management education.

Our highly successful two and a half year part-time MBA is directed towards experienced managers from the public and private sectors.

The programme follows a core group of modules and workplace based assignments, followed by electives and a dissertation.

A full-time programme is currently being designed.

Specially tailored consortium programmes for organisations are also available.

For further information please contact Kath Hemsworth, MBA Administrator, on 061-247 3713/3717, or write to her at The Manchester Metropolitan University, Faculty of Management and Business, MBA Office, Aytoun Building, Aytoun Street, Manchester M1 3GH.

MANCHESTER SCHOOL OF MANAGEMENT, UMIST

Location and Contact Details:

Address	UMIST
	P O Box 88
	Manchester M60 1QD
	UK
Telephone Number	061 200 3500
Facsimile Number	061 200 3505
Contact Names	M Greatorex

School Description:

The school has a number of specialist MSc courses, in Marketing, Personnel Management and Industrial Relations; Accounting and Finance; Technology Management; Operations Management and Organisational Psychology. There is a large faculty and scope for specialisation. The part-time MBA is offered jointly with Manchester Business School.

School Details:

MBA Courses	Full-time	Part-time
Duration	1 year	3 years
Class Contact	300 hours	1 day/week; some week-ends
Dissertation or Project	yes	yes
Assessment	exams/coursework/dissertation	
Final date for applications:		
	on-going	on-going

Estimated Fees 1992/1993 Academic Year:

UK	£2,250	£5,000
overseas	£5,000	

1992 Student Intake:

Intake	120	48
UK	66	47
Other EC	20	
Non-EC	34	1
Women	54	12

Faculty Details:

Full professors	8
Visiting lecturers/professors	2
With Master's degree	20
With PhD	40

Facilities:

Library hours	09.00-21.45 weekdays
	09.00-11.45 Saturdays
IT availability	65 pcs and terminals
Other facilities	audio-visual aids

International Affiliations:

Penn State University; ESC-Lyon; ESADE

MIDDLESEX UNIVERSITY BUSINESS SCHOOL

Location and Contact Details:

Address	The Borroughs
	London NW4 4BT
	UK
Telephone Number	081 362 5000
Contact Name	Miss B Turner

School Description:

Middlesex Business School is proud of its European links both at undergraduate and post-graduate level. The course is currently under review for modularisation, semesterisation and credit accumulation and transfer.

School Details:

MBA Courses	Full-time ✓	Part-time ✓
Duration	1 year	2 years
Class Contact	20 hours/week	6 hours/week
Dissertation or Project	either	either
Assessment	exam/course	exam/course
Final date for applications:		
	30th August	30th August
Estimated Fees 1993/1994 Academic Year:		
	£5,800	£1,900

1992 Student Intake:

Intake	42	34
Women	37%	24%

Faculty Details:

Dedicated MBA programme teaching staff	8
Full professors	5
Visiting lecturers/professors	10
With Master's degree	30
With PhD	21

Facilities:

Library hours	10.00-20.30 Mon-Thurs;
	10.00-17.00 Fri; 10.00-16.00 Sat
IT availability	164 terminals
Other facilities	language laboratory facilities are
	available to part-time students

International Affiliations:
None

NAPIER BUSINESS SCHOOL

Location and Contact Details:

Address	Department of Management Studies
	Redwood House, 16 Spylaw Road
	Edinburgh EH10 5BR
	UK
Telephone Number	031 455 5016
Facsimile Number	031 346 8553
Contact Name	Vacancy

School Description:
The school offers full exemptions to CIM Diploma holders (other than Core Study). Work-based projects, transfers on to Business Schools Network. Exemptions for Professional Qualifications. New 3-tier format to be introduced 1993.

School Details:

MBA Courses	Part-time	Open learning
Duration	2 years	2 years
Class Contact	1 aft/1 eve/wk	1 week
		10 weekends/yr
Dissertation		
or Project	dissertation	dissertation
Assessment	course assessment and exam	
Final date for applications:		
	end September	end August

Estimated Fees 1993/1994 Academic Year:

£1,500	£2,500

1992 Student Intake:

Intake	50	50
UK	50	50
Women	40%	40%

Faculty Details:

Dedicated MBA	
programme teaching staff	30
Visiting lecturers/professors	10
With Master's degree	20
With PhD	5

Facilities:

Library hours	7 days a week, 09.00-20.00
IT availability	20 terminals on Redwood site,
	100+ on other sites
Cultural	University clubs/orchestra etc.
opportunities	

International Affiliations:
Haarlem, Holland.

NENE COLLEGE, FACULTY OF MANAGEMENT AND BUSINESS

Location and Contact Details:

Address	Park Campus
	Moulton Park
	Northampton NN2 7AL
	UK
Telephone Number	0604 735500
Facsimile Number	0604 720636
Contact Names	FT: David Shuttleworth
	PT: David Hillyard

School Description:
The courses are validated by the University of Leicester. The part-time programme allows intakes in January and September each year and can be completed over a maximum of 5 years. In the full-time MBA (Europe) programme students from the UK and France study Stage 1 (1st semester) in Poitiers, France and Stage 2 at Nene College, Northampton. Students must be able to offer adequate standard French to enter the course.

School Details:

MBA Courses	Full-time	Part-time
Duration	1 year	2-5 years
Class Contact	500 hours	400 hours
Dissertation		
or Project	yes	yes
Assessment	assignments and exam	

Individual courses approved by AMBA are indicated by a 'tick'.

PART TWO   123

Final date for applications:

	September	September/ January

Estimated Fees 1993/1994 Academic Year:

	£5,000	£1,900

1992 Student Intake:

Intake	12	22
UK	5	22
Other EC	6	
Non-EC	1	
Women	42%	18%

Faculty Details:

Dedicated MBA programme teaching staff	20
Visiting lecturers/professors	10
With Master's degree	36
With PhD	2

Facilities:

Library hours	08.30-22.00 Mon-Thurs
	08.30-17.00 Fri
	10.00-13.00 Sat
IT availability	ratio of approximately 8:1 terminals
	7 days/week, 14 hrs/day

NEWCASTLE BUSINESS SCHOOL

Location and Contact Details:

Address	University of Northumbria at Newcastle
	Northumberland Building
	Newcastle on Tyne NE1 8ST
	UK
Telephone Number	091 227 4942
Facsimile Number	091 227 4560/4684
Contact Name	Tracy Chandler

School Description:

Joint residential courses with Groningen and MA in European Business Administration; Information Management, Management Development, Public Sector, wide range of Masters degree level electives, eg Consultancy, HRM, Marketing. MAs in Marketing, Business Information Technology, Travel and Tourism.

School Details:

MBA Courses	Full-time	Part-time
Duration	1 year	3 years (change to 2 proposed)
Class Contact	400 hours	200 hours/year
Final date for applications:		
	August	August
Estimated Fees 1993/1994 Academic Year:		
	£5,500	£2,500

1992 Student Intake:

Intake	25
UK	24
Other EC	1
Women	40%

Faculty Details:

Total MBA programme teaching staff	25
Full professors	1
Visiting lecturers/professors	8
With Master's degree	66
With PhD	11

Facilities:

Library hours	09.00-21.00/09.30-17.00 Sat
IT availability	Dedicated to MBA FT 20, PT 25 open access terminals. 164 classroom based plus University VAX, JANET
Cultural opportunities	Access to full range of culture in Newcastle, pivotal city of the Northeast; open country, close to Borders, Hadrian's Wall, Scotland.

International Affiliations:

Strathclyde Graduate Business School; Gronigen – Hansa Polytechnic.

UNIVERSITY OF NEWCASTLE UPON TYNE

Location and Contact Details:

Address	School of Business Management
	University of Newcastle upon Tyne
	Newcastle upon Tyne NE1 7RU
	UK
Telephone Number	091 222 6150/6188
Facsimile Number	091 222 8131
Contact Name	Jayne Barrass (Secretary Joan Harvey (Director, MBA programme)

School Description:

Contacts with local business and industry, electives.

School Details:

MBA Courses	Full-time ✓	Part-time ✓	Company Consortium
Duration	1 year	2⅔ years	3 years
Class Contact	6 per week	6 per week	420 hours for total
Dissertation or Project	dissertation	dissertation	dissertation
Assessment	exam/ course	exam/ course	exam/ course
Final date for applications:			
	July/Aug	July/Aug	end Aug
Estimated Fees 1993/1994 Academic Year:			
Home & EC	£5,834	£2,076	
Overseas	£7,742		

1992 Student Intake:

Intake	20	18
UK	7	18
Other EC	2	
Non-EC	11	
Women	30%	

Faculty Details:

Dedicated MBA programme teaching staff	11
No of full professors	1
Visiting lecturers/professors	5/5
With Master's degree	2
With PhD	8

Individual courses approved by AMBA are indicated by a 'tick'.

UNIVERSITY OF
NEWCASTLE UPON TYNE

THE NEWCASTLE UNIVERSITY MBA

Newcastle University's School of Business Management has a commitment to a practical, integrated approach to post-graduate studies. We are renowned for excellence in academic scholarship and management education and all students benefit from our long and close links with local, national and international companies, as well as from our active interest in research. The School has strong links with business schools in France and Denmark.

FULL-TIME MBA: An extensive 12-month course which will develop your management potential and enhance your career opportunities. As places are limited, entry to the programme is competitive.

PART-TIME MBA: A well-established 2½ year programme designed for participants to continue their careers without interruption, whilst putting new knowledge into practice straight away.

Both courses start in October.

If you would like to find out more, please contact: MBA Secretary, School of Business Management, Armstrong Building, University of Newcastle upon Tyne, NE1 7RU. Tel: (091) 222 6150.

Facilities:

Library hours	University library 09.00-21.00
IT availability	Extnsive – available in library, computing area (Central Campus and in school.
Cultural opportunities	Theatre, concerts, nightclubs, unspoilt countryside, opportunities for sports of all kinds including windsurfing, sailing, climbing, etc.

International Affiliations:
ESC Grenoble, EDHEC Lille, ESC Toulouse, ESC Marseilles, Aarhus Business School

---

NOTTINGHAM BUSINESS SCHOOL

Location and Contact Details:

Address	Nottingham Trent University Burton Street Nottingham NG1 4BU UK
Telephone Number	0602 418418 ext.2920
Facsimile Number	0602 486512
Contact Names	Chris Prince (Dir.) Helen Beeby (Admin.)

School Description:
NBS offers an MBA with appropriate interim awards – the Certificate in Management and the DMS. Suitably qualified and experienced candidates will be able to join the second year of the programme. The first two years of the programme are also offered on Saturdays. Specialist routes for Public Sector Management and Business Information Management. Particular strengths in Business Development, International Business and Human Resource Management. Programme is CAT rated and Specific M level credits gained elsewhere will be accepted.

Schools offering an AMBA-approved course are indicated in this section by the AMBA 'roundel'.

School Details:

MBA Courses	Part-time/Modular/Company/ Consortium
Duration	up to 3 years
Class Contact	Av. 6 hours/week
Dissertation or Project	dissertation
Assessment	mainly assignments, some exams
Final date for applications:	September

Estimated Fees 1993/1994 Academic Year:

Years 1/2	£1,555
Year 3	£2,295

1992 Student Intake:

Intake	120 (year 1)
Women	30%

Faculty Details:

Dedicated MBA programme teaching staff	30

Full professors	8
Visiting lecturers/professors	12
With Master's degree	18
With PhD	10

Facilities:

Library hours	08.30-20.30 Mon-Fri 09.00-17.00 Sat
IT availability	Nottingham Business School runs 120 pcs across a much larger academic network
Cultural opportunities	Residential week in final year spent outside UK focussed on in-company project
Other facilities	Alumni association with programme of visiting lecturers

International Affiliations:

EAE Barcelona, Ecole Supérieure de Commerce, Toulouse, Brno Business School, Czech Republic, Wielkopolska Business School, Poznan, Poland.

SCHOOL OF MANAGEMENT AND FINANCE, NOTTINGHAM UNIVERSITY

Location and Contact Details:

Address	University of Nottingham University Park Nottingham NG7 2RD UK
Telephone Number	0602 515500
Facsimile Number	0602 515503
Contact Name	Admissions Tutor for relevant MBA

School Description:

All full-time students attend management interpersonal skills course and undertake a group project, normally a practical consultancy exercise for a local organisation. Strengths are in finance and financial services, and there are language and foreign institutions modules, including Japanese. Specialist MBA programmes in Financial Studies, Education, and Health are available; strengths include Finance, Publis Services Management, General Management and International aspects of Management.

School Details:

MBA Courses	Full-time Modular ✓	Part-time Modular ✓	Company/ Consortium
Duration	12 months	2-5 years	2-5 years
Class Contact	average 15 hours/week	varies	varies
Dissertation or Project	both	both	project and often dissertation
Assessment	exam/course		
Final date for applications:			early application is advised

Estimated Fees 1993/1994 Academic Year:

£6,500   £542 per module

1992 Student Intake:

	General MBAs	Financial MBAs
Intake	80	63
UK	44	29
Other EC	5	4
Non-EC	31	30
Women	29%	35%

(Full-time and part-time courses are taught together)

Faculty Details:

Dedicated MBA programme teaching staff	43
Full professors	11
Visiting lecturers/professors	1
With Master's degree	22
With PhD	19

Facilities:

Library hours	09.00-21.45 Mon-Fri 09.00-16.45 Sat

Individual courses approved by AMBA are indicated by a 'tick'.

IT availability	25 terminals for MBA course members in dedicated suite, many more elsewhere; 24-hour computer access is possible within the University
Cultural opportunities	Numerous: MBA Society, excellent theatres etc. nearby in the City
Other facilities	MBA resource room, full social facilities

International affiliations:
ESC PAU, France.

THE OPEN BUSINESS SCHOOL
Certificate · Diploma · MBA

The Open
University

MBA
PROGRAMME FROM
THE OPEN BUSINESS SCHOOL

If you're looking for the business qualification which opens doors to higher management, here's your chance.

The Open Business School MBA.

A modular programme with a range of options which allows you to reach for an MBA without dropping out from your job.

Over 6,000 managers are currently studying on the Open Business School MBA. Course content and materials have been developed in consultation with practising managers and business education experts.

And you can study anywhere in the UK, the EC and increasingly through-out the rest of Europe.

The Open Business School MBA is open to all. Even with no qualifications you can still complete Stage 1 by passing the OU Professional Certificate and Diploma in Management.

For a full prospectus, call the 24 - hour OBS Hotline

 **(0908) 373077**

or write to the The Customer Service Centre,
The Open Business School, PO Box 222, Milton Keynes MK7 6YY.

OPEN BUSINESS SCHOOL

Location and Contact Details:

Address	The Open University, Walton Hall
	Milton Keynes MK7 6AA
	UK
Telephone Number	0908 653361/653186
Facsimile Number	0908 563744
Contact Name	Alison Robinson

School Description:

The programme features strong strategic and international focus, and high level of choice, with many interdisciplinary courses and public sector/manufacturing option. The face-to-face element (some 300 hours) is far higher than normal for distance learning. Direct entry to stage 2 is possible for some students with an approved DMS or other equivalent qualifications.

School Details:

MBA Courses	*Distance learning*
Duration	2.75-7 years
Class Contact	1260 total study hours. Face-to-face
contact varies.	

Dissertation		
or Project	optional project	
Assessment		exam/course

Final date for applications:
20/9/93 for February 1993 start

Estimated Fees 1993/1994 Academic Year:
£2,050 year 1
£2,350 year 2
£2,200 year 3

1992 Student Intake:

Intake	1,500
UK	1280
Other EC	170
Non-EC	50
Women	20%

Faculty Details:

Dedicated MBA	
programme teaching staff	27
Full professors	5
Visiting lecturers/professors	6
With Master's degree	49
With PhD	8

Facilities:

IT availability	pc access assumed; computer conferencing available and teaching software provided with many courses
Other facilities	network of 13 regional centres in UK, offices throughout Europe, and 500+ tutors provide an exceptional level of tuition and support

International Affiliations:

programme offered throughout Western Europe and Hungary via own offices; Eurocontact NVT, Brussels.

OXFORD BROOKES UNIVERSITY, SCHOOL OF BUSINESS

Location and Contact Details:

Address	Wheatley
	Oxford OX33 1HX
	UK
Telephone Number	0865 485920
Facsimile Number	0865 485830
Contact Name	c/o The Course Manager

School Description:

The course aims to develop personal effectives, personal skills, management activities and sensitivity to the environment. Transferability between 3 modes (FT, PT, OL); full CATS rating of all modules. School strengths lie in innovation, dissemination of management practices in Eastern Europe and Services Management.

School Details:

MBA Courses	*Full-time*	*Part-time*	*Open-learning*
Duration	12 months	36 months	36 months
Class Contact	15 hours/wk	6 hours/wk	
Dissertation			
or Project	project	project	project
Assessment	exam/course		
Final date for applications:			
	June	July	December (For Jan); June (for July)
Estimated Fees 1993/1994 Academic Year:			
	£6,000	£2,000	£2,000

Schools offering an AMBA-approved course are indicated in this section by the AMBA 'roundel'.

1992 Student Intake:

Intake	30	30	200
UK	25	28	130
Other EC	2	2	40
Non-EC	3		30
Women	20%	30%	30%

Faculty Details:

Dedicated MBA programme teaching staff	16
Full professors	3
Visiting lecturers/professors	10
With Master's degree	70
With PhD	19

Facilities:

Library hours	until 21.00; Sat until 12.30
IT availability	24-hour access, 75 terminals in the school + 590 in the University
Cultural opportunities	Oxford, Cotswolds and London
Other facilities	shared common room; personal tutors; access to Bodleian Library.

UNIVERSITY OF OXFORD, SCHOOL OF MANAGEMENT STUDIES

Location and Contact Details:

Address	Templeton College
	Kennington
	Oxford OX1 5NY
	UK
Telephone Number	0865 735422
Facsimile Number	0865 736374
Contact Name	Dr K. J. Blois

School Description:

Emphasis on small group teaching and individual tuition.

School Details:

MBA Courses	*Full-time*
Duration	2 years
Dissertation or Project	dissertation
Assessment	exam
Final date for applications:	
	31st March
Estimated Fees 1993/1994 Academic Year:	
	£2,200 UK; £5,320 Non-UK, both plus College Membership £1,339-£1,730

1992 Student Intake:

Intake	27
UK	6
Other EC	3
Non-EC	18
Women	30%

Faculty Details:

Dedicated MBA programme teaching staff	23
Visiting lecturers/professors	29
With PhD	9

Facilities:

Library hours	08.30-20.00 Mon-Fri 09.00-12.00 Sat
IT availability	10 terminals including word processing and accessing to many databases, company data, external networks.
Cultural opportunities	membership of University of Oxford
Other facilities	Information Centre and Library covers all aspects of management and business studies and includes materials from related subjects such as economics, psychology and sociology.

Individual courses approved by AMBA are indicated by a 'tick'.

OXFORD
BROOKES
UNIVERSITY

School of Business

MASTER OF BUSINESS ADMINISTRATION

This challenging programme aims to blend theory with practice, provide you with effective managerial competences, and promote personal development.

- Study in Oxford for the MBA
- Develop your management potential and prepare yourself for senior management
- Three modes of study

   Full-time *(12 months starting in September)*

   Part-time *(3 years starting in September)*

   Open Learning *(3 years starting in July and January)*

The programme is flexible and may allow transfer between full-time and part-time and open learning modes if your circumstances change.

MPhil/PhD

Register full-time or part-time for research degrees in a wide range of business and other disciplines.

*For an information pack
(MBA or MPhil/PhD) contact:*

MBA Secretary, School of Business, Oxford Brookes University, Wheatley Campus, Oxford OX33 1HX.

Tel: 0865 485920 *(Full-time and Part-time)*
Tel: 0865 485783 *(Open Learning)*

PLYMOUTH BUSINESS SCHOOL

Location and Contact Details:

Address	Drake Circus
	Plymouth
	Devon PL4 8AA
	UK
Telephone Number	0752 232800
Facsimile Number	0752 232853
Contact Names	John Russell-Hodge

School Description:
Plymouth Business School is the Major provider of Business and Management West of Bristol. It is located in a new purpose designed building, part of the city centre campus. Plymouth is an historic city with a high quality of life which has attracted world-class companies such as Wrigley, Toshiba, Murata and Plessey. The MBA is a general programme with central themes of Managing in a Competitive Environment, Managerial Skills and Effectiveness & IT.

School Details:

MBA Courses	Full-time	Part-time	Modular
Duration	12months	2½ years	1-5 years
Class Contact	c. 480 hours	480 hours	480 hours
Dissertation or Project	yes	yes	yes
Assessment	exam/ course	exam/ course	exam/ course
Final date for applications:			
	1st Sept	1st Sept	1st Sept
Estimated Fees 1993/1994 Academic Year:			
	£5,400	£1,800 pa	£5,400 total

1992 Student Intake (total):

Intake	75
UK	67
Other EC	4
Non-EC	4
Women	20%

Schools offering an AMBA-approved course are indicated in this section by the AMBA 'roundel'.

Faculty Details:

Dedicated MBA programme
   teaching staff   16
Full professors   3
Visiting lecturers/professors   4
With Master's degree   7
With PhD   67

Facilities:

Library hours   08.00-22.00 daily

IT availability	Postgrad centre 12 486 pcs dedicated to programme
Other facilities	dedicated MBA suite including pcs, refreshments, small reference library
Cultural opportunities	Theatre, sailing & watersports, language development

PORTSMOUTH UNIVERSITY

Location and Contact Details:

Address	Portsmouth Business School
	Locksway Road
	Milton, Southsea
	Hampshire PO4 8JF
	UK
Telephone Number	0705 844039
Facsimile Number	0705 844059
Contact Name	Chris Fill/Richard Christy

School Description:

The Portsmouth MBA is orientated to the needs of employers and organisations. Students should therefore have at least three years' full-time work experience to derive benefit from the programme. All Portsmouth MBA programmes are registered with the CATS Scheme. There are specialist electives in Transport and Distribution, and a total of 28 electives are available. The programme centres upon managing uncertainty and complexity and is orientated very closely to the needs of organisations and employees.

School Details:

MBA Courses	Full-time	Part-time	Modular	Company/ Consortium
Duration	1/3 years	2/3 years	various	as agreed
Class Contact	14 hrs/ week	6 hrs/ week	various	as agreed
Dissertation or Project	project	project		project
Assessment	exam/ course	exam/ course	exam/ course	exam/ course

Final date for applications:
          31st Aug   15th Sept 15th Sept open
Estimated Fees 1993/1994 Academic Year:
UK/EC   £4,500   £1,500   various
overseas   £6,500

1992 Student Intake:

Intake	185
UK	148
Other EC	12
Non-EC	25

Faculty Details:

Dedicated MBA programme
   teaching staff   24
Full professors   3
Visiting lecturers/professors   11
With Master's degree   13
With PhD   11

Facilities:

Library hours	09.00-21.00
IT availability	dedicated suites total 165 pcs; full range of business software

International Affiliations:

HES Rotterdam; Vic Barcelona; Escole Superieur de Commerce Bordeaux; Fachhochschaule Munster; University of Georgia.

PUTTERIDGE BURY BUSINESS SCHOOL

Location and Contact Details:

Address	Hitchin Road, Luton
	Bedfordshire LU2 8LR
	UK
Telephone Number	0582 482555
Facsimile Number	0582 482689
Contact Name	Andrew Moore

School Description:

Dedicated Management Centre; strong consultancy arm; Management Charter Initiative Regional Centre. CATS scheme operative + Accreditation of Prior Achievement. The MBA is very applied in nature and the majority of assignments are work based. Most tutors are actually carrying out research/consultancy in their subject specialisms.

School Details:

MBA Courses	*Part-time*
Duration	2 years
Class Contact	360 hours
Dissertation or Project	dissertation
Assessment	exam/course

Final date for applications:
September 1993
Estimated Fees 1993/1994 Academic Year:
£2,400

1992 Student Intake:

Intake	50

Faculty Details:

Dedicated MBA programme teaching staff	15
Full professors	2
Visiting lecturers/professors	3
With Master's degree	15
With PhD	3

Facilities:

Library hours	09.00-21.00 Mon-Fri
IT availability	45 terminals
Cultural opportunities	Putteridge Bury Association

International Affiliations:
ESC-Lyon; ESADE Barcelona.

UNIVERSITY OF READING, THE MANAGEMENT UNIT

Location and Contact Details:

Address	P.O. Box 225
	Whiteknights
	Reading RG6 2AY
	UK
Telephone Number	0734 318591
Facsimile Number	0734 316539
Contact Name	Judi Elvy (Dir.)

School Details:

MBA Courses	*Open Learning*
Duration	18 months
Class Contact	90 hours formal workshops and residential courses
Dissertation or Project	Project and approx 60 hours informal study groups
Assessment	exam/course. NB exam in the form of a case study to be received in advance

Final date for applications:
N/A 3 or 4 programmes a year
Estimated Fees 1993/1994 Academic Year:
£4,405

1992 Student Intake:

Intake	17
UK	16
Other EC	
Non-EC	1
Women	25%

Faculty Details:

Dedicated MBA programme teaching staff	4
Visiting lecturers/professors	22
With Master's degree	13
With PhD	7

Facilities:

Library hours	09.00-22.15
IT availability	Plentiful throughout campus. Word processing facilities also available in library and computer centre
Cultural opportunities	Beautiful campus. Music, arts, theatre museums.
Other facilities	Sport: including water sports facilities, good restaurants, arts cafe and pubs.

International Affiliations:
The programme is linked to Henley Distance Learning Ltd which is an internationally-based organisation.

Schools offering an AMBA-approved course are indicated in this section by the AMBA 'roundel'.

MBA by Open Learning

This stimulating and practical programme enables and empowers managers to develop their potential as **proactive, responsive** and **responsible** individuals.

* Develops **mastery** in its widest sense
* Commitment to **excellence** and **quality**
* At the frontier of **theory** and **practice**
* Based on **action learning**
* Supports development of **learning organisations**
* Develops **flexibility, adaptability** and **innovation**
* Facilitates **transfer of learning** from **individual to organisation**

Unlimited counselling and tutorial support is available. Monthly half-day workshops and residential periods facilitate the development of interpersonal skills as well as maintaining momentum and enthusiasm.
Informal evening workshops are also offered, strengthening the establishment of networks. Company mentors act as lynchpins, ensuring maximum benefit to the organisation from delegate's learning.

Further information from:
Judi Elvy, Director of MBA
The Management Unit
University of Reading
P O Box 225
Whiteknights
Reading
RG6 2AY
Tel: (0734) 318591 Fax: (0734) 316539

Royal County of
BERKSHIRE
Berkshire Business Training
Award Winner 1991

ROFFEY PARK MANAGEMENT INSTITUTE

Location and Contact Details:

Address	Forest Road
	Horsham
	West Sussex RH12 4TD
	UK
Telephone Number	0293 851644
Facsimile Number	0293 851565
Contact Name	Mac Bolton

School Description:
Roffey Park offers a unique programme: two modes – weekends only or one week blocks. A special feature is self- managed learning using learning sets to design learning contracts whose achievement is assessed by the sets and by the individual. No credit transfers.

School Details:

MBA Courses	*Part-time*
Duration	2 years
Class Contact	Variable
Dissertation or Project	project
Assessment	no exams

Final date for applications:
none
Estimated Fees 1993/1994 Academic Year:
£5,400 + VAT

1992 Student Intake:

Intake	21
UK	21
Women	12%

Faculty Details:

Dedicated MBA programme teaching staff	15
Visiting lecturers/professors	27
With Master's degree	18
With PhD	12

Facilities:

Library hours	always open
IT availability	2 terminals

Individual courses approved by AMBA are indicated by a 'tick'.

Faculty Details:

Dedicated MBA programme teaching staff	50
Full professors	4
Visiting lecturers/professors	25
With PhD	7

Facilities:

Library hours	08.45-21.00 Mon-Thurs
	08.45-18.00 Fri
	weekend opening by special arrangement
IT availability	50 terminals

Concentrations/Specialisations:

Finance; General Management; International Business; Management Information Systems; Marketing; Operations Management; Organisational Behaviour; Public Policy; 3 electives

Overview of Course Details:

full-time places (1992/93)	18
part-time places (1992/93)	160
% of women students	30
% international students	3
Bi-lingual requirement	No
Exchange with overseas	Yes
TOEFL required	Yes
GMAT average	550

UNIVERSITY of SALFORD

THE MANAGEMENT SCHOOL

MBA DEGREE

This is a broadly based degree offering those with no previous qualifications in business the opportunity to gain this widely recognised qualification. The course is offered on a part time or full time basis and introduces you by stages to the foundation subjects of business a series of core courses in business strategy and offers a range of specialist electives.

MSc DEGREE

This specialist degree programme offers those who have had some undergraduate experience of business studies the opportunity to specialise in some depth in an area of their choice. Courses are offered on a part time and a full time basis and cover Human Resource Management, Finance, Marketing, Information Technology Transport, Management Application and Management Development.

For full details write to:
Head of the Management School
University of Salford, Salford, M5 4WT. Fax: 061 745 5022

SHEFFIELD BUSINESS SCHOOL

Location and Contact Details:
Address	The Old Hall
	Totley Hall Lane
	Sheffield S17 4AB
	UK
Telephone Number	0742 532904
Facsimile Number	0742 532870
Contact Names	Mr Nick Foster (f/t)
	Mr John Shipton (pt)
	Ms Jean Smith

School Description:
Particular strengths of the programme are courses in Change Management and Crisis Management.

School Details:

MBA Courses	Full-time ✓	Part-time ✓	Company/ Consortium
Duration	1 year	3.5 years	3 years
CLass Contact	15 hrs/ week	6.5 hrs/ week	variable
Dissertation	yes	yes	yes
Assessment	course assessment		

Final date for applications:

	September	September	n/a

Estimated Fees 1993/1994 Academic Year:

	£6,000	£1,400

1992 Student Intake:
Intake	29	170
UK	6	170
Other EC	8	
Non-EC	15	
Women	30%	30-40%

Faculty Details:
Dedicated MBA programme teaching staff	50
Full professors	7
Visiting lecturers/professors	25
With Master's degree	48
With PhD	9

Facilities:
Library hours	08.45-21.00 Mon-Thurs
	08.45-18.00 Fri
	weekend opening by special arrangement
IT availability	60 terminals
Cultural opportunities	Theatres, cinemas, adjacent to open country, cultural exchanges, visits to Prague, Moscow, France and Germany

International Affiliations:
Technical University, Prague

SHEFFIELD UNIVERSITY MANAGEMENT SCHOOL

Location and Contact Details:
Address	P O Box 598, Crookesmoor Building
	Conduit Road
	Sheffield S10 1FL
	UK
Telephone Number	0742 768555 ext.6763
Facsimile Number	0742 725103
Contact Name	Mrs E. Davidson

School Description:
The University has invested approximately £2.5 million in a purpose-built Management School to be opened in July 1993. The new school will have excellent computing facilities, study space, be close toits own library and have a cafeteria and social recreation area. School specialisations include General Management, Marketing Management and European Business Management.

School Details:
MBA Courses	Full-time ✓
Duration	1 year
Class Contact	c. 22 hrs/week
Dissertation or Project	dissertation
Assessment	exams and course assessment

Final date for applications:

	1st July 1993

Estimated Fees 1993/1994 Academic Year:

UK/EC	£5,800	
overseas		£7,000

1992 Student Intake:
Intake	72
UK	34
Other EC	19
Non-EC	19
Women	34%

Faculty Details:

Dedicated MBA programme
teaching staff 26
Full professors 7
Visiting lecturers/professors 2
With Master's degree 5
With PhD 12

Facilities:

Library hours   09.00-21.30 Mon-Thurs
                 09.00-17.00 Fri
                 09.00- 13.00 Sat (term-time);
                 09.00-17.00 weekdays (vacation)

IT availability   30 Novell networked workstations
                   running MS Word, Lotus 123, rbas
                   3.1 and other relevant business
                   packages

International Affiliations:

RVB Maastricht (Netherlands); Groupe ESC Rennes
(France); University of Aalborg (Denmark); University
of Uppsala (Sweden).

SOUTH BANK UNIVERSITY

Location and Contact Details:

Address   103 Borough Road
           London SE1 0AA
           UK
Telephone Number   071 815 8209
Facsimile Number   071 815 8280
Contact Names   Alison Morgan (Admin.)
                    Bronagh Power (Dir.)

School Description:

The school offers a strong Public Sector Management course, and specialises in Small Business Sector. CATS recognition. Exemption from Stage 1 for students with good DMS, but it is by no means automatic. MBA (Europe) and MBA (Education) also offered.

School Details:

MBA Courses	Full-time	Part-time
Duration	18 months	30 months
Class contact	144 hrs +	144 hrs
Project	Dissertation 1 semester i.e. 6 months approx.	
Assessment	exam/course	

Final date for applications:
           Applications and interviews all year round.

Estimated Fees 1993/1994 Academic Year:
           £5,000   £5,000

1992 Student Intake:

Intake	73
Women	25%

Faculty Details:

Dedicated MBA programme teaching staff	45
Full professors	4
Visiting lecturers/professors	10
With Master's degree	30
With PhD	15

Facilities:

Library hours	09.00-21.00 daily; Saturday by arrangement
IT availability	facility available to 21.00 Mon-Thurs; Saturday by arrangement
Cultural opportunities	Wide range of multicultural societies and clubs; sports complex.

SOUTHAMPTON UNIVERSITY MANAGEMENT SCHOOL

Location and Contact Details:

Address   Home Farm
           Leigh Road, Eastleigh
           Hants SO5 4EU
           UK
Telephone Number   0703 620911
Facsimile Number   0703 620911
Contact Name   C. Wilkinson

School Description:

The flexible modular structure allows students to construct their own sequence and effort of study over four school terms per annum. Modules are offered in various modes of attendance including evening work. There are four entry points per annum. The school also offers a DBA, which is company-based, part-time study and research – details are available on request. The school specialises in Accounting, Economics, Finance, General Management, International Business Management, Information Systems Marketing, Operations Management, Organisational Behaviour and offers 25 electives.

School Details:

MBA Courses	Full-time	Part-time	Modular	Company/ Consor ium
Duration	12 months	2-5 years		
Class Contact	500 hours	500 hours		
Dissertation or Project	yes	yes		
Assessment	exams/course assessment			

Final date for applications:
           30th Sept   30th April
                        30th June
                        30th Sept
                        31st Dec

Estimated Fees 1993/1994 Academic Year:
           £5,800   £2,900

1992 Student Intake:

Intake	32	60
UK	25	60
Non-EC	5	
Women	22%	20%

Faculty Details:

Dedicated MBA programme teaching staff	6
Full professors	1
Visiting lecturers/professors	60
With Master's degree	all
With PhD	all

Facilities:

Library hours	08.30-21.30
IT availability	3 teaching laboratories plus open learning centre (interactive teaching media)
Other facilities	fitness centre; sports and recreation facilities

UNIVERSITY OF STIRLING

Location and Contact Details:

Address	Stirling
	FK9 4LA
	Scotland, UK
Telephone Number	0786 467415
Facsimile Number	0786 450776

Facilities:

Library hours	80 hours/week
IT availability	55 networked PCs

School Description:

The Stirling MBA programme is taught by specialist staff drawn from disciplines throughout the School of Management. The school comprises departments of Accountancy and Finance, Computing, Economics, Management Science and Marketing. Specialist variants in Banking, Finance, Human Resources Management, International Business, Management Information Systems, Marketing and Retail Management.

School Details:

MBA Courses	Full-time ✓
Duration	12 months
Class Contact	450 hours
Dissertation or Project	either
Assessment	exam/continuous assessment
Final date for applications:	continuous
Estimated Fees 1992/1993 Academic Year:	£4,750 EC/Home; £7,050 non-EC

1992 Student Intake:

Intake	116
UK	12
Other EC	34
Non-EC	70
Women	39%

Faculty Details:

Dedicated MBA programme teaching staff	36
Full professors	7
With Master's degree	18
With PhD	17

Schools offering an AMBA-approved course are indicated in this section by the AMBA 'roundel'.

STRATHCLYDE GRADUATE BUSINESS SCHOOL

Location and Contact Details:

Address	199 Cathedral Street
	Glasgow G4 0GU
	UK
Telephone Number	041 553 6000
Facsimile Number	041 552 2501
Contact Names	Candace Greensted

School Description:

The school's new 11.6m complex provides state-of-the-art learning facilities and accommodation, and more than doubles the school's capacity. The degree is structured so that students have the choice of specialising in certain areas or keeping the degree broad based. Total flexibilty across all routes.

School Details:

MBA Courses	Full-time ✓	Part-time ✓	Open-learning	Compan y/Consortium
Duration	1 year	3 years	2-5 years	2-5 years
Class Contact	500 hours	500 hours	500 hra equivalent	500 hours
Assessment	exam/course			
Final date for applications:				
	Approx July	Approx August	n/an/a	

Estimated Fees 1993/1994 Academic Year:

£7,500	c. £2,250	c. £2,250

1992 Student Intake:

Intake	89	100	145	230
UK	46			
Other EC	10			
Non-EC	33			230
Women	15%			

Faculty Details:

Dedicated MBA programme teaching staff	60
Full professors	11

Facilities:

Library hours	09.00-21.00 Mon-Thurs; 09.00-17.00 Fri; Saturday pm
IT availability	60 PCs within SGBS, full access to all University IT facilities

International Affiliations:

Groupe ESC, Nantes & Groupe ESC, Toulouse, France; Universidad D'Eusto, Bilbao, Spain

---

SUNDERLAND BUSINESS SCHOOL

Location and Contact Details:

Address	1-4 Thornhill Park, Sunderland
	Tyne and Wear, SR2 7JZ
	UK
Telephone Number	091 515 2330
Facsimile Number	091 515 2308
Contact Name	Mr Ian Paterson

School Description:

The programme, which is in three stages (each of which lead to qualifications), is intended for practising managers. Learning is achieved by a combination of distance learning, college workshops and work-based activities. Private and Public Sector Module Options; CAT; APA Unit (Assessment of Prior Achievement)

School Details:

MBA Courses	Part-time
Duration	3 years
Class Contact	3 hours/week
Dissertation or Project	Work-based project
Assessment	continuous assessment

Final date for applications:

November

Estimated Fees 1993/1994 Academic Year:

£1,500 year 1
£1,700 year 2
£2,150 year 3

1992 Student Intake:

Intake	190
UK[TAB190	
Women	25%

Faculty Details:

Dedicated MBA programme teaching staff	6
Visiting lecturers/professors	4
With Master's degree	6

Facilities:

Library hours	08.30-22.00 Mon-Fri; 08.30-17.00 Sat; 10.00-18.00 Sun
IT availability	100 terminals
Other facilities	Video and sound facilities, cinema

Individual courses approved by AMBA are indicated by a 'tick'.

SURREY EUROPEAN MANAGEMENT SCHOOL

Location and Contact Details:

Address	University of Surrey
	Guildford
	Surrey GU2 5XH
	UK
Telephone Number	0483 509347
Facsimile Number	0483 440807

School Description:

Credit transfer acceptable; Accreditation of Prior Learning; open access route. Relevant modules may also be followed in the rest of the University. Extensive range of focus modules.

School Details:

MBA Courses	Full-time	Part-time	Distance-learning
Duration	1 year	2 years	2 years
Class Contact	225 hours	225 hours	225 hours
Dissertation or Project	dissertation	dissertation	dissertation
Assessment	exam/course assessment		
Final date for applications:	none	none	none

Estimated Fees 1992/1993 Academic Year:

	£5950	3300	depends on mode and location

1992 Student Intake:

Intake	26	32	71
UK	13	32	14
Other-EC	6		
Non-EC	7		57
Women	50%	16%	38%
Dedicated MBA programme teaching staff	11		
Full professors	3		
Visiting lecturers/professors	variable		
With Master's degree	4		
With PhD	3		

Facilities:

Library hours	09.00-22.00
IT availability	throughout university
Other facilities	CD-Rom, Extel, Language Centre

TEESSIDE BUSINESS SCHOOL

Location and Contact Details:

Address   University of Teesside
Flatts Lane Centre, Normanby
Middlesbrough, Cleveland, TS6 0QS
UK

Telephone Number   0642 342920
Facsimile Number   0642 324925
Contact Name   Dr Hedley Malloch

School Description:

The MBA course is part of the Linked Management Development Programme. Members progress to MBA via the Certificate in Management (2 Semesters) and Masters of Business Administration (3 semesters). There is a good range of interesting, non-standard electives.

School Details:

MBA Courses   *Part-time*
Duration   3.5 years
Class Contact   600 hours
Dissertation
 or Project   dissertation
Assessment
Final date for applications:
    August 1993

Estimated Fees 1993/1994 Academic Year:
    £1,000

1992 Student Intake:

Intake   42

Faculty Details:

Dedicated MBA
 programme teaching staff   27
Visiting lecturers/professors   3
With Master's degree   22
With PhD   12

Facilities:

Library hours   09.00-21.00 Mon-Thurs;
    09.30-17.00 Fri-Sat
IT availability   3 terminals to prime mainframe; 24 PCs with 3 printers, 24 Apple Macintosh with 3 printers
Cultural   One week residential in The
 opportunities   Hague, Holland; theme: International Management

International Affiliations:

The Haagse Hogeschool, Netherlands.

THAMES VALLEY UNIVERSITY SCHOOL OF MANAGEMENT

Location and Contact Details:

Address   St Mary's Road, Ealing
London W5 5RF and
Wellington Street, Slough
Berks, SL1 1YG, UK

Telephone Number   081 231 2501/0753 697581
Facsimile Number   081 566 1353/0753 697 557
Contact Name   Michael Cuming (Dir.)

School Description:

The Thames Valley University MBA has developed effective student-centred "Live Case" and seminar courses and case work is topical and up-to-date. There are options in Project Management, European Studies and Corporate Relations. Special features include Entrepreneurships and School strengths lie in Operations and Project Management, European Management and Human Resource Management.

School Details:

MBA Courses   *Part-time*   *Company/ Consortium*

Duration   2.5 years

Class Contact   479 hours
Dissertation
 or Project   both
Assessment   exam/course
Final date for applications:
    10th September 1993
Estimated Fees 1993/1994 Academic Year:
    £1,950 Stages½ c. £1,250 Stage 3

1992 Student Intake:

Intake   38
UK   36
Other EC   1
Non-EC   1
Women   9%

Faculty Details:

Dedicated MBA
 programme teaching staff   7
Full professors   2
Visiting lecturers/professors   14
With Master's degree   18
With PhD   3

Facilities:

Library hours	09.00-20.45 Mon-Thurs;
	09.45-17.00 Fri; 10.00- 15.45 Sat
IT availability	200 terminals
Cultural opportunities	Use of language labs, London College of Music concerts

International Affiliations:
(pending)

ULSTER BUSINESS SCHOOL

Location and Contact Details:

Address	Shore Road
	Newtownabbey
	County Antrim BT37 0QB
	Northern Ireland
Telephone Number	0232 365060 ext.3107
Facsimile Number	0232 365117
Contact Name	Mr Gavin McWhinney

School Description:

The school offers several skill-based workshops, outward bound team building week and overseas workshops on the full- time and International MBA programmes. There is a large faculty to draw on for staff resources, and links with the local business community. Details of the 15-18 month International MBA are available on request.

School Details:

MBA Courses	Full-time	Part-time
Duration	1 year	3 years
Class Contact	18 hours/week	7 hours/week (44 weeks)
Dissertation or Project	dissertation	dissertation
Assessment	exams/coursework	
Final date for applications:		
	April 1993	April 1993

Estimated Fees 1993/1994 Academic Year:
yet to be confirmed

1992 Student Intake:

Intake	45	300
UK	42	270
Other EC	2	30
Non-EC	1	
Women	40%	30%

Faculty Details:

Dedicated MBA programme teaching staff	25
Full professors	4
Visiting lecturers/professors	3

Ulster Business School

MBA IN INTERNATIONAL BUSINESS

This unique international 15 month programme is designed to combine the personal and business skills needed by the international business leaders of tomorrow with the practical needs of industry and commerce today.

Features:
- Gain first hand experience of European business cultures
- Intensive summer school in USA, Europe, or Asia.
- Workshops on European Business practices in Belgium, and on financial markets in Dublin and London.
- Top level briefings from business leaders from UK and abroad.
- Study of a European language.
- International corporate project.

This rigorous programme is restricted to mature, highly motivated and enthusiastic executives with a minium of 2 years' business experience, who wish to work and study with an international peer group drawn from across the world.

For further information, please contact the Course Director:
Professor Alan Fox
Ulster Business School
University of Ulster at Jordanstown
Shore Road
Newtownabbey
Co Antrim BT37 0QB
U.K.
Tel: (44-232) 365060 Ext. 3109
Fax: (44-232) 365117

University of Ulster

Schools offering an AMBA-approved course are indicated in this section by the AMBA 'roundel'.

UNIVERSITY OF WALES, ABERYSTWYTH

Location and Contact Details:

Address	MBA Programme, Llandinam Building
	Penglais Campus
	Aberystwyth, Dyfed SY23 3DB
	WALES
Telephone Number	0970 622523
Facsimile Number	0970 622524
Contact Name	Mr N Perdikis

School Description:

The school offers an MBA for students who wish to continue higher education without having acquired business experience. A new MBA, in Agribusiness, is now available, specialising in Agriculture and Food Marketing; Agribusiness Management, Agrifood Marketing Policy in Developed and Less Developed Countries. The MBA at Aberystwyth affords students the facilities of the National Library of Wales; many and varied cultural activities; a busy and interesting sports club with a wealth of facilities available and beautiful countryside to spend leisure time.

School Details:

MBA Courses	*Full-time*
Duration	1 year
Class Contact	35 hours
Dissertation or Project	dissertation

Assessment   exam/course

Final date for applications:
    May/June

Estimated Fees 1993/1994 Academic Year:

UK/EC	£3,700
overseas	£5,300

1992 Student Intake:

Intake	42
UK	7
Other EC	6
Non-EC	29
Women	50%

Faculty Details:

Dedicated MBA programme teaching staff	25
Full professors	5
With Master's degree	16
With PhD	7

Facilities:

Library hours	08.30-17.30 (term-time)
IT availability	100 terminals
Cultural opportunities	many and varied

WARWICK BUSINESS SCHOOL

Location and Contact Details:

Address	University of Warwick
	Coventry CV4 7AL
	UK
Telephone Number	0203 523922
Facsimile Number	0203 523719
Contact Name	Stuart Chambers

School Description:

The school also offers distance learning and Consortium MBAs – details are available on request.

School Details:

MBA Courses	*Full-time* ✓	*Part-time* ✓	*Distance-learning*	*Company/Consortium*	
Duration	12 months	3 years	3-4 years	3 years	15 months
Class Contact	30 hrs/ week	6 hrs/ week	8 days pa	5 wks pa	
Dissertation or Project	project	project	project	projec t	

Assessment   exam/course

Final date for applications:

30th June	31st Dec	30th April/315th Oct	
		30th Sept	

Estimated Fees 1993/1994 Academic Year:

EC	£8,300	£2,680	£1,690	£3,500
overseas	£9,500		£1,920	

1992 Student Intake:

Intake	120	72	321
UK	72	65	196
Other EC	17	3	25
Non-EC	31	4	100
Women	30%	13%	21%

Faculty Details:

Dedicated MBA programme teaching staff	75
Full professors	19
Visiting lecturers/professors	30

| With Master's degree | 52 |
| With PhD | 33 |

Facilities:

Library hours	09.00-21.30 Mon-Fri
	14.00-18.00 Sat
	14.00- 21.30 Sun

IT availability	18 dedicated MBA terminals plus additional 54 postgraduate terminals
Cultural opportunities	Major arts centre on campus, close to Stratford
Other facilities	foreign language laboratory, excellent arts centre, full sports and social facilities

WOLVERHAMPTON BUSINESS SCHOOL

Location and Contact Details:

Address	University of Wolverhampton
	Compton Park Campus, Compton Road West
	Wolverhampton WV3 9DX
	UK
Telephone Number	0902 323604
Facsimile Number	0902 323755
Contact Name	Mr Glenn Richer
	Mr Chris Cooper

School Description:

The School has a significant range of In-Company Programmes, involving major Private and Public Sector Organisations. Flexible Modular Structure allowing Credit Transfer and Accreditation of Prior Learning. Integrative Pan-European modules drawing on the School links with Russia and with Western Europe. Strengths in Marketing, Personal Skills Development, Enterprise and Pub;ic Sector Management.

School Details:

MBA Courses	Full-time	Part-time	Modular	Company/ Consortium
Duration	1 year	3 years	3 years	3 years
Dissertation or Project	project	project	project	project
Assessment	exam/ course	exam/ course	exam/ course	exa m/ course
Final date for applications:				
	Dec	Sept	Sept	variable

(Jan start)

Estimated Fees 1993/1994 Academic Year:

£5,000 £1,400/£2,000/£200 as p/t

1992 Student Intake:

Intake	22	107	as p/t
UK	6	101	
Other EC	3		
Non-EC	14	6	
Women	20%	35%	

Faculty Details:

Dedicated MBA programme teaching staff	21
Full professors	4
Visiting lecturers/professors	12
With Master's degree	47
With PhD	8

Facilities:

Library hours	09.00-20.30 Mon-Fri; 09.30-12.30 Sat
IT availability	150 terminals; PRIME network with worldwide library databases
Cultural opportunities	Residentials and links with local industry
other facilities	Pleasant campus setting on two sites. Easy access to language courses.

Schools offering an AMBA-approved course are indicated in this section by the AMBA 'roundel'.

MBA

Wolverhampton Business School

Wolverhampton Business School has offered Management Development Programmes for many years and offers a flexible and innovative approach to post experiential learning.

Full time: this is an intense one year course building on the foundations of functional management to lead to a comprehensive grasp of strategic issues. The course runs over a calendar year so as to fit in with the needs of the business community. The participant can tailor their individual programme to cover specialisms in the public sector, financial services and manufacturing. This is an international course in terms of both content and participants.

Part time: designed for practising managers, this course allows participants and employers to match management development with the working environment. Again, the programme can be tailored to meet individual needs in a way which reflects Wolverhampton Business School's flexible approach to business courses.

Both programmes offer the option of obtaining a Post Graduate Certificate or Diploma in Management as an alternative to a full MBA.

For further details contact Glenn Richer (Full time) or Chris Cooper (Part time), Wolverhampton Business School, University of Wolverhampton, Compton Park Campus, Compton Road West, Wolverhampton WV3 9DX. Tel. 0902 323688 (Full time); 0902 323652 (Part time). Fax. 0902 323755.

UNIVERSITY OF WOLVERHAMPTON

Schools offering an AMBA-approved course are indicated in this section by the AMBA 'roundel'.

ESADE (Escuela Superior de Administración y Dirección de Empresas)

Location and Contact Details:

Address   Avenida de Pedralbes, 60-62
              08034 Barcelona
              SPAIN
Telephone Number   34 3 280 61 62
Facsimile Number   34 3 204 81 05
Contact Name   Mr. Josep Mila

School Description:

ESADE is a founding member of the EFMD and the CEMS (Community of European Management School), a member of the PIM since 1975, member of CLADEA, AACSB, FINC and numerous other international associations. The course structure consists of three clearly differentiated points: Introduction to Business, the Core Programme and Majors. Other programs offered at ESADE: 5 year combined BBA/MBA program; Ph.D. program; Executive Development Programs; In- Company Training Programs; Language School. Concentrations/Specialisations include: Finance; General Management; Health; International Management; Management Information Systems; Marketing; Operations Management; Public Policy; Small business; Tax Management; 80 electives

School Details:

MBA Courses	Full-time ✓	Part-time
Duration	2 years	3 years
Class Contact	1,300 hours	1,300 hours
Dissertation or Project	no	no
Assessment	exam/course	exam/course
Final date for applications:		
	15th June	15th June
Estimated Fees 1993/1994 Academic Year:		
	1,886,000 Pta	959,000 Pta

1992 Student Intake:

Intake	150	150
UK	5	-
Spain	70%	95%
Other EC	15	5%
Non-EC	10	-
Women	34%	15%

MBA

Bilingual Master's Programme

**A two year full-time general management programme.
Students can opt to do the first year in either English or Spanish**

For entreprising individuals with a gift for organisation, sensivity to current events, demonstrated leadership qualities and good learning capacities

Application forms and further details
ADMISSIONS OFFICER MBA Programme
ESAD. Avda de Pedralbes.
60-62 08034 Barcelona, Spain.
Tel (34 3) 280 61 62 · Fax (34 3) 204 81 05

ESADE
School of Management
Barcelona

Individual courses approved by AMBA are indicated by a 'tick'.

Faculty Details:

Dedicated MBA programme teaching staff	120
Full professors	90
Visiting lecturers/professors	15
With Master's degree	60
With PhD	50

Facilities:

Library hours	08.00-22.00 weekdays
	09.30-20.00 Saturdays
IT availability	140 pcs linked with 2 mainframes (hours: 08.00- 02.00 weekdays, 08.00-18.00 Saturdays)
Other facilities	mail delivered to pigeonholes, repository for official publications (EC, ILO, World Bank, IMF and others), international on-line service, European Information Centre, Behavioural Sciences laboratory and language school

International Affiliations:

CESMA MBA, Groupe ESC, Lyon; Cranfield School of Management, England; Edwin L. Cox School of Business, Southern Methodist University, Texas; HEC, Montréal; Indiana University, USA; Instituto Tecnológico y de Estudios Superiores de Monterrey, Mexico; ISA MBA-Groupe HEC, France; Manchester Business School, England; Norwegian School of Economics and Business Administration; Pennsylvania State University, USA; University of British Columbia, Vancouver; University of Florida, USA; University of Illinois at Urbana-Champaign, USA; University of Southern California, USA; Wissenschaftliche Hochschule für Unternehemensführung- Koblenz, Germany; York University, Canada.

CESMA MBA – GROUPE ESC LYON

Location and Contact Details:

Address	23 Av Guy de Collongue
	69132 ECULLY
	FRANCE
Telephone Number	33 72 20 25 25
Facsimile Number	33 78 33 61 69
Contact Name	Ms Jacqueline del Bello

School Description:

Lyon is France's second city, located in the Rhone-Alpes, and is France's second most important industrial region, in particular in high tech and research. There are numerous cultural and business associations, an integrated programme comprising a strong muticultural and humanistic approach to management, and extensive use of case studies, business games and involvement of practising managers; double MBA with Cranfield School of Management. There are also focused seminars on Environment, European Management, Crisis Management, Negotiation, Personal Development & Leadership.

School Details:

MBA Courses	Full-time ✓
Duration	12 months
Class Contact	700 hours
Dissertation or Project	project
Assessment	exams/course

Final date for applications:
10th June
Estimated Fees 1993/1994 Academic Year:
FF 90,000

1992 Student Intake:

Intake	79
UK	0
France	66
Other EC	6
Non-EC	7
Women	22%

Faculty Details:

Dedicated MBA programme teaching staff	35
Full professors	8
Visiting lecturers/professors	4
With Master's degree	19
With PhD	16

Facilities:

Library hours	09.00-19.00 Mon-Fri ;09.00-12.00 Sat
IT availability	40 desktop PCs at computer centre, one portable computer for each study group (total: 20)
Cultural opportunities	Proximity to Lyon city centre; Opera, Theatre, Symphony Orchestra

Schools offering an AMBA-approved course are indicated in this section by the AMBA 'roundel'.

International M.B.A. Programme

In Madrid, Spain

Further information should be requested from:

INSTITUTO de EMPRESA
Dirección de Cursos.
María de Molina, 11, 13 y 15. 28006 Madrid.
Tels.: (341) 562 81 00/08/09 y (341) 411 65 11/94
Fax: (341) 411 40 82.

INSTITUTO de EMPRESA

Course Outline

The International MBA is an intensive Spanish-English bilingual programme, in which the participants, after having completed twelve months of course work and a 3-4 month management internship with public or private firms, are incorporated into key positions in multinational or leading industrial companies.

The programme includes courses using the case method, lectures and seminars, visits to companies and institutions relevant to the business field, and the completion of a Business Plan for creating a new business.

Participant Profile

Candidates of any nationality may attend the programme upon successful completion of a rigorous selection process and having demonstrated leadership skills. Latin-American and Philippino candidates may apply for grants awarded by El Instituto de Cooperación Iberoamericana. The average age of those taking part is 26-27 years old and they normally have one to three years work experience and top degrees from leading universities.

The Instituto de Empresa

The Instituto de Empresa is a private independent institution founded in 1973 for the purpose of teaching Business Administration and Top Management training programs. Its academic staff is composed of 49 full-time, 23 associates, 118 part-time and 32 visiting professors.

The Instituto de Empresa is centrally located in Madrid, Spain, and housed in five large villas (9,000 sq. m.) set in spacious garden surroundings.

Other facilities | Own common room, documentation centre and European depository library, data-bases, language laboratory, multi- purpose gymnasium, tennis courts. Proximity to French Alps: skiing and other sports; French Riviera, Switzerland and Italy a few hours away.

International Affiliations:
Cranfield School of Management (UK), ESADE (Spain), HEC Montréal (Canada).

IESE – UNIVERSITY OF NAVARRA

Location and Contact Details:

Address	Avenida Pearson 21
	08034 Barcelona
	SPAIN
Telephone Number	34 3 204 4000
Facsimile Number	34 3 280 1177
Contact Name	Paul J. McDonough

School Description:

IESE values the diversity of nationalities, as well as previous academic and work experience represented in its student body. The school offers a unique opportunity to become fluent in two major commercial languages (English and Spanish), while enhancing business skills in a traditional rigorous full-time MBA programme.

School Details:

MBA Courses	Full-time ✓
Duration	21 months
Class Contact	19 hours/week
Assessment	exam/course

Final date for applications:
1st May
Estimated Fees 1993/1994 Academic Year:
1,875,000 Pta

1992 Student Intake:

Intake	210
UK	3
Other EC	144
Non-EC	63
Women	20%

Faculty Details:

Dedicated MBA programme teaching staff	112
Full professors	43
Visiting lecturers/professors	3
With Master's degree	63
With PhD	60

Facilities:

Library hours	until 21.00
IT availability	25 Apple Macintosh computers connected in a network. An Apple laser printer, 4 Apple impact printers, 5 IBMs with 3 Epson printers. VAX-3800 and VAX3100 connected in cluster, to which all students have access. International E-Mail and possibilities to connect with IESE computers from home.
Other facilities	new library building with additional work rooms and a self-service cafeteria to supplement the main dining facilities

International Affiliations:

UC Berkeley, Chicago, Columbia, Dartmouth, Duke, IPADE, ISA, Keio, Northwestern, London Business School, UCLA, Western Ontario, Wharton.

EUROPE'S OLDEST TWO-YEAR MBA PROGRAMME

INTERNATIONAL
GRADUATE SCHOOL
OF MANAGEMENT

UNIVERSITY OF NAVARRA

Barcelona - Madrid

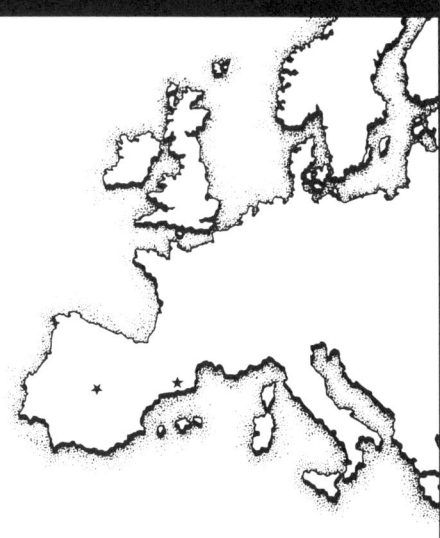

In 1964 IESE started the first two-year MBA Programme in Europe.

Since 1980 this Programme has been bilingual in Spanish and English. The Programme is a truly international one, attended by students from more than thirty countries, the majority coming from Europe and North America. This Bilingual Programme is a major opportunity to become fluent in the two main commercial languages of the western world, whilst enhancing management skills and capabilities.

The select group of highly motivated multicultural students joining IESE each year is one especially valued for its diversity of nationalities, previous academic background and international experience.

If you hold a completed university degree, see yourself as a hard-working adaptable individual capable of competing successfully in our internationally oriented environment and would like more information, contact:

Paul J. McDonough
Director, MBA Admissions
IESE
Avenida Pearson 21
08034 Barcelona, SPAIN
Tel.   (34.3) 204 40 00
Telex   50924 IESB E
Telefax   (34.3) 280 11 77

Individual courses approved by AMBA are indicated by a 'tick'.

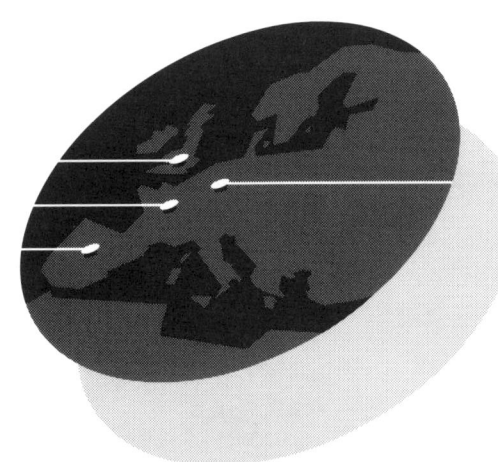

FOCUS YOUR BUSINESS CAREER FOR A CHANGING WORLD

For information, please contact:

MBA Admissions Office
EAP Paris
6 ave de la Porte de Champerret
75838 Paris Cedex 17
Phone: (+33 1) 44 09 33 32
Fax: (+33 1) 44 09 33 35

EAP Oxford
12 Merton Street
Oxford OX1 4JH
Phone: (+44 865) 72 45 45
Fax: (+44 865) 25 19 60

EAP Berlin
Europa Center, Breitscheidplatz
1000 Berlin 30
Phone: (+49 30) 254 80 20
Fax: (+49 30) 254 80 231

EAP Madrid
Arroyofresno, 1
28035 Madrid
Phone: (+34 1) 38 62 511
Fax: (+34 1) 37 39 229

For twenty years EAP has run leading edge management programmes from four learning centres in Europe.

The joint expertise and resources of these learning centres combine to make EAP a leader in multicultural management development in Europe.

EAP's **European MBA** focuses on developing the leadership skills, attitudes and business knowledge to operate across Europe and around the world.

This is the focus that more and more companies are looking for. The focus that you will require to build your career potential. EAP's **European MBA** provides this focus through its international curriculum, faculty from 14 countries, multinational student body and European Project.

If you want to shape your career to meet the challenges of a complex and changing business world, join our one year, full time **European MBA** in Paris.

EAP Oxford and EAP Madrid offer part time versions of the European MBA programme.

EAP is a 'Grande Ecole' in France and has university status in Germany.

CHAMBRE DE COMMERCE ET D'INDUSTRIE DE PARIS

Schools offering an AMBA-approved course are indicated in this section by the AMBA 'roundel'.

IMD

Location and Contact Details:
Address   P O Box 915
             1001 Lausanne
             SWITZERLAND
Telephone Number   41 21 618 01 11
Facsimile Number   41 21 618 07 07
Contact Name   Ms Aurélie Morel

School Description:
International general management school: 30 nationalities in a typical class of 82 participants; faculty: 18 nationalities in 1993; international course materials. The course has an integrative approach to general management; practical multi-disciplinary problem-solving and decision- making under uncertainty. It has unique international consulting projects that enable participants to apply the material taught in the programme.

School Details:
MBA Courses   Full-time ✓
Duration   1 year
Class contact   900 hours
Dissertation
  or Project   both: International Consulting Project
Assessment   continuous

Final date for applications:
           31st August
Estimated Fees 1993/1994 Academic Year:
           SFr 38,000 (individual);
           SFr 58,000 (sponsored)

1992 Student Intake:
Intake	83
UK[TAB11	
Other EC	22
Non-EC	49
Women	18%

Faculty Details:
Dedicated MBA programme teaching staff	24
Full professors	24
Visiting lecturers/professors	4
With Master's degree	4
With PhD	24

Facilities:
Library hours	24 hours, 7 days/week
IT availability	1 per student, either desktop or portable and laser printers
Cultural opportunities	Other executive programs

INSEAD

Location and Contact Details:
Address   Boulevard de Constance
             77305 Fontainebleau Cedex
             FRANCE
Telephone Number   33 1 60 72 40 00
Facsimile Number   33 1 60 72 42 42
Contact Name   Helen Henderson

School Description:
INSEAD is genuinely international: it has a combination of multi-national participants, faculty and course material, and guarantees a truly global approach.

School Details:
MBA Courses   Full-time ✓
Duration   10 months
Class contact   540 hours
Dissertation
  or Project   mixture of exams, projects, group work and class participation
Final date for applications:
           April (Sept entry)
           Aug (Jan entry)

Estimated Fees 1993/1994 Academic Year:
           FF 1240,000

1992 Student Intake:
Intake	466
UK	73
Other EC	200
Non-EC	193
Women	17%

Faculty Details:
Dedicated MBA programme teaching staff	79
Full professors	79
Visiting lecturers/professors	50
With Master's degree	79
With PhD	75

Facilities:
Library hours	08.00-20.00
IT availability	60 work stations available

ISA (Institut Superieur Des Affaires)

Location and Contact Details:

Address   HEC School of Management
1, rue de la Libération
78350 Jouy-en-Josas
FRANCE

Telephone Number   33 1 39 67 73 83
Facsimile Number   33 1 39 67 74 65
Contact Name   Christine Luckx

School Description:

ISA offers a generalist bi-lingual programme which stresses the global dimensions of business. Strong emphasis is placed on teamwork. The innovative programme experiential learning features include Sextant, Euro-Challenge and numerous self-development seminars. ISA also offers one of the largest student exchange programmes with the most distinguished MBAs in the USA, Canada, Europe and Asia.

School Details:

MBA Courses   *Full-time* ✓
Duration   16 months
Class Contact   14 months
Project   yes, depends on concentration
Assessment   exams 80%
continuous 40%
presentations 20%
Final date for applications:
1st Jan, 1st March, 1st May
Estimated Fees 1993/1994 Academic Year:
FF 82,500

1992 Student Intake:

Intake   115
UK   11
Other EC   85
Non-EC   19
Women   25

Faculty Details:

Dedicated MBA
  programme teaching staff   110
Full professors   94
Visiting lecturers/professors   30
With Master's degree   47
With PhD   47

Facilities:

Library hours   08.30-22.00 3 times a week;
    08.30-19.30 other times
IT availability   08.00-00.00, Saturday 09.00-17.00.
Mainframe IBM 9370 plus 76 micros, including Macintosh, HP and IBM
Other facilities   Housing available on campus, restaurant, theatre, extensive sports facilities; wooded hills and lake ideal for hiking or jogging

International Affiliations:

USA: Columbia, Kellogg, Stern, UCLA, Wharton; Canada: Western Ontario, McGill; London and Manchester Business Schools; Europe: Rotterdam, Bocconi, IESE; Keio in Japan; and G. Vargas in Brazil.

ROTTERDAM SCHOOL OF MANAGEMENT – ERASMUS UNIVERSITY

Location and Contact Details:

Address   P O Box 1738
3000 DR Rotterdam
THE NETHERLANDS

Telephone Number   31 0 10 408 2222
Facsimile Number   31 0 10 452 9509
Contact Name   Ms Connie Tai

School Description:

The Rotterdam School of Management offers two full-time MBA Programs. The MBA Program covers all aspects of general management and includes such subjects as finance, marketing, R&D, human resource management and strategic management. The MBA/MBI Program combines study in information technology (IT) to the traditional MBA courses. MBA/MBI students follow the required courses in general management during the first year, followed by an eight-week summer program of required MBI courses. In the second year students complete both required and elective MBA and MBI courses.

The international character is reflected by the international student body (nearly 40 different nationalities are represented), an international faculty, the exchange programs and a strong focus on the global market. The language of instruction is English; no other languages are required.

The classes illustrate the varieties in cultural and educational backgrounds and are rearranged several times throughout the year, allowing students to work

ISA
AN OUTSTANDING
BILINGUAL MBA
IN FRANCE

Europe provides unique opportunities and challenges for managers. At ISA we are shaping international business leaders to meet those challenges head-on.

ISA offers:

• the leading bilingual French/English MBA programme.

• the strength and resources of the HEC School of Management, France's most prestigious management training institution since 1881.

• a sound training for a career in international management, as recognized by the several hundred companies recruiting from the school annually.

• a renowned permanent faculty, whose members have significant research and consulting interests.

• an intensive 16 month programme in an ideal study environment, just 15 kilometers from the centre of Paris.

• the opportunity to gain wider international experience by participating in an exchange programme with leading North American, Japanese, and European schools.

If you wish to know more about the ISA MBA, we invite you to telephone, or send for a brochure.

Please fill out this form to receive an application in French ☐
or in English ☐

Name: _____

Address: _____

City: _____

Country: _____

Degree Earned: B.A. ☐   B.E. ☐
B.S.C.☐ L.L.B.☐   M.S.☐ Ph.D.☐

INSTITUT SUPÉRIEUR DES AFFAIRES

Please address your inquiries to:
Institut Supérieur des Affaires
Admissions Department
78351 Jouy-en-Josas Cedex, France
Phone: (33-1) 39 67 73 82

 CHAMBRE DE COMMERCE ET D'INDUSTRIE DE PARIS

---

closely with all fellow students and to enrich the "MBA experience": it is not only what you learn, but also what you can contribute in class. Teaching methods are diverse and have a strongly practical nature: lectures, case studies, field trips, teamwork, management games and independent work are important in enhancing the learning process. The RSM stresses teamwork because it is a realistic model for the way in which management issues are handled in the business world.

School Details:

MBA Courses	Full-time	MBA/MBI	In-company
Duration	20 months	20 months	Varies
Class Contact	60 weeks	68 weeks	
Dissertation or Project	project	project	
Assessment	exam/ course	exam/ course	

Final date for applications:
	1st May	1st May	

Estimated Fees 1993/1994 Academic Year:
	Dfl18,000	DFl22,500	

1992 Student Intake:
Intake	108	24
UK	10	
Other EC	62	
Non-EC	60	
Women	20%	

Faculty Details:

Dedicated MBA programme teaching staff	73
Full professors	18
Visiting lecturers/professors	50
With Master's degree	71
With PhD	39

Facilities:

Library hours	Erasmus University: Mon-Fri 0900-22.30; Sat 0900-14.00 RSM: Mon-Thurs 0900-21.00; Fri 0900-1700
IT availability	200 terminals; mainframe and network are available to students
Other facilities	RSM has 25 classrooms of its own, plus the facilities of the Erasmus University, including classrooms, audotorium, library etc. The RSM classrooms are built-in amphitheater style. There is a language laboratory.
Cultural opportunties	Many social events. Many sports facilities, tennis courts, squash courts and a sports centre.

International Affiliations:

Wharton Business School, Kellogg Graduate School of Management, Western Ontario, MIT, ISA, SDA Bocconi, Manchester Business School, etc.

SDA BOCCONI

Location and Contact Details:

Address	Divisione Master Via Balilia 16/18 20136 Milano ITALY
Telephone Number	39 2 5836 6605/6606
Facsimile Number	39 2 5836 3275
Contact Name	Ms Gabriella Aliatis

School Description:

SNA Bocconi, the Graduate School of Management, operates in the field of post-experience management. It meets the need of companies by offering more than 400 courses and seminars anually attended by 10,000 managers. The bilingual MBA is a general management course with interfunctional approach. Emphasis is put on in-company projects. During the last 4 months of the programme ther si opportunity to focus on Information Systems. MIEM: entirely taught in English with strong interdisciplinary and international approach.

School Details:

MBA Courses	Full-time ✓	MIEM
Duration	16 months	12 months
Class Contact	16 months	12 months
Dissertation or Project	project with final report	MIEM case studies
Assessment	exam/course	

Final date for applications:
	15th April	31st May

Estimated Fees 1993/1994 Academic Year:
	Lit 28,000,000	14,000 ECU

1992 Student Intake:

Intake	127	49
UK	7	2
Other EC	80	24
Non-EC	40	23
Women	20%	40%

In a place you can't pronounce, in a 13th century castle, in a tiny country, below sea level, they crafted the biggest little International MBA programme you'll ever find.

Be very careful when Dutch business people, academics and politicians start telling you how small their country is. It's a trick. It's their way of softening up prospects and disarming the competition.

If they try it on you ask them how The Netherlands got to be the number two global food exporter (number one is the USA). Or what gave them the right to have the world's largest seaport. Or what enables their multi-nationals and retail brands to blend into the local scene wherever they operate. Or the reasons why leading international companies relish managers trained in The Netherlands.

Alternatively ask for details of Nijenrode University's International MBA Programme.

But take care, again. It's not for everyone. Members of a typical Nijenrode IMBA class
- representing some twenty nationalities -
have an excellent university track record and five years substantial business experience.

Average age is 28, GMAT scores range from 580 to 740.

Only the best are accepted.

Major international stakeholders help select Nijenrode's International MBA candidates. And the higher the standards, the better their next generation of general managers.

For details of Nijenrode's International MBA Programme '93 - '94 call, write or fax:
International MBA Office, Nijenrode University, The Netherlands Business School, Straatweg 25, 3621 BG
BREUKELEN The Netherlands, Tel. int. 31 3462 91603 Fax. int. 31 3462 50595.

Nijenrode University
THE NETHERLANDS BUSINESS SCHOOL

Individual courses approved by AMBA are indicated by a 'tick'.

Faculty Details:

Dedicated MBA
  programme teaching staff   73
Full professors   45
Visiting lecturers/professors   26

Facilities:

Library hours	until 23.00 weekdays; 00.30 Saturdays
IT availability	75 PCs available until 21.00; Saturday and Sunday on request

Cultural opportunities	Seminars and encounters with leading speakers from the social political and cultural world. Italian and English language courses.
Other facilities	shared common room; mail delivered to pigeonholes

International Affiliations:

No affiliations – exchanges of international students and faculty are organized with other main European and US business schools.

TRINITY COLLEGE DUBLIN, SCHOOL OF BUSINESS STUDIES

Location and Contact Details:

Address	Trinity College, College Green Dublin 2 EIRE

Telephone Number01 702 1632/1024
Facsimile Number 01 6799503
Contact Name   Ms Estelle Feldman

School Description:

"Trinity College, one of Europe's oldest universities, offers a year MBA which is intensive and intimate, and attracts students of diverse backgrounds from all over the world. The School of Business Studies, an integral part of the University, is noted for its undergraduate and senior management programmes and its commitment to an innovative independent-minded and internationally-oriented approach to management." *Fortune Magazine, 24/08/92.* The course is for those with at least three years work experience who wish to develop the abilities appropriate to an international career in middle and senior management. The coure offers small class sizes, a strong interconnection dimension, a 7-month company project, Business Culture and individual research option.

School Details:

MBA Courses	Full-time
Duration	11 months
Class Contact	c. 700 hours
Dissertation or Project	project
Assessment	exam/course assessment

Final date for applications:
   Round 1 31st January
   Round 2 31st March
Estimated Fees 1993/1994 Academic Year:
   on request

1992 Student Intake:

Intake	30
UK	6%
Other EC	64%
Non-EC	30%
Women	25%

Faculty Details:

Dedicated MBA
  programme teaching staff   23
Full professors   4
Visiting lecturers/professors   2
With Master's degree   13
With PhD   10

Facilities:

Library hours	6 day week access
IT availability	24-hour access to computer labs
Cultural opportunities	Dublin, the capital of Ireland, provides a stimulating environment for the student. The city is famous for its cultural activities, particularly theatre. Many of the most famous thinkers and writers in the English language not only lived in Dublin but studied at Trinity College.
Other facilities	Dublin is a cosmopolitan city which maintains a friendly if not village-like sense fo community. Students have easy access to fine shopping and recreational facilities. The seashore and the countryside are within thirty minutes by public transport.

International Affiliations:

MBA programme has visiting international faculty, permanent linkages are indirect through business school.

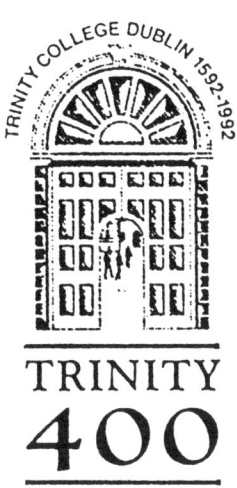

University of Dublin
Trinity College 1592 – 1993
Celebrating over 400 years of
International Academic Excellence

offers

AN OUTSTANDING EUROPEAN MBA

Trinity's School of Business Studies, an integral part of the university, is noted for its commitments to an innovative, independent-minded and internationally oriented approach to management.

THE TRINITY MBA

This intensive one-year full-time programme is for those with at least three years' experience who wish to develop the abilities appropriate to an international career in middle and senior management.

For further information and application form contact:

MBA Programme Secretary, School of Business Studies, Trinity College, Dublin 2, Ireland
Tel: (intl. code 353-1) 7021024 / 7020127   Fax: (intl. code 353-1) 6799503

Individual courses approved by AMBA are indicated by a 'tick'.

THE UNIVERSITY OF CHICAGO GRADUATE SCHOOL OF BUSINESS

Location and Contact Details:

Address   Office of Admissions and Financial Aid
            1101 E. 58th Street
            Chicago Illinois 60637
            USA
Telephone Number   312 702 739
Facsimile Number   312 702 9085
Contact Name   William W, Kooser, Assistant Dean of
Management.

School Description:

The University of Chicago, recognised internationally for research and teaching, is located in the multi-cultural Hyde Park neighbourhood of Chicago. It is the second oldest American school of business, and the only one with two Nobel Laureats. Other courses offered include Weekend and Executive Courses, details of which are available on request. Strengths lie in: Accounting; Behavioural Science; Business Economics; Econometrics; Financial Management; Industrial Relations and Human Resource Management; International Business; Marketing Management; Policy Studies; Production Management; Quality Management; Statistics.

School Details:

MBA Courses	Full-time ✓	Part-time
Duration	2 years	2.5 years
Class Contact	day	evening
Dissertation or Project	no	no
Final date for applications:		
	25th March	2 months before starting quarter

Estimated Fees 1993/1994 Academic Year:

	$36,000	$2,020/course

1992 Student Intake:

Intake	1200	1200

Faculty Details:

Dedicated MBA programme teaching staff	150
Full professors	45 tenured; 56 associate/assistant
Visiting lecturers/professors	49
With Master's degree	10
With PhD	140

Facilities:

Library hours	08.00-01.00 Mon-Thurs; 08.00-22.00 Fri-Sat; 12.00- 01.00 Sun
IT availability	students are required to own a pc; computing laboratories are readily available

International Affiliations:

Universities of Melbourne and NSW; Katholieke Universiteit Leuven; Pontificia Universidad Católica de Chile; ESSEC, Groupe HEC; LBS, LSE and University of Manchester; Chinese University of Hong Kong; Universita Commerciale Luigi Bocconi; Waseda; Erasmus; Yonsei; IESE; Handelshgskolan I Stockholm; Hochschule St Gallen.

CORNELL UNIVERSITY JOHNSON GRADUATE SCHOOL OF MANAGEMENT

Location and Contact Details:

Address   315 Malott Hall
            Ithaca, New York 14853-4201
            USA
Telephone Number   1 607 255 2327
Facsimile Number   1 607 254 4590
Contact Name   Anne Coyle - Director of
                    Administration

School Description:

The aim of the Johnson Graduate School is to prepare students for general management careers; therefore, no one pedagogical approach dominates, cases and more theoretical approaches are combined. Joint Degree Programs offered in conjunction with schools of Law, Engineering, Asian Studies, and Industrial and Labour Relations.

School Details:

MBA Courses	Full-time ✓
Duration	2 years
Class Contact	20 courses
Dissertation or Project	no

Individual courses approved by AMBA are indicated by a 'tick'.

Assessment varies
Final date for applications:
 1st March
Estimated Fees 1993/1994 Academic Year:
 c. $19,000

1992 Student Intake:
Intake 261
Women 24%

Faculty Details:
Dedicated MBA
 programme teaching staff 41
Full professors 24
Visiting lecturers/professors 2
With PhD all

Facilities:
Library hours 08.00-24.00
IT availability 20 IBM and 18 Macintosh pcs with connection to central VAX network, 5 VAX network terminals, 5 laser printers
Cultural opportunities International Student Organisations; Located in rural and scenic wine country, the Fingerlakes region. Only 4 hours' drive to New York City. Praised for its collegial atmosphere. Skiing, sailing and rock climbing readily available.
Other facilities various online news retrieval services

International Affiliations:
London Business School, University of Groningen, Hochschule St Gallen, Norwegian School of Economics and Business Administration, Universite Catholique de Louvain, Ecole Superieure des Sciences Economiques, SDA-Bocconi, IESA Caracas.

DARTMOUTH COLLEGE – THE TUCK SCHOOL

Location and Contact Details:
Address 100 Tuck Hall
 Hanover, New Hampshire 03755-9030
 USA
Telephone Number 1 603 646 3162
Facsimile Number 1 603 646 1308
Contact Name Henry F. Malin

School Description:
Located in beautiful northern New England; residential campus; two-hour drive to Boston, 4½ hours to New York City. New international research centre established in 1992.

School Details:
MBA Courses *Full-time* ✓
Duration 2 years
Class Contact 26 hours
Dissertation
 or Project project
Assessment exam/course
Final Date for applications:
 15th April
Estimated Fees 1993/1994 Academic Year:
 $33,500 inclusive ($19,950 tuition only)

1992 Student Intake:
Intake 185
UK 4
USA 144
Other 37
Women 22%

Faculty Details:
Full professors 19 full; 9 assoc; 5 asst.
Visiting lecturers/professors 10
With Master's degree 33
With PhD 33

Facilities:
Library hours 08.00-24.00
IT availability 54 terminals
Cultural opportunities Hopkins Centre, Hood Museum of Art

International Affiliations:
London Business School, IESE, International University of Japan.

HARVARD UNIVERSITY GRADUATE SCHOOL OF BUSINESS ADMINISTRATION

Location and Contact Details:

Address   Soldiers Field Road
Boston, MA 02163
USA
Telephone Number   617 495 6127
Facsimile Number   617 496 9272

School Description:

Harvard University has a renowned faculty, with extensive resource and campus facilities. The general management curriculum is taught using the case method of study.

School Details:

MBA Courses   Full-time ✓
Duration   2 years
Class Contact   17 hours - case study format
Assessment   exams/class participation
Final date for applications:
8th March

Estimated Fees 1993/1994 Academic Year:
c. $36,000

1992 Student Intake:

Intake	1600
UK	60
Other EC	112
Non-EC	231
Women	29%

Faculty Details:

Dedicated MBA programme teaching staff	193
Full professors	93
Visiting lecturers/professors	8

Facilities:

Library hours   09.00-22.00 Mon-Thurs;
09.00-17.00 Fri; 12.00- 17.00 Sat;
12.00-22.00 Sun

UNIVERSITY OF MICHIGAN SCHOOL OF BUSINESS ADMINISTRATION

Location and Contact Details:

Address   701 Tappan Street
Ann Arbor
Michigan 48109-1234
USA
Telephone Number   313 763 5769
Facsimile Number   313 763 5688
Contact Name   Judith A. Goodman

School Description:

The school offers a strong global business programme; strong ties with the community – many student projects are community-based; very diverse student body and faculty; opportunities for specialisation; world-class computer and library facilities; leadership skills from its top-ranked executive education group.

School Details:

MBA Courses	Full-time ✓	Part-time
Duration	2 years	4 years
Class Contact	60 hours	60 hours
Dissertation or Project	no	no
Assessment	varies – exams, projects, papers	

Final date for applications:
    1st March   15th April/
    1st November
Estimated Fees 1993/1994 Academic Year:
    $18,600 $460/credit hour

1992 Student Intake:

Intake	440	300
US	85%	98%
Women	24%	26%

Faculty Details:

Dedicated MBA programme teaching staff	128
Full professors	43
Visiting lecturers/professors	25
With Master's degree	135
With PhD	130

Facilities:

Library hours   08.00-24.00
IT availability   145 advance microcomputers housed in a student lab and two classrooms

---

Individual courses approved by AMBA are indicated by a 'tick'.

Other facilities
One of the nation's largest business libraries with over 210,000 volumes, almost 369,000 microfilms, 3,200 serials and periodicals

International Affiliations:
Wirtschaftsuniversität Wien; National University of Singapore; Erasmus University; Ecole des Hautes Etudes Commerciales' Universita Commercial Luigi Bocconi; London Business School; Stockholm School of Economics; Universitaet des Saarlandes Saarbruecken; St Gallen; ESADE.

MIT SLOAN SCHOOL OF MANAGEMENT

Location and Contact Details:

Address   50 Memorial Drive, Room E52-112
Cambridge, MA 02142
USA
Telephone Number   1 617 253 3730/1 617 253 0449
Facsimile Number   1 617 253 6405
Contact Name   Rod Garcia, Acting Director of
Admissions

School Description:
This Seprember 1993 the Sloan School is embarking on a revised curriculum. The new core calls for the creation of three new subjects to introduce behavioural, economic, and mathematical perspectives on management. It seeks to connect theory and practice more tightly than before and provides for considerably more student choice. Additionally, the thesis will become optional and a series of innovative management tracks is being developed to help link students' professional interests more closely with their Sloan School experience.

School Details:

MBA Courses   *Full-time* ✓
Duration   2 years
Dissertation
 or Project   Thesis/project
Assessment   exam/course/class participation/group
projects
Final date for applications:
    4th February 1994
Estimated Fees 1993/1994 Academic Year:
    $35,000

1992 Student Intake:
Intake   200-245/year
Women   25%

Faculty Details:
Dedicated MBA
 programme teaching staff   118
Full professors   106
Visiting lecturers/professors   12
With Master's degree/PhD   100%

Facilities:
Library hours   five divisional libraries as well as several branch libraries and special service units make up the MIT libraries; the hours vary
IT availability   Own centre: 24-hour, 7-day access to Macintosh (30) and pc (30) labs
Cultural
 opportunities   Extensive contact with students; over 35% are international.

International Affiliations:
London Business School.

STANFORD GRADUATE SCHOOL OF BUSINESS

Location and Contact Details:

Address	Stanford University
	Stanford, California 94305-5015
	USA
Telephone Number	415 723 2766
Facsimile Number	415 725 1668
Contact Name	Marie Mookini

School Description:

Enjoys a West Coast location near Silicon Valley and San Francisco, with proximity to Pacific Rim nations. Diverse student body, strong alumni network. The distinguished faculty includes a Nobel Prizewinner and a former Secretary of State. There is a strong international alumni network, the class size is relatively small, the student body is diverse with strong academic and professional backgrounds. It is one of the most selective schools and usually admits 1 out of every 11 applicants. The school also offers a variety of executive programmes; Public Management Programs, Joint Degree Programs with Law, Engineering etc.

School Details:

MBA Courses	Full-time ✓
Duration	2 years
Class Contact	25 credits
Final date for applications:	
	3 filing periods – Mid November, Early January, Early March

Estimated Fees 1993/1994 Academic Year:
$20,195

1992 Student Intake:

Intake	359
US	278
Non-US	81
Women	27.8%

Faculty Details:

Dedicated MBA programme teaching staff	120
Tenure-track professors	78
Visiting lecturers/professors	42
With PhD	100%

Facilities:

Library hours	08.00-23.00 weekdays
	08.00-21.00 weekends
IT availability	more than 90 in lab; additional on-line in library
Cultural opportunities	Full range both on-campus events and in surrounding community.
Other facilities	Stanford located in Silicon Valley near many high- tech businesses, and near proximity to San Francisco.

STERN SCHOOL OF BUSINESS/NEW YORK UNIVERSITY

Location and Contact Details:

Address	Management Education Centre
	44 W 4th Street, Suite 10-160
	New York, New York 10012
	USA
Telephone Number	212 998 0600
Facsimile Number	212 995 4231
Contact Name	Hallie Kuiper, Associate
Director/Manager	International Admissions

School Description:

The MBA program at the Stern School is designed to produce complete managers-individuals who can cope successfully with the rapidly changing circumstances of today's business world. Our program stresses the international dimensions of management education within both our core and elective courses. Stern's approach to management education is two- fold: we ensure students of a solid management base through our strong core program and allow them to tailor additional coursework to their professional and personal goals. Because of the depth and breadth of the electives we offer, Stern provides students with the unparalleled opportunity to pursue their particular professional interests.

School Details:

MBA Courses	Full-time ✓	Part-time
Duration	2 years (fall)	4 years
	16 months (spring)	
Assessment	exams/projects	exams/projects
Final date for applications:		
	15th April	15th May
	1st August	

Estimated Fees 1993/1994 Academic Year:

$18,028	$914 first credit, $546 each additional credit	

1992 Student Intake:

Intake	400	420

Faculty Details:

Dedicated MBA programme teaching staff	198
Full professors	198
Visiting lecturers/professors	10
With Master's degree	3
With PhD	195

Facilities:

Library hours	Open stacks 08.30-23.00 Mon-Thurs; 08.30-19.00 Fri; 10.00-23.00 Sat; 08.30-22.00 Sun. Study areas 08.30- 01.00 Sun-Fri; 10.00-01.00 Sat
IT availability	extensive IT available; entire library automated
Other facilities	Stern School open 24 hours a day, 7 days a week

THE JOHN E. ANDERSON GRADUATE SCHOOL OF MANAGEMENT AT UCLA

Location and Contact Details:

Address	405 Hilgard Avenue Los Angeles, California 90024-1481 USA
Telephone Number	310 825 6944
Facsimile Number	310 825 8582
Contact Name	Linda Baldwin, Director,

School Description:

UCLA has developed several innovative programs to complement its general management curriculum. They include: Entrepreneurial Studies, International Studies, International Business and Comparative Management, Arts Management, Real Estate and Finance, public and Not-for- Profit Management, Entertainment Management, and Technology Management. The programs afford numerous opportunities for students to interact with venture capitalists, real estate and entertainment industry people. The Los Angeles area is especially attractive for such student/professional interaction. Special topics courses addressing these areas, internships, active special interest organisations, as well as study abroad opportunities for those in the International Management Fellows Program provide ample opportunity for students to experiment in these fields. School strengths include: Accounting; Economics; Finance; General Management; International Business; Management Information Systems; Marketing; Non-Profit Organisations; Operations Management; Organisational Behaviour; Public Policy; Quantitative Analysis; Small Business; 11 electives.

School Details:

MBA Courses	Full-time ✓	Part-time
Duration	2 years	3 years
Dissertation or Project	Field Study	Consulting Field Study
Assessment	examinations	

Final date for applications:

	1st April	15th April

Estimated Fees 1993/1994 Academic Year:

CA residents	$4,300	$15,300
non-residents	$14,000	$24,000

1992 Student Intake:

Intake	705	240
UK	8	
Other EC	21	
Non-EC	97	3
Women	30%	26%

Faculty Details:

Dedicated MBA programme teaching staff	160
Full professors	84 + 4 emeritus recalled
Visiting lecturers/professors	72
With Master's degree	2%
With PhD	98%

Facilities:

Library hours	08.00-22.00 Mon-Thurs 08.00-17.00 Fri 09.00- 17.00 Sat 12.00-18.00 Sun

Schools offering an AMBA-approved course are indicated in this section by the AMBA' roundel.

WELCOME TO THE FUTURE.
WELCOME TO STERN.

WHERE YOU'LL EARN AN M.B.A. THAT GIVES YOU ALL THE TOOLS YOU'LL NEED TO EXCEL IN THE GLOBAL MARKETPLACE.

The Stern School offers you: **a globally-focused curriculum,** with concentrations in nine functional areas; **a new Management Education Center,** the largest investment in classrooms, computer facilities, and audiovisual technology by any U.S. business school; **a diverse community** with 33 percent international enrollment; **Manhattan location,** the center of global commerce, finance, and culture; **and a superb reputation** -- NYU is ranked second only to Harvard by Standard & Poor's as a source of top executives in major corporations.

Graduates of New York University's Stern School of Business are equipped with skills needed to excel in a rapidly changing international market. Chief executive officers and business school deans recently polled by *U.S. News and World Report* rank Stern's International Business department No. 2 and Department of Finance No. 5.

Find out more about the Stern School's M.B.A. program. Full time program starts in September and January.

Stern School of Business
New York University
Management Education Center
44 West 4th Street
Suite 10-160
New York, NY 10012
Telephone 1-212-998-0600
Fax 1-212-995-4231

NEW YORK UNIVERSITY

THE STERN SCHOOL OF BUSINESS
WHERE TOMORROW'S BUSINESS
LEADERS LEARN TODAY.

Individual courses approved by AMBA are indicated by a 'tick'.

| IT availability | 108 terminals |
| Cultural opportunities | Distinguished Speakers Program; Firm Night; Days on the Job to Tokyo, Paris, New York City, to name a few; MBA Interchange |

International Affiliations:
ISA, ITSEM, Stockholm School of Economics, Chinese University of Hong Kong, SDA Bocconi University, IESA, ITAM, National University of Singapore, Pontificia Universidad Catolica de Chile, National Taiwan University in Taipei, and The Washington Campus, a one-month programme either in Washington, DC or on a 5-city tour of Europe.

COLGATE DARDEN GRADUATE SCHOOL OF BUSINESS ADMINISTRATION

Location and Contact Details:
Address	University of Virginia
	Box 6550
	Charlottesville, VA 22906-6550
	USA
Telephone Number	804 924 7281
Facsimile Number	804 924 4859
Contact Name	A. Jon Megibow, Director

School Description:
The school has an innovative Strategic Management and Leadership required course in the second year. The first year has an integrated curriculum.

School Details:
MBA Courses	*Full-time*
Duration	2 years
Class Contact	500 students
Dissertation or Project	required
Assessment	50% class participation 50% exams
Final date for applications:	
	1st Dec/15th Jan/15th Mar
Estimated Fees 1993/1994 Academic Year:	
VA residents	$6,855
non-residents	$14,227

1992 Student Intake:
Intake	233
UK	1
Other EC	10
Non-EC	15
US	218
Women	81

Faculty Details:
Dedicated MBA programme teaching staff	100
Full professors	69
Visiting lecturers/professors	20
With Master's degree/PhD	90%

Facilities:
| Library hours | 06.00-24.00 |
| IT availability | approximately 30 IBM, 12 Macintosh |

International Affiliations:
Stockholm School of Economics; University of Melbourne.

Schools offering an AMBA-approved course are indicated in this section by the AMBA' roundel.

KENAN-FLAGLER BUSINESS SCHOOL

Location and Contact Details:
Address	CB 3490 Carroll Hall
	University of North Carolina at Chapel Hill
	Chapel Hill, NC 275999-3490
Telephone Number	919 962 3236
Facsimile Number	919 962 0898
Contact Name	Anne-Marie Summers

School Description:
With a focus on business issues and problems, not functional areas, courses at Kenan-Flagler are taught from an integrated point of view. Emphasis also is placed on implementation, with workshops and seminars on professional skills.

School Details:
MBA Courses	*Full-time* ✓	*Part-time*
Duration	2 years/18 months (4 Semesters)	
Class Contact	15 hrs/wk	
Dissertation		
or Project	project	
Assessment	exam/course	

Final date for applications:
                1st March
Estimated Fees 1993/1994 Academic Year:
                £3,118.70 NC resident $8,702.70 other

1992 Student Intake:
Intake	367
UK	2
Other EC	18
Non-EC	25
Women	25%

Faculty Details:
Dedicated MBA programme teaching staff	60
Full professors	35 full; 22 Assoc; 9 Asst
Visiting lecturers/professors	f/t 10; p/t 11
With Master's degree	SPA = 8; EPA = 9
With PhD	82 (78 Faculty, 4 staff)

Facilities:
Library hours	08.00-24.00 Mon-Thurs;
	08.00-20.00 Fri; 10.00- 18.00 Sat;
	12.00-24.00 Sun
IT availability	19 terminals
Cultural opportunities	International speakers

International Affiliations:
McGill University, Manchester Business School, ESSEC, GROUPE-HEC, IESA, KUL-Leuven.

J.L. KELLOGG GRADUATE SCHOOL OF MANAGEMENT, NORTHWESTERN UNIVERSITY

Location and Contact Details:
Address	Leverone Hall
	2001 Sheridan Road
	Evanston, IL 60201
	USA
Telephone Number	708 491 8696
Facsimile Number	708 491 4960
Contact Name	Michele Y. Rogers

School Description:
Specialises in Organisational Behaviour, Marketing, Finance, Manufacturing Management, Health Services Management, Public/Non-profit, Transportation, Entrepreneurship.

School Details:
MBA Courses	*Full-time* ✓	*Part-time*
Duration	1/2 years	2.5-5 years
or Project	exam/course	exam/course

Assessment	March 30th	

Final date for applications:

Estimated Fees 1993/1994 Academic Year:
                £19,000   £1,850/course

1992 Student Intake:
Intake	11	1,300

Faculty Details:
Dedicated MBA programme teaching staff	87
Full professors	
Visiting lecturers/professors	
With Master's degree	
With PhD	90%+

Facilities:
Library hours	09.00-22.00

Individual courses approved by AMBA are indicated by a 'tick'.

IT availability   Numerous DOS and Apple

Cultural   Arts, music, theatre and dance
   opportunities   programs

International Affiliations:
SASIN, Thailand.

Useful contacts

United Kingdom

General

Association of MBAs, 15 Duncan Terrace, London N1 8BZ. Tel: 071-837 3375

Services to MBA members. Offers general information. Administers Business School Loan Scheme. Does NOT offer scholarships.

Association for Management Education & Training in Scotland (AMETS), The Cottrell Building, University of Stirling, Stirling, FK9 4LA Tel 0786-450906

Organisation for Scottish schools. Provides MBA fact sheet on Scottish schools. Details on Management Training.

Career Development Loans, Career Development, Employment Department, Steele House, Room 711, Tothill Street, London SW1H 9NF. Tel: 0800-585 505

Loans for vocational courses. Available for one year of study only.

Chartered Institute of Bankers, LoMBArd Scheme, 10 Lombard Street, London EC3V 9AS. Tel: 071-929 4301

For details about LoMBArd Scheme -- MBA courses for Associates of the Institute.

Foundation for Management Education, Sun Alliance House, New Inn Hall Street, Oxford, OX1 2QE. Tel: 0865-251 486

Provides information about Management Teaching.

MBA & GMAT Advice Centre, Pastest, Rankin House, Parkgate Estate, Knutsford, Cheshire, WA16 8DX. Tel: 0565-755 226 Fax: 0565-650 264

Publications etc. GMAT Bulletins for those studying outside the USA.

Women in Management, 64 Marryat Road, London SW19 5BN. Tel: 081-944 6332

A network for women in management. Provides training and development and offers advice.

Scholarships & Awards

Association of Commonwealth Universities, John Foster House, 36 Gordon Square, London, WC1H OPF. Tel: 071-387 8572

Scholarships for study within the Commonwealth. Information on Commonwealth universities. Publications on undergraduate and postgraduate courses.

Economic & Social Research Council (ESRC), Polaris House, North Star Avenue, Swindon, SN2 1UJ. Tel: 0793-413 000

Funding for research degrees and some masters courses in the UK. Funding NOT available for MBA study. Provides Management Teaching/Conversion Fellowships.

The Grants Register, Globe Book Services Ltd., Macmillan Publishers Ltd., Brunel Road, Basingstoke, Hants RG21 2XS. Tel: 0256-817 245

Comprehensive listing of grants, scholarship and awards. Available in all academic and large libraries.

London Chamber of Commerce & Industry,
Charles R E Bell Fund, Examinations Board,
Marlow House, Station Road, Sidcup, Kent
DA15 7BJ. Tel: 081-302 0261
Scholarships tenable in the UK or abroad.

Rotary International of Great Britain &
Ireland, Kinwarton Road, Alcester,
Warwickshire B49 6BP. Tel: 0789-765 411
Scholarships for study outside one's own country.

The Royal Academy of Engineering, Grants &
Awards Office (MFS), 2 Little Smith Street,
London SW1P 3DL. Tel: 071-222 2688
Scholarships for professionally qualified engineers
between ages of 26--34. Tenable only at
international schools.

United States

General Information

Graduate Management Admissions Council
(GMAC), 11601 Wilshire Boulevard, Suite
1060, Los Angeles, CA 90025, USA
Umbrella organisation for US schools. MBA
forums. Publications.

Educational Advisory Service, Fulbright
Commission, (US-UK Educational
Commission), Fulbright House, 62 Doughty
Street, London WC1N 2LS.
Tel: 071-404 6994 or for Test Information:
071-404 6854.
General information of study in the USA. Library
of university catalogues. Provides list of awards
and GMAT Bulletins for those wishing to study
in USA. Must send an A4 s.a.e. stamped for 80
grams.

Scholarships

American Association of University Women
USA, Educational Foundation Programs,
1111 16th Street North West, Washington,
DC 20036-4873, USA. Tel: 202 785 7700
Scholarships for women currently studying in the
USA.

British Universities North America Club
(BUNAC), 16 Bowling Green Lane, London
EC1R 0BD. Tel: 071-251 3472
'Topping up' awards for study in North America.

English Speaking Union of the Commonwealth,
37 Charles Street, London W1X 8AB. Tel:
071-493 3328
Scholarships for study in the USA.

Frank Knox Fellowships, 16 Great College
Street, London SW1P 3RX.
Tel: 071-222 1151
Scholarships for Harvard only.

Fulbright Awards, Fulbright Commission,
Fulbright House, 62 Doughty Street, London
WC1N 2LS. Tel: 071-404 6880
Scholarships for study in the USA. Academic
exchanges.

Kennedy Memorial Trust, Kennedy
Scholarships, 16 Great College Street,
London SW1P 3RX. Tel: 071-222 1151
Scholarships for Harvard and MIT only.

Thouron Awards, Office of the Registrar,
University of Glasgow, Glasgow G12 8QQ.
Tel: 041-339 8855
Scholarships for University of Pennsylvania only.

Thomas Angear Scholarship, The Dean, Office
of Admissions, Johnson Management School,
Cornell University, Ithaca, NY 14853, USA.
Tel: 607 255 8915
For study at Cornell only. Open to EC nationals.
Worth $5,000 in 1991. Renewable for 2nd year.

Research assessment – business and management studies

The Universities Funding Council is responsible for distributing government grants to universities. In 1992 it was to distribute £600 million of research funding. It achieved this on the basis of rankings in an assessment.

Column 1: Ranking

A top ranking of '5' in the first column indicates some research of international excellence with the rest of national excellence.

A '4' equals research of national excellence 'in virtually all sub-areas of activity, possibly showing some evidence of international excellence, or to international level in some and at least national level in a majority'.

A '3' signals research equating to national excellence in a majority of areas, or to international level in some.

A '2' indicates research equating to national excellence in up to half the areas.

A '1' indicates research of national excellence in none, or virtually none, of the areas.

Column 2: Staff Participation

A five point scale of excellence is matched by a second ranking reflecting size. This runs from A to F.

'A' signals that 100 to 95 per cent of a department's staff were included in the research submission:

'B'   94–80 per cent
'C'   79–60 per cent
'D'   59–40 per cent
'E'   39–20 per cent
'F'   less than 20 per cent

The ranking below offers the intending student objective knowledge as to the quality of the research carried out at an individual school. It is not, however, a ranking of MBA programmes.

The table below only includes those institutions which offer an MBA degree.

University	Ranking	Staff
Anglia Polytechnic University	2	E
Aston University	3	B
University of Bath	3	B
University of Birmingham	3	B
Bournemouth University	2	F
University of Bradford	5	B
University of Brighton	2	D
University of the West of England, Bristol	1	F
Buckinghamshire College of Higher Education	1	E
City of London Polytechnic	1	F
City University	4	B
Coventry University	2	E
Cranfield Institute of Technology	3	D
De Montfort University	2	E
Derbyshire College of Higher Education	1	E
University of Durham	2	C
University of Greenwich	1	C
University of Hertfordshire	2	E
University of Huddesfield	2	E
University of Hull	3	A
University of Humberside	1	F
University of Keele	3	A
University of Kent at Canterbury	3	B

University	Ranking	Staff
Kingston University	2	E
University of Central Lancashire	1	E
University of Lancaster	5	B
University of Leeds	2	A
Liverpool John Moores University	2	E
London Business School	5	A
Imperial College of Science and Technology	3	A
Loughborough University of Technology	4	B
Luton College of Higher Education	1	F
University of Manchester	3	A
Manchester Metropolitan University	2	E
UMIST	5	A
Middlesex University	2	D
Nene College	1	F
University of Newcastle upon Tyne	2	B
University of North London	1	D
University of Northumbria at Newcastle	1	F
University of Nottingham	3	A
Nottingham Trent University	1	E
University of Oxford	3	A
Oxford Brookes University	1	E
University of Plymouth	1	D
University of Portsmouth	2	E
University of Salford	2	C
University of Sheffield	3	A
Sheffield Hallam University	3	F
University of Southampton	4	B
University of Surrey	3	C
University of Teesside	1	E
Thames Valley University	1	F
University of Warwick	5	A
University of Westminster	2	F
University of Ulster	3	E
University of Aberdeen	1	A
Dundee Institute of Technology	1	D
University of Edinburgh	3	A
Glasgow Polytechnic	1	D
University of Glasgow	3	B
Heriot-Watt University	3	C

University	Ranking	Staff
Napier University	1	F
Robert Gordon University	1	E
University of Stirling	2	C
University of Strathclyde	5	B
University of Glamorgan	1	E
University College of North Wales, Bangor	3	A
University of Wales College of Cardiff	4	A

Index of Schools

Specialist MBAs

Courses available in the United Kingdom carry a 'specialist' label (i.e., MBA in ...) are listed below. You should note that other schools will offer optional courses in many of these subject areas.

SPECIALIST MBA	UNIVERSITY
Agribusiness	Aberystwyth
Banking and/or Finance	Birmingham, City, Dundee University, Greenwich College, Hull, Nottingham University
Biotechnology Management	Birmingham
Construction Management	Dundee University
Education	Keele, Nottingham University, South Bank
Engineering Management	City
European MBA	Canterbury, Derbyshire, Dorset, Keele, Middlesex, Nene College, Sheffield University, South Bank
Health	Canterbury, Durham, Nottingham
Human Resource Management	City
Information Technology	City, Hull
International Business	Birmingham, University of Bristol, City, Glasgow University, Ulster
Marketing	City, Sheffield University
Mineral Resources	Dundee University
Oil and Gas Management	Dundee University
Project Management	Dundee University, Henley
Public Sector Management	Aston
Technology Management	Brighton